José María de Pereda

TWAS 354

José María de Pereda

LAWRENCE H. KLIBBE

New York University

TWAYNE PUBLISHERS

A DIVISION OF G. K. HALL & CO., BOSTON

Library of Congress Cataloging in Publication Data

Klibbe, Lawrence Hadfield, 1923-
José María de Pereda.

(Twayne's world authors series, TWAS 354. Spain)
Bibliography: p. 175.
1. Pereda, José María de, 1833-1906.
PQ6554.P3Z7   863'.5   74-17390
ISBN 0-8057-2687-X

TO MY PARENTS

Contents

About the Author

Lawrence H. Klibbe received his Ph.D. from Syracuse University and is currently on the Romance Languages faculty of New York University. He contributed the volume on *Fernán Caballero* for the Twayne's World Authors Series. He has also published *James Russell Lowell's Residence in Spain, 1877-1880,* and has coedited an edition of Gustavo Adolfo Bécquer's *Rimas y leyendas.* He has written for various journals, such as *Hispania, The Modern Language Journal,* and *Thought,* and reviews books regularly in *Books Abroad.* He also works for the New York City Board of Education as an examiner in foreign languages.

Preface

José María de Pereda still maintains a very respectable place within the history of Spanish literature, especially the novel, during the nineteenth century. However, critics have not always been kind to him during the twentieth century, and his contributions as a writer generally win historical rather than aesthetic praise. Pereda represents the culmination of a certain development in Spanish prose fiction beginning with local-color sketches and progressing clearly in the direction of regionalism at the service of traditionalism through the definitive efforts of Fernán Caballero. Pedro Antonio de Alarcón and Juan Valera, although in disagreement at times with Fernán Caballero's methods and ideology, composed stories with an implicit defense of the rural, conservative, orthodox viewpoints; and the three authors used Andalusian backgrounds very often in their works. Pereda follows in their footsteps by accepting uncompromisingly the ideological premises of these fellow artists, but his rigid, dogmatic attitude toward Spain and the Spaniard became increasingly extreme and outmoded — because of the rapidly changing circumstances, political, economic, and social — as the twentieth century approached. The antipathy and opposition of Pereda's literary colleagues to the problems of the age, such as urbanization, industrialization, liberalism, democratic reforms, and the rise of the middle class, faced only the initial challenges of these nineteenth-century movements. Pereda also published his outstanding novels, such as *Sotileza* (Fine Spun) and *Peñas arriba* (The Upper Peaks), at the time when Spanish and European literatures were about to come to grips with the convulsions of the twentieth century. Spanish literature would soon reflect the reactions of the "Generation of 1898" to the traumatic consequences of military defeat and national unrest; and the European literary heritages would experience the impact of the innovative, dynamic theories, like those of Freud, as well as the shock of World War I, on realistic and naturalistic patterns. All these outside ideas and events, of course, made themselves felt in Spain and explain further the decline in Pereda's stock among readers and critics during this century.

Nevertheless, Pereda offered some original approaches and certainly stressed the importance of style and artistic form in the nineteenth-century novel and short story. Pereda, for example, transferred the action from the more familiar area of southern Spain to the mountains and coast of his native *patria chica* ("little homeland") in the North. He thereby provided a very different dimension to a prevailing impression of "Sunny Spain," obtained from the usual narrative backgrounds of Fernán Caballero, Alarcón, and Valera, and from the reports of romantic writers like Irving and Hugo. Pereda blended realistic and naturalistic characteristics in his writings, although he would forcefully deny any direct influence of naturalism as alien to his philosophic and religious beliefs. But his stylistic achievement, most of all, and the lengthy, loving, and detailed descriptions of the northern regions in Spain justify Pereda's acceptance as a master in the use of the Spanish language. This linguistic success and artistry should balance the scale for Pereda against the frequent criticism of his myopic convictions regarding a country, a people, and a way of life isolated happily and tranquilly from the historical present. With contemporary trends, Pereda may be due for a more appreciative recognition and new readers thanks to his love of nature, his rejection of urban encroachments upon the wilderness, his desire for a simple existence, his respect for the beauties of solitary surroundings, and his unyielding attack upon unrestrained materialism as destructive of the exemplary, enduring qualities found in a simple land and its inhabitants.

After the first chapter, which traces the general facts of his life and the place of individual works within this framework, Pereda's works are treated chronologically. Each of the two major novels, *Sotileza* and *Peñas arriba*, receives extensive analysis and commentary in separate chapters. Pereda's last works and the vicissitude of his fortunes in the reading and critical audiences of the twentieth century are discussed in the last two chapters. All translations from the Spanish are my own throughout the text.

Appreciation is owed New York University and my colleagues for

Preface

their cooperation and help, Professor Gerald E. Wade for his encouragement and suggestions, and the Twayne staff during all the stages of this book.

LAWRENCE H. KLIBBE

New York University

Chronology

1833 February 6: Born at Polanco, province of Santander, Spain.
1840 Family moves to Santander, the provincial capital, where José María finishes elementary school.
1852 Graduates from secondary school in Santander. Leaves for Madrid to enter artillery school in Segovia.
1853 Gives up interest in a military career and writes a short story, "La suerte de un sombrero" (The Fate of a Hat).
1854 Returns to Santander because of disillusionment and home-sickness. Changes in the northern city further depress Pereda.
1855 Mental depression increases after mother's death, and his illness from cholera causes concern for his life by the family.
1856 Takes an extended vacation in the southern province of Andalusia to recuperate from the effects of cholera.
1857 Returns to Santander completely recovered physically and psychologically. Begins to work for a local magazine, *La Abeja Montañesa* (The Mountain Bee).
1858 Writes articles for the same magazine under the signature of "P." Founds his own journal, *El Tío Cayetano* (Old Cayetano), and publishes his own articles, sketches, notes, etc.
1859 *El Tío Cayetano* ceases publication after thirteen issues.
1862 Pereda's father dies.
1864 Pereda continues collaboration with *La Abeja Montañesa* and writes some theatrical pieces for local audiences without any great success.
1864 *Escenas montañesas* (Mountain Scenes), Pereda's first book, a collection of previously published articles and sketches, with a prologue by Antonio de Trueba, wins little critical recognition.
1865 A brief residence in Paris with unfavorable reactions about the city. Secretary of the Ateneo Científico y Literario (Literary and Scientific Atheneum) in Santander. Preoccupation

with politics increases shortly before the Revolution of 1868.

1869   Marries Diodora de la Revilla Huidobro. Adherence to the Carlist cause after the abdication of Isabel II and another attempt to publish *El Tío Cayetano* as an outlet for his political opinions.

1871   Traditionalist, or Carlist, deputy to the Cortes (Parliament) in Madrid. Second book, *Tipos y paisajes* (Types and Landscapes), a continuation of *Escenas montañesas*, helps to establish friendship with Benito Pérez Galdós, who visits Pereda's home province that summer.

1872   Quits Madrid for Santander, disgusted with politics and depressed generally by lack of any notable achievements as a writer. Retreats to the security of his family, friends, and native surroundings. Friendship with a fellow countryman from Santander, Critic Marcelino Menéndez Pelayo.

1876   Contributes to a new magazine, *La Tertulia* (The Club). *Bocetos al temple* (Sketches in Distemper), a collection of three short novels, *La mujer de César* (Caesar's Wife), *Los hombres de pro* (Men of Worth), and *Oros son triunfos* (Diamonds Are Trump).

1877   *Tipos trashumantes* (Nomadic Types), short stories and sketches.

1878   *El buey suelto* (The Bachelor), his first long novel.

1879   *Don Gonzalo González de la Gonzalera* (Don Gonzalo González of Gonzalera), a thesis novel.

1880   *De tal palo, tal astilla* (A Chip off the Old Block), a novelistic answer to Galdós's, *Gloria* (Glory).

1881   *Esbozos y rasguños* (Outlines and Sketches), a series of scenes and characters from the neighborhoods of Santander.

1882   *El sabor de la tierruca* (Redolent of the Soil), a novel with prologue by Galdós.

1883   *Pedro Sánchez*, a novel, published.

1884   Publication of the first volume of the *Obras completas* (Complete Works) with a critical introduction by Menéndez Pelayo. Makes tour of Spain; the receptions are consistently enthusiastic and laudatory.

1885   *Sotileza* (Fine Spun), his best novel to this date, published. Trip to Portugal with Galdós.

1888   *La Montálvez* (The Lady Montálvez), a novel criticized more harshly than any previous work as too naturalistic.

1889   *La puchera* (The Stew), a novel.

1890   Deaths in family and ill health.

1891   Two ineffective, weak novels, *Nubes de estío* (Summer Clouds) and *Al primer vuelo* (On the First Flight). A literary polemic with Emilia Pardo Bazán.

1893   Suicide of oldest son, Juan Manuel.

1895   *Peñas arriba* (The Upper Peaks), an immediate bestseller, dedicated "to the holy memory of my son," accepted as the rival of *Sotileza* for the most outstanding novel.

1896   Election to the Real Academia Española (Royal Spanish Academy). *Pachín González*, his last novel.

1897   Acceptance speech to the Real Academia Española on the regional novel with the reply by Galdós on the same topic.

1900   Renewed efforts in the theater reminiscent of youthful illusions.

1901   Failure or lukewarm reception of some plays. Defense of Galdós's controversial drama, *Electra*.

1902   Ceases writing extensively but travels in Spain to see family and acquaintances.

1903   Grand Cross of Alfonso XII awarded to Pereda and Menéndez Pelayo as two distinguished compatriots of Santander.

1904   Noticeable decline in health.

1906   Death at Santander on March 1.

CHAPTER 1

Man of the North

JOSÉ María de Pereda is probably associated more closely with one particular region, the province of Santander, than any other Spanish writer of the nineteenth century. His regional or country novels favor completely the way of life in the northern province of Spain; his urban or Madrid novels portray little merit and a great deal of unhappiness associated with the large city. Pereda's life reflects unfailingly the same theses as his works, and this philosophy influenced his decision to spend most of his years in his *patria chica* ("little homeland"). A life active in literary, political, social, and personal interests developed within the confines of wholehearted acceptance of tradition. Pereda, in short, decided to tread the sure, secure road of the past, following contentedly and successfully the signposts already established by another generation and another age.

I *Coming of Age*

Pereda's parents, Juan Francisco de Pereda y Haro and Bárbara Sánchez de Porrúa, natives respectively of Polanco and Comillas (villages in the province of Santander), belonged to the proud heritage of the minor nobility in this mountainous land. Both parents possessed modest but adequate incomes, showed an appreciation and respect for books and culture, entered without difficulty as a matter of birthright into the society of Santander, and certainly exemplified standards of traditionalism and orthodox beliefs. Religion played a major part in the Pereda household, and the couple made annual retreats in a nearby monastery where the wife once witnessed her own future funeral rites, in imitation of Charles V's ceremony at Yuste in the sixteenth century.[1]

The marriage produced twenty-two children of whom only nine survived to maturity, and José María was the last child born to this union, when his mother was almost fifty years old. The parents, of course, had married at an early age: the father was eighteen and the mother fifteen. There seems little doubt that José María was naturally the spoiled member of this large family throughout his childhood and adolescence. His oldest brother, Juan Agapito, acted as a second father for José María, and this fraternal loyalty served the younger Pereda to decisive advantage on several occasions until his brother's death in 1870. Juan Agapito, in fact, rescued and guided the entire Pereda household when his mother's expected inheritance after her mother's death in 1822 did not materialize. Juan Agapito, although he was only eighteen years old, left for Havana where he quickly and successfully entered the business world. From Cuba he sent money to Santander, enabling his parents to maintain their respected position among their neighbors. The influential role of this mature, intelligent, and wealthy son grew with the years; and his faithful and dutiful service to the Pereda family cannot be overestimated in tracing José María's life and career.

José María spent the first seven years after 1833 in the *Montaña* ("Highlands"), the familiar classification for the area near the Pereda homes in Polanco and la Requejada, where his childhood provided happy memories, which are reflected in his use of this background in several works, particularly *Peñas arriba* (The Upper Peaks). Again, the financial security resulting from Juan Agapito's good fortunes and devotion gave José María these advantages of security and material satisfactions, which were not always available to the children in Pereda's stories. The distant intervention of José María's brother in Cuba, around 1840, persuaded the parents to move to the city of Santander because of the better facilities and opportunities available for the education of all the children, especially José María. The change from country to city, probably regretted at the time by José María, nevertheless became a happy, profitable experience for the boy. Once more, no exceptional events and no family problems marred the youthful and adolescent years in Santander.

José María's years in school at Santander, terminating with the *bachillerato* (the approximate equivalent of the baccalaureate degree in the United States) in 1852, were marked by no outstanding scholastic or intellectual achievements; but his academic record was respectable enough for him to gain entrance to a university. His personal activities likewise offered no noticeable variation from the usual adventures, episodes, and pranks common to the young men of his age and class. The education in the Spanish schools in Santander, as elsewhere in Spain, reflected the rigid society of the time; but Pereda evidently acquiesced in the aims of this school training. An emphasis upon rote learning, with reliance upon the classics and the teachings of Catholicism, provoked no overt rebellion on his part, although Pereda objected to the "tough" program in secondary school as opposed to the "soft" studies of the elementary level. Also, he, like all students, disliked some courses and some teachers. Pereda, in brief, seemed to have survived the first nineteen years of his life very normally and with no very interesting, exceptional adventures or misadventures.[2]

II   *Two Years in the Big City*

After coming of age at nineteen, indicated not only by the conclusion of secondary studies but likewise by a rather formal introduction to Santander society, Pereda departed for Madrid in the fall of 1852 in order to prepare himself, especially in mathematics, for entrance to the artillery school in nearby Segovia. This decision to select a military career seems to have been one of mutual determination on the part of both the family and the young Pereda. The vocational choice was not surprising in Spain at that period: opportunities for advancement in life were limited, the sons of large households often found paths open only in the church or the armed forces, and José María's background and training predisposed him to adhere to such a traditional career in service to the nation. Pereda's own youthful glow undoubtedly suggested this course of action or accepted readily the familial idea. There is certainly no evidence that he left Santander with anything but high hopes for a vast change in his prosaic existence and for an exciting experience as an officer in the Spanish army.

The two years spent by Pereda away from Santander and in the capital of Madrid were formative and decisive in two apparently contradictory ways. Residence in the city revealed his true vocation, that of a writer, and enabled him to observe at first-hand the literary and cultural currents of the Spanish scene. However, his trenchant, conclusive reactions to these observations alienated and disturbed him to such an extent that his departure — or flight — from the metropolis signaled the beginning of a lifelong antipathy to urban civilization as well as an immediate, serious psychological crisis. This near nervous breakdown was consequently a compound of disillusionment and homesickness. It is pertinent at this point to remember the reactions of José María's older brother, Juan Agapito, who, at the same age, boldly and resolutely left Spain for Cuba to restore the family fortune by his acumen and hard work. Juan Agapito pursued vigorously a realistic and practical program, although he probably suffered from the same loneliness and melancholy at times as his younger brother. The contrast is also significant because Juan Agapito's counsel and example was ultimately responsible for José María's psychological and physical restoration in this worsening situation, the most dangerous of his life. Certain revelations emerge rather clearly in this problem of challenge and response, indicative of the author's character and personality.

What happened during this relatively short residence in Madrid that so disturbed Pereda and altered so totally his entire outlook on life and literature? One explanation may lie in the common occurrence of a young man, born and bred to a rural or small-town atmosphere, going to the big city to make his fame and fortune and experiencing an entirely new way of life. The shock resulting from a swift transfer from a secure, predictable way of life to a kaleidoscopic pace, without the support of family and friends, has been chronicled and analyzed throughout literature. If one accepts Horatio Alger's formula that the youth in such a dilemma must either "sink or swim," then the accurate, perhaps cruel, conclusion might be advanced that Juan Agapito "swam" and José María "sank" in their confrontations with the city and change. However, further explanations could be offered about the events of these two years, so essential and important for the comprehension of Pereda's later development. José María's selection of a military career never rested on solid bedrock, and he devoted himself to the many cultural and social opportunities of Madrid almost immediately upon becoming acquainted with the geographical dimensions of his new quarters. He similarly felt no qualms about abandoning preliminary glimpses into the complex phases of mathematics. There is the inescapable conclusion, therefore, that his true interests and enthusiasms were aroused by the proximity of an active cultural, especially literary, atmosphere.

These new activities in Pereda's case were not characterized by the deviance or dissipations associated with a great deal of the romantic spirit, still in vogue and yielding slowly to the realistic ideas coming principally from France. Pereda's rigid upbringing and puritanical nature, on the contrary, directed his nascent literary curiosities not to Bohemianism but into the world of books, the theater, conversations at the cafés, and friendships with young men of his own class. Soon, however, Pereda could not escape the encroaching web of politics and government. His initial interest in the color and stimulation of theatrical ventures yielded to the excitement of the Spanish political arena. Another reason for this shift in his attention may be due to the fate of an early and obscure attempt as a writer. During this stay in Madrid, he seemed to have composed a short story, "La suerte de un sombrero" (The Fate of a Hat), but little is known about this endeavor.[3] If Pereda's failure initially as an author discouraged him into turning to politics, the choice was no less unhappy at this turbulent time of the national panorama.

Spanish history is full of unrest from 1833, when Fernando VII's death had ushered in the unexpected accession of his daughter to the throne, until 1868, when the disastrous reign of this same woman, Isabel II, finally erupted in a revolution with the demand for her abdication. During these years the country enjoyed little domestic peace and suffered from the failure to keep apace with the material progress of the other European powers. Don Carlos, Fernando VII's brother, had rallied to his cause (the claim that only males and not females could inherit the crown) all the traditional, conservative, and aristocratic elements of the nation. The *carlistas* ("Carlists") launched a series of civil wars and insurrections from 1833 until their conclusive defeat in 1876, and after the Pretender's death, the partisans of Don Carlos lent their warlike enthusiasms to his heirs, even though their hopes for victory were never rooted optimistically in reality. The Carlist cause injured a nation already dangerously divided because of the animosities revealed by the ideological and political differences during the Napoleonic occupation of the peninsula. Although the Carlists probably represented a minority of the Spanish population, they were very popular in the rural areas, particularly the North of Spain. Obviously, the Pereda family adhered without question to the Carlist ideals, and in Madrid José María found himself caught between a party which he admired, and his recent acquaintances, few of whom shared his sentiment. The cities, with Madrid as the logical center, supported the party of the queen; although Isabel II's party was actually a divided, quarreling assortment of politicians, long on ambition but short on power (as governmental changes unfortunately demonstrated). The liberal and progressive elements in Spain were concentrated in the cities, especially Madrid; urban liberals preferred the turbulent, chaotic circus of the disunited, vaguely idealistic parties (owing a shadowy allegiance to the not very exemplary royal personage of Isabel II) to the reactionary Carlists.

There are a few recognizable strands in the tangled web of the political situation which Pereda, however he might have tried, could not have traced easily. The *progresistas* ("progressives") and *moderados* ("moderates") were the principal parties of liberals and conservatives, respectively; but both factions declared themselves to be constitutional or faithful to a semblance of democratic procedures. The *apostólicos* ("apostolics") were absolutists, favoring a strong monarchy and church; and the *exaltados* ("exalted") were radicals, demanding immediate and sweeping changes in the social, political establishments. The progresistas and moderados generally controlled the government, and the ministries were dominated for the most part by representatives of these majority groups. The apostólicos and exaltados won little popular support because of their extreme views. Other divisions of the confusing spectrum appeared and disappeared, and the above parties often broke into smaller sections because of constant feuds and disagreements. Due to this splintering, the real power resided in the generals, who, relying upon their command of the troops, could become the prime minister or dispose of a rival officer, holding the reins of government, if the latter's forces were smaller or weaker. *Pronunciamientos* ("pronouncements"), calling for insurrection or a quick, decisive overthrow of the incumbent regime by a military leader, became so frequent and commonplace that the term acquired an international status for this type of political change.

Pereda received a lasting negative impression of the dangerous and tragic course of events in nineteenth-century Spain, and Madrid in particular, when he witnessed the so-called Revolution of 1854 or *La Revolución de Julio* ("The July Revolution"). This complicated and ultimately insignificant uprising (futile in the repetitious, inconclusive character of the actions) was the outgrowth of the increase of popular unrest during the early spring, rumors of uprisings in other parts of the country, an authentic rebellion in the outskirts of Madrid, and devious, comic-opera maneuvers between military leaders and politicians, culminating in an inexplicable outburst of violence on the part of a mob. The masses in the middle of July set up barricades, burned royal and other official properties, looted private residences and stores, and terrorized the citizens of the capital until two generals, Espartero and O'Donnell, restored law and order with soldiers under their authority. The officers' reward for their salvation of the people and the city was forthcoming: Espartero was appointed prime minister, and O'Donnell was named minister of war. Their luck lasted only two years, and Espartero, out-maneuvered by O'Donnell, resigned; but the latter soon fell into Isabel II's disfavor, and she replaced him with Narváez, an officer returning to power.

Pereda utilized this background in his novel *Pedro Sánchez* in 1883. The story of the picaresque hero resembles closely the author's own traumatic experiences thirty years previously, as well as his observations about people caught in the whirligig of these historical and political events. This novel is perhaps the most accurate source about Pereda's few years in Madrid, especially the culminating episode of the Revolution of 1854, which determined him to return to Santander. Although many of Pereda's novels portray the pitfalls of the city, which is present as a force and a background, if not always the setting, in his books, *Pedro Sánchez* is the single novel where the action is centered completely in an urban environment. The evident autobiographical input suggests that Pereda was shocked and shaken by the failures of liberalism and democratic idealism and the incipient dangers to his noble, chivalric tradition.

Before witnessing the excesses of mob rule (in which he may have come close to death in a shooting fray), Pereda had already prepared himself psychologically to return home. "Here, rightly or wrongly, there are always attractions that pull one in pursuit of the court and that one looks at too fondly," Pereda wrote to his cousin at the end of 1853, "and a day will come on which one may regret to exchange them for the rainy and dull Highlands."[4] But the cultural pleasures of Madrid, pursued and praised by Pereda in this letter, are tempered by nostalgic memories and thoughts of the *Montaña*. In any case, by the end of the summer of 1854, Pereda's disillusionment was complete, and he left for Santander, desirous to resume the way of life he had so happily exchanged only two years earlier for the glamour of the big city.

III   *You Can't Go Home Again*

The lesson for Pereda, which he challenged for his remaining years both personally and in his writings, is the simple explanation that time alters all things, nothing stands still, and a man must make a reconciliation between his impossible wish for stability and the onward steps of time. Pereda, entering his home town of Santander after an enervating, demoralizing period in Madrid, noticed with some dismay that this city was also accepting nineteenth-century civilization. Santander was awakening to a possible role in the development and growth of Spanish economic, commercial, and industrial power. The new physical features of the city reflected the change to a utilitarian, middle-class culture instead of the familiar division into aristocratic and humble structures. Interests and activities revolved around business enterprises, the acquisition of wealth, and the power that money could effect in the society of the province. Another sudden and unexpected encounter with urbanization, change, and the passing of one order for another unnerved Pereda so completely that he retreated into a state of withdrawal, apathy, and dour reactions about everyone and everything.

In the following year, 1855, Pereda suffered the severest crisis of his life. The previous signs of an approaching nervous breakdown were augmented by the effect of his mother's death in March. Fortunately, however, Juan Agapito had rejoined the Pereda household after many years abroad, and he again took an especial interest in his youngest brother. Juan Agapito is credited with discovering, orienting, and encouraging the literary interests of José María, although these proclivities had already become noticeable during the latter's two years in Madrid.[5] Toward the end of this same year, José María fell victim to a cholera epidemic rampant in the province so that there were serious worries about his body and mind. It is obvious that his mental condition affected his physical health, and in turn, the effects of cholera further depressed him.

José María recovered slowly but not fully from the attack of cholera, and Juan Agapito then insisted upon a change of setting to restore his unlucky brother. An extended vacation in Andalusia with its hospitable, warm climate worked miracles for José María; and he recovered from his mental depression as well as from the aftermath of the bout with cholera. This is the sole instance in Pereda's life when he prospered in body and spirit away from the secure settings of Santander. Perhaps his close call with death, or at least his existence as an invalid, represented the bottom of the pit, and he naturally had to climb upward and out of this doleful condition. Another explanation may be found in the Andalusian background, people, and environment. It is true that the climate is preferable to the harsh weather of the North, except for northern natives and convinced fans of the region. In the South, where the regionalists were first describing the sort of traditional virtues and characteristics also practiced in the province of Santander, Pereda may have noticed that a pleasant, positive atmosphere could exist in other parts of Spain. Theoretically, Pereda may have decided at this time to write about the North in the same fashion that some of his compatriots, such as Fernán Caballero, Antonio de Trueba, Pedro Antonio de Alarcón, and Juan Valera, were utilizing Andalusia in local-color sketches, short stories, and novels.

Pereda's return to Santander left no uncertainties about his full recovery, mentally and physically; and he also showed a zest for activity which must have pleased Juan Agapito, by now the most influential person in Pereda's life. The most permanent contribution of Juan Agapito to José María's life came when the former rejected any intentions of the latter to enter the business world or to follow in the footsteps of the successful older brother. Apparently, José María showed some enthusiasm about a place in the family management, certainly a practical, undramatic, and realistic answer to the question of exactly what he intended to do in Santander. It is necessary to keep in mind that, from the viewpoint of finances and material security, José María de Pereda probably was the wealthiest Spanish author of the nineteenth century. Thanks to Juan Agapito's success and solicitude, José María could devote himself entirely to a career of his own choice. His prominent background, the family residences in the city of Santander and the countryside of Polanco and la Requejada, and the power of a happy combination of nobility and money afforded him leisure, opportunities, and influence. Credit is due to Pereda for setting himself high standards of work and achievement when he could have slipped effortlessly into years of enjoyment and mediocrity; and credit is likewise due to Juan Agapito for his role in rejuvenating José María's enthusiasm for writing and for the almost paternal manner in which he guided and helped his younger brother.

IV A Try at Journalism and the Theater

The following years as a literary neophyte from 1858 until 1864, when Pereda published his first book and left the friendly but limited audience of Santander, are important personally and intellectually, despite the lack of any outstanding creative literary endeavors. He suffered one family loss in the death of his father in 1862. Relations within the household continued to be very congenial, in particular with Juan Agapito, always ready to encourage and help the *niño mimado* ("spoiled child") or baby of the large group of Pereda offspring. This support and security provided by the family represents another major advantage for Pereda, for whom financial means alone were insufficient impetus. Outside the Pereda homes in and around the city of Santander, José María now traveled back and forth as he pleased for a change from the routine or for his own interests. The young writer renewed his friendships socially and culturally in the province, and added to the number of his acquaintances by reason of his social standing and the moderate size of Santander.

Pereda's prime activity during these years revolved around a local literary journal, *La Abeja Montañesa* (The Mountain Bee), founded in 1857 by a friend of the Pereda family, Castro Gutiérrez de la Torre. All the collaborators in the magazine were of about the same age and background as Pereda so that, in many instances, this journalistic effort constituted a fortunate projection of childhood background and adolescent experiences. Surprisingly, money did not create any problems for this publishing enterprise. The writers contributed without any compensation, as far as one can determine, and the review seemed to exist rather soundly on some sales and perhaps a discreet subsidy from the editor and other participants, including Pereda. His initial contributions constituted a mixture of news items, local gossip, and literary commentaries in which he, like any aspiring journalist, gained confidence and training for a writing career.

His self-assurance evidently increased quickly because by February 28, 1858, he wrote his first long article, "La gramática del amor" (The Grammar of Love) for the magazine, signing the humorous piece with the capital letter, "P." A second article, "Ya escampa" (There You Go Again), appeared in *La Abeja Montañesa* (The Mountain Bee) during the summer of the same year; but Pereda continued until 1864 to conceal his identity, perhaps not very seriously or successfully, by not using his full name. By December of 1858, Pereda and some of his other associates had decided to found their own journal, *El Tío Cayetano* (Old Cayetano), named after one of the more appealing beggars of the city of Santander; but the magazine only lasted thirteen issues, ceasing publication on February 27, 1859. Perhaps the competition with *La Abeja Montañesa*, the loss of interest by the writers, or the realization that the new venture demanded too much time and effort compelled the staff to return to their first publishing undertaking. No hard feelings seemed to ensue, and the young men returned to *La Abeja Mon-*

tañesa, although they had never stopped fully their collaboration with that journal.

Pereda's role in the short-lived magazine, in addition to whatever financial and editorial assistance he may have given, afforded him a major opportunity for publishing significant items, exclusive of notes and theatrical reviews. The *costumbrista* ("local-color") sketches, included in his first book, were initially printed in *El Tío Cayetano*. The reception of these *cuadros de costumbres*, as these "pictures of customs" were designated popularly, must have encouraged Pereda to feel that he had at last found a way to embark upon a more significant literary future. But upon his renewed concentration for *La Abeja Montañesa*, Pereda succumbed again to his preoccupation with the theater. Throughout his life, in fact, he wanted to win recognition as a dramatist; and he indulged at various times an unrequited attraction for the stage. In Madrid, he had enjoyed the theater and probably, as a result of seeing many performances and reading various dramas, acquired the chronic urge to make his contribution to literature in that genre. The irony is that Pereda failed completely in all his dramatic endeavors; and his few plays are generously excluded from any serious evaluation of his work. He is seldom, if ever, mentioned as a playwright; and the theatrical efforts can be considered briefly as a sort of by-product of the total activity of Pereda as an artist.

Nevertheless, Pereda labored assiduously during this time in various facets of the dramatic field until, in 1864, he wisely collected and edited the more durable *cuadros de costumbres*. A partial explanation may be that Pereda was perhaps the most learned among the group at *La Abeja Montañesa* about theater, or at least he was the one who had seen at first hand the dramatic presentations in Madrid. In any case, Pereda took charge of the theatrical reviews for the magazine as he had also done for the few issues of *El Tío Cayetano*. He then tried his hand at dramatic composition without any significant recognition. In 1861 he produced *Tanto tienes, tanto vales* (Your Wealth Is Your Worth) in honor of a visit to Santander by Isabel II, and in December of that year he wrote the libretto for a light comedy in verse, *Palos en seco* (Whacks Without Reason). In 1863 he composed a humorous skit, *Marchar con el siglo* (To Be with the Times), and a *zarzuela* ("musical comedy"), *Mundo, amor y vanidad* (World, Love, and Vanity). Finally, in 1866, Pereda ended temporarily his dramatic endeavors with another *zarzuela, Terrones*

y pergaminos (Farms and Parchments), in which he more happily
fused an average dramatic sense with his winning device of local-
color sketches, portraying vividly the atmosphere of Santander.

V *A Questionable Success*

The stage was set for Pereda to progress beyond the literary
limelight of Santander, which he had been entertaining in print and
on the stage since 1858, to the rest of Spain and particularly the
capital, scene of his disillusioning adventures ten years earlier. His
first article, signed with his full name, was published by *La Abeja
Montañesa* in July of 1864; and this essay, "Los zánganos de la Pren-
sa" (The Drones of the Press), shows traces of his wry humor and
penetrating observations in the forthcoming book. Shortly
thereafter, Pereda published *Escenas montañesas* (Mountain Scenes)
with a prologue by Antonio de Trueba, a popular author of *costumbrista* articles generally describing the Basque region. Trueba's introductory essay provided Pereda with a questionable success in this
initial lengthy work intended for a wider audience than the expected
friendly readers of Santander. Trueba, sincerely expressing his
honest feelings about Pereda's representation of Santander, con-
cluded that this neophyte author from the North had supplied only
the harsh, unfavorable side of life in his home province. It is true
that Pereda's eighteen sketches are not only realistic but verge on
the naturalistic, although he would have denied this. Actually,
Pereda had departed significantly from the romantic formulas in
constant usage. Later, Marcelino Menéndez Pelayo, Pereda's compatriot from Santander and staunch friend, criticized Trueba's interpretation as an ineffective reading of the texts. Pereda never again
called upon Trueba for the latter's dubious support, and he dis-
creetly omitted the prologue by "my renowned literary godfather"
in the edition of his *Obras completas* (Complete Works).

The damage was done, however, and Pereda's first attempt to use
Santander as literary material failed completely to attract any attention outside his home province. He had dedicated this book to Juan
Agapito, in gratitude for the older brother's faith and solicitude; and
therefore this apparent failure must have been more painful for
Pereda. Hartzenbusch and Mesonero Romanos, a romantic and a
costumbrista writer, respectively, offered the sole major sources of
approval for the discouraged author of *Escenas montañesas;* but
their encouraging comments arrived in the form of personal letters
rather than in the desired form of newspaper and magazine articles.

The ultimate blow for Pereda came from the readers of Santander, whom he knew warmly and regarded as a sympathetic public for his pictures of the *Montaña*, because the predominantly middle-class public reacted against the selection of types, scenes, and situations showing poor, unfortunate aspects of their society. These readers of the new middle class desired not only a realistic panorama of their province but a vision of the Highlands in which the spirit was happy, optimistic, humorous, and light. In short, the reaction of Santander proved unflattering to Pereda because of his supposedly injurious and unjust interpretations of the North. Trueba's prologue, coinciding in general with these unhappy and bitter conclusions of the people of Santander, may have been a partial cause for the reaction against Pereda. Some explanation can be also offered in the mentality of the new rising bourgeoisie who wanted only pleasant publicity about Santander for commercial, social, and political advantages.

Pereda's pride and sensitivity compelled him to react silently but effectively in a way that he must intimately have dreaded: a trip abroad, away from the illusory security of Santander. He left for Paris in December of 1864, where a residence of several months resulted in the predictable unhappiness, homesickness, and disillusion with the life of a large city. Paris, enjoying increasing fame as the capital of the Second Empire, seemed to Pereda a spiritual and moral trap, probably more so than Madrid during his sojourn a decade earlier. Little is definitely known about Pereda's experiences in Paris during the early months of 1865, but the general impressions of biographers and commentators, despite the author's reticence, are convincing as to the influential results of this disturbing confrontation with the exciting, strenuous Parisian activities. Pereda, all are agreed, read widely as usual, certainly made or renewed his acquaintance with the realists, such as Balzac, and perhaps came into contact with the emerging naturalists.[6]

The return to Santander, somewhat like the dejected return from Madrid, found Pereda dissatisfied with conditions in his home city and province. The memories of *Escenas montañesas* seemingly had endured and hardened during his absence or, at least, his highly sensitive nature perceived a cool reception among the social circles of Santander. Pereda was elected secretary of the newly organized Ateneo Científico y Literario (Literary and Scientific Atheneum) in Santander, but he felt that this post was an insult rather than an honor because the presidency of this society appeared the more worthy reward for his devotion to the city. Obviously, such a delicate sense of honor looked for, and found, more causes of presumed scorn. Pereda read two papers before the Atheneum entitled "La Romería del Carmen" (The Pilgrimage of Our Lady of Mount Carmel) and "Mi primer sombrero" (My First Hat), a series of minor reminiscences in a light vein to which listeners failed to show any enthusiasm or appreciation. A local newspaper printed a derogatory column about Pereda's two lectures, and he retreated from the unsympathetic world of Santander. Pereda's extreme and often unjustified reactions to unfavorable criticism constitute a definite pattern, unfortunately, and throughout his life Pereda showed an excessive concern for immediate, favorable attention, overtly solicited approval from friends and supporters, and tended to sulk in an isolated retreat when the critical brickbats come. This psychological mannerism is illustrated in Pereda's refusal to collaborate further in the columns of *La Abeja Montañesa*, in his temporary abandonment of writing in favor of more reading, and in the withdrawal from the Atheneum.

The political situation, which Pereda had previously scorned as a malady of his age, again attracted his attention, perhaps in compensation for the supposed slights of the Atheneum and Santander, in general. Also, the end of Isabel II's reign was rapidly approaching because of the national consensus about her incompetency as a ruler and unexemplary behavior as a woman. All groups, despite their lack of cooperation and internecine disharmony, concurred in the demand for her removal and a different government. Pereda had witnessed in 1854 an early manifestation of the revolutionary spirit which now spread throughout the country, resulting in the queen's forced abdication in 1868. The decision, therefore, cannot be solely attributed to Pereda's pique when he veered toward the maelstrom of Spanish politics after the questionable success of *Escenas montañesas* and the attendant coolness of his neighbors in the Highlands.

VI   *No Hope in Politics*

Pereda's renewed enthusiasm for politics, sparked by his fear of liberal, radical inroads against the traditionalism of the *Montaña*, lasted for almost five years, from the end of 1867 until the last months of 1872. Happily, other personal and literary interests succeeded in bringing him satisfaction and recognition, and the disillusionments of this renewed tilt at the windmills of the outside world did not cause Pereda such anguish as in the past. The first failure of this period came with his collaboration for the resurrected version of *El Tío Cayetano,* a journalistic mouthpiece for Carlism. By now Pereda had decided that the Carlists represented the only hope for Spain as he wanted the nation — a bulwark against the progressive ideas of the nineteenth century. Although Pereda's writings for the newspaper lack any important literary substance, these journalistic efforts nevertheless demonstrate clearly and effectively the philosophy and ideology he would later espouse more successfully in his novels. The strident, fanatical note of Pereda's contributions surpassed the intentions of his collaborators, and few were ready to follow him on the warpath for Carlism when he seemingly preferred another civil war in the unrealistic hope of restoring Don Carlos to the throne. Calmer observers, even in the staunchly conservative North, realized that the more logical solution for their ideals would be a Bourbon monarchy with Alfonso XII, son of Isabel II, as the king.

Thus, *El Tío Cayetano* enjoyed only a brief second life from November 9, 1867 until July, 1869, despite Pereda's frequent columns and sustained zeal. However, he had secured an audience, pro and con, which recognized his abilities as a writer and his attitudes, emerging as a political entity on the rapidly changing scene; and Pereda also found his prestige restored in Santander, despite the unwillingness of the majority to follow him completely in renewed battle with the rulers in Madrid. In 1870 Pereda accompanied Fernando Fernández de Velasco, a prominent Carlist citizen of Santander, on a trip to Vevey, Switzerland, for the purpose of establishing contact with Don Carlos, the pretender to the shaky throne. The strategy for the Carlists, in opposition to Pereda's original views as expounded in *El Tío Cayetano,* centered around victory in the elections, an ironic dependence for success upon a procedure which these traditionalists really wanted to eliminate.

From 1868 until 1875, Spain witnessed the coming and going of six types of government: the monarchy of the Bourbons, a provisional committee, a regency, an elective kingship, a republic, a military directorate, and again, the monarchy of the Bourbons. The succession of governments was kaleidoscopic: the forced abdication of Isabel II in 1868; the comic-opera reign of an Italian prince, Amadeo of Savoy, 1870-73; the abortive First Republic, lasting barely a year until 1874; another *pronunciamiento* by a disgruntled general at the end of that experiment; and at last, the restoration of the Bourbons under Alfonso XII in 1875. Salvador de Madariaga ex-

presses the puzzlement of many Spaniards when he asks of this era:
"What could they do? They had lost half a century fighting: fighting
against the French; fighting among themselves; fighting the
hostility of a despicable court; fighting — the hardest fight, perhaps,
of all — against their own political shortcomings."[7]

Pereda, however, continued to enjoy this confusing and
frustrating internal struggle; and he eagerly accepted designation as
the Carlist candidate for election from the district of Cubiérnaga to
the Cortes in Madrid. The Carlists had adopted an astute — and
winning — plan of action because the leading promoters of the
cause, after the conferences with the exiled pretender, had organized
in the province a political club, a *Círculo Tradicionalista*
("Traditionalist Circle"), in Santander. These "traditionalists"
rallied to their banner the numerous partisans in Santander, and
they "got out the vote" enthusiastically, assuring Pereda's election.
Pereda abandoned his usual preference for isolation by traveling
throughout the region, to the exclusion of his familiar concentration
upon reading. He later utilized these experiences and his reactions in
the early political novelette *Los hombres de pro* (Men of Worth). In
1871, therefore, Pereda, as the Traditionalist, or Carlist, deputy to
the Cortes once more journeyed to Madrid, where he soon became
disgusted with the futile maneuvers of politicians and the inept
governments. After the dissolution of the Cortes in 1872, Pereda
returned to Santander and turned away from politics, at least from
any further solicitation of governmental participation, for the rest of
his life. Again, the psychological effects of this additional disillusionment in the city and in national events pained Pereda greatly, and he
slipped once more into a mood of vexation, retreat, and depression.
He recovered quickly, however, thanks to the fact that the people of
Santander still accepted Pereda as a honored citizen of the *Montaña*
and that devoted friends and family supported him.

VII *First Literary Phase*

During these fruitless years spent in the morass of Spanish internal
strife Pereda had little time to devote to writing, and his depressed
mood at the end of 1872 extended to his failure as an author. Almost
forty years old, Pereda considered himself a failure because he had
published only two books with very limited success: *Escenas montañesas*, ignored by audiences outside Santander and disliked by
most of the province's inhabitants; and *Tipos y paisajes* (Types and
Landscapes), essentially a continuation of the first work, which

gained some limited critical favor but little popular attention, after publication in 1871. It is possible that Pereda's presence in Madrid at this time as a Carlist delegate, where the traditionalists enjoyed little support, may have contributed to the loss of a greater audience. Nevertheless, the attention that he did receive certainly helped his later fame and erased the unhappy memories of his ardent espousal of the Carlist cause. For example, two recognized authors, Gaspar Núñez de Arce and Benito Pérez Galdós, congratulated Pereda on his achievement in *Tipos y paisajes*. Pereda's lifelong friendship with Galdós, a major literary acquaintanceship of nineteenth-century Spanish literature, started at this date. There is no doubt that Galdós, who traveled to Santander in the summer of 1871 for the purpose of meeting Pereda in person and seeing the *Montaña*, stimulated and encouraged the dejected writer of Santander. Both writers, opposed so obviously in spirit, style, and subject, nevertheless provide the notable example of artists exchanging views and differences on a friendly basis. The visit of Galdós to Pereda, who introduced him to the life of Santander, revealed an immediate empathy between the two men, and both authors rejoiced in the mutual cordiality of this initial encounter.[8]

Again, Pereda was fortunate at this critical and decisive moment of his life and career in having friends whom he could rely upon for generous encouragement. This period also marks the beginning of the close ties between Pereda and Marcelino Menéndez Pelayo. The latter, a native of Santander like Pereda, was about to publish his first critical studies that established his name as the foremost scholar of nineteenth-century Spain. Menéndez Pelayo shared Pereda's conservative philosophy and love of the *Montaña*, and he, like Galdós, revived Pereda's lagging vocation as a writer. More than Galdós, in fact, who lived almost all the time in Madrid, Menéndez Pelayo, as a neighbor and compatriot of Pereda, enjoyed more direct contact with the older and more influential citizen of Santander.[9]

During these same years, the end of the first literary phase, Pereda (who had suffered the loss of his father in 1862) was grieved by Juan Agapito's death in 1870. Happily, Pereda had married in 1869 a woman who complemented him perfectly, incarnating his concept of the traditional Spanish wife and mother. Diodora de la Revilla Huidobro, a lady belonging to the same aristocratic society as Pereda, adhered to the conservative, religious, and rural loyalties; and she silently served her husband throughout his life by her love, devotion, attention, and understanding of his dejected moods and writing agonies. There seems no question that Pereda's marriage on both sides exemplified the best hopes of the traditionalist society that husband and wife sincerely and enthusiastically advocated. For Pereda, the union secured him stability in his personal struggle against apparent failure as an author and politician, and his personal future looked more promising as he embarked upon an intensive period of reading and social life in his retreats at Polanco and San- tander.[10]

VIII   *The Second Phase*

The rather gloomy conclusion to Pereda's first literary phase, definitely a failure in his eyes, neglected alike by the critics and public, was followed by four years of silence until 1876. Family and friends saved Pereda from any possible repetition of the dangerous crisis of his youth, and he seemed more disposed to slip gently into a life of comfort and ease. It appears, however, from the remaining evidence of Pereda's activities during these four years of artistic hibernation that he was stirred from the doldrums not so much by his own ambition as by the efforts of many friends. particularly Galdós and Menéndez Pelayo.[11] Pereda's return to the literary arena in 1876 may be more than accidental because this year witnessed a shift in the direction of Spanish politics and literature.

Although Pereda was not tempted to renew his bout with the politicians of Madrid, he must have been very satisfied with the accession of Alfonso XII to the throne and the success of a conser- vative government which slowly defeated any liberalizing forces in the Cortes and in the other national institutions, such as the univer- sities. This period, known as the Restoration in Spanish history, lasted with little effective opposition and only minor domestic dis- turbances until 1898, when the disastrous war with the United States revealed the convenient but deteriorating façade of the régime. Pereda's popularity and esteem were at a peak in the same two decades between 1876 and 1898, and his fame started to decline sharply in the aftermath of "the splendid little war" (in the words of Theodore Roosevelt), along with the fortunes of a majority of the literary stars of the nineteenth century.

If, however, Pereda's happiness as a husband, father, and solid citizen of Santander assured him of an idyllic background and source of inspiration for renewed attack upon his goal of literary greatness, the development of the Spanish novel by 1876 also showed him the way to imitate and emulate his contemporaries. Fernán Caballero, who dominated the novelistic genre from 1849 until approximately

1870, had clearly influenced and impressed Pereda.[12] In 1870, Galdós experimented with the historical novel and by 1876 had found a successful formula with his series of *Episodios nacionales* (National Episodes), which were based upon nineteenth-century Spanish history. Also, Galdós in 1876 published two of his several outstanding *novelas contemporáneas* ("contemporary novels"), *Doña Perfecta* and *Gloria*. In 1874, the renaissance of the Spanish novel emerged assuredly with Juan Valera's *Pepita Jiménez* and Pedro Antonio de Alarcón's *El sombrero de tres picos* (The Three-Cornered Hat). Pereda's silence between the years 1872 and 1876, or at least his failure to publish any book between *Tipos y paisajes* (Types and Landscapes) in 1871 and the appearance of three short novels in a collection in 1876, cannot be blamed upon a lack of knowledge of the Spanish novel during this time.

The second phase of Pereda's career as a writer, comprising the years when he progressed logically and surely from short stories and novelettes to the lengthy, current vogue of the modern nineteenth-century novel, coincides with his establishment as an important author. Pereda could have stopped publishing works in 1884, the end of this second period, when he began the preparation of the *Obras completas* (Complete Works), and he would have remained in literary history as a noteworthy contributor to the realistic novel. This intensive period, from 1876 until 1884, gained for Pereda critical and popular acclaim for which he had yearned in previous years, although doubts persisted as to his ability and energy to produce works of the first category, novels that would transcend the boundaries of literary history and merit aesthetic, intrinsic respect and immortality. Nonetheless, the books of this second phase reveal long hours of preparation in terms of length and skilled organization.

In 1876, Pereda had joined with some friends in Santander, including Menéndez Pelayo, to start a new magazine, *La Tertulia* (The Club), under the leadership of Francisco Mazón. Pereda's collaboration, augmented by the urgings of his friends and admirers, finally impelled him to publish in that year *Bocetos al temple* (Sketches in Distemper), a collection of three short novels, *La mujer de César* (Caesar's Wife), *Los hombres de pro* (Men of Worth), and *Oros son triunfos* (Diamonds Are Trump). Actually, the first two novels had been published before in 1870 and 1871, respectively, in magazines in which they had received little recognition. The third novel, probably completed in 1875, was included to provide thematic continuity and to allow the volume to compete in size with the standard novels of the age. Pereda, in his biting satire of contemporary politics and the hypocritical formulas of polite social circles, certainly drew blood from his opponents, who realized the seriousness of his critical attacks upon liberal ideas throughout the three stories, in addition to his pointed references to the vices and defects of city life. Menéndez Pelayo wrote a penetrating commentary on *Bocetos al temple*, which added to the savor of this first true success for his countryman from Santander.

This success of 1876 served as a catalyst for Pereda, who, in the following year, prepared a second edition of *Escenas montañesas* and published *Tipos trashumantes* (Nomadic Types), short stories and sketches, based on impressions of summer tourists in Santander. The shrewd depictions of city dwellers swarming over the tranquil landscape of the *Montaña*, satirical portrayals for the most part, again won Pereda both attention and attacks, which he undoubtedly preferred to omission or polite disregard; and his loyal compatriot, Menéndez Pelayo, printed another meritorious review of *Tipos trashumantes*. In the meantime, Galdós had defended *Bocetos al temple* although Pereda's attitudes were not in agreement with his own vision of the Spanish problem; and Galdós had also urged liberal foes of Pereda to accept the challenge of seeing in print the ideas of conservatives and traditionalists, such as the writer from Santander. By now, however, Pereda had decided to undertake a positive defense of his ideals and those of the *Montaña* instead of the negative (although highly successful and respected) criticisms of the city and contemporary life.

Once more, Menéndez Pelayo played an affirmative part in Pereda's decision, and later, further impelled the latter to a still more lasting contribution to the novelistic genre in Spain. Pereda, encouraged by Menéndez Pelayo's observation that the theme was unexploited, prepared his first long novel, which he published in 1878. *El buey suelto* (The Bachelor) is more correctly transcribed as *El buey suelto . . .*, an abbreviation for the Spanish expression *El buey suelto bien se lame* ("The loose ox licks himself well"), referring to the independence and self-reliance of the single person, or bachelor. Pereda, however, took the opposite approach in this first novel, defending the advantages of the married state for men and showing the shallowness of single life. More indirectly, and certainly more astutely, Pereda was thereby praising a cornerstone of a stable, conservative, religious society in this literary treatment of marriage as good and necessary for all young men. A thesis novel, therefore, became the vehicle for Pereda's sustained beliefs in traditionalism as essential for the rebirth of true Spanish greatness. No reviews appeared immediately, and Pereda complained bitterly to Menéndez Pelayo about this neglect; but when the commentaries finally started to appear, Pereda was equally distressed because the reactions were very unfavorable. The general tone of the reviews, led by the prestigious voice of "Clarín" (the pseudonym of Leopoldo Alas), one of the most important critics of the nineteenth century, expressed disapproval of Pereda's portrayals, overt didacticism, and lack of impartiality about the questions of bachelorhood and marriage.

For the first time, however, Pereda reacted aggressively and more maturely (and fortunately for the world of Spanish literature) by publishing the next year another — and better — *novela de tesis.* This new thesis novel, *Don Gonzalo González de la Gonzalera* (Don Gonzalo González of Gonzalera) conveys in the humorously poetical, pompous title all the invective of Pereda against the *indianos,* or Spaniards who made their fortunes in the New World and returned to Spain, expecting to enter quickly into the aristocratic social circles. The political barbs stood out in this second novel, and Pereda, instead of weakening before the adverse criticism of *El buey suelto,* increased his scorn of the ineffective liberal, democratic attempts at government. Pereda, then, no longer retreated and sulked when he failed to win acclaim; he had psychologically matured enough that strongly held viewpoints were maintained but were refined by a first-rate style and technique. And the critics, although still in disagreement with Pereda's ideas, greeted this new novel warmly and approvingly. Clarín, for example, welcomed Pereda into the ranks of the leading novelists of this important decade in the history of the Spanish novel. *Don Gonzalo González de la Gonzalera,* although not one of the two best, most lasting novels of Pereda, is nevertheless proof that Pereda, both personally and as a man of letters, was achieving artistic stability and carving a niche in the wider area of literature beyond the limits of Santander. If one point or one year could be indicated when Pereda's success was solidly determined, the date of publication of *Don Gonzalo González de la Gonzalera* can be defended as evidence of decisive self-confidence and energetic endeavor for further work by the novelist.[13]

IX *A Successful Literary Routine*

The next five years of Pereda's second phase brought all the success — critical, popular and financial — desired by the author. Inspired by a winning formula, he worked long hours at the composition of his novels, planning more works illustrating his theses about the structure of Spain, good and bad. He was likewise fortunate in his friendships because Menéndez Pelayo in 1878 had secured the Chair of Spanish Literature at the Universidad Central, or University of Madrid, and Galdós was acclaimed as the most promising novelist of nineteenth-century Spain. Pereda's relationships with the two men were warmer than ever, and Galdós continued to spend part of the summer in Santander. But the growing importance of Galdós as the literary spokesman for liberal ideas and against traditional values, especially the church, forced Pereda to the attack. Thanks to the graciousness and courtesy of the two authors, the argumentative discussions, orally and in writing, never caused such rancor that an estrangement resulted. In 1897, Galdós, upon replying to Pereda's acceptance speech in the Real Academia Española, mentioned this aspect of their friendship:

> I remember that, in the early times of our relationship, twenty-five years ago, when we used to speak of literary matters or of the various political questions connected with them, we saw our spirits of fraternal concord confused so soon, as if separated by a deep and wide furrow which I saw no way to fill. Our delightful conversations often ended in arguments, but their animation never went beyond the limits of cordiality. Pereda never yielded. He is uncompromising, with a homogeneous character, and of a temperament which excludes any alteration. He conquered from me territories relatively vast more easily than I won any inches of terrain. But it is correct to say candidly that he lost them again as soon as we separated, and the inch of ground, if by chance I succeeded in winning it with great effort, was recovered by my opposite; and at the first interview again, we found ourselves in the same position, he with his beliefs and I with my opinions.[14]

Certainly, in 1880 the closest approach to a breach between the literary and social friends occurred when Pereda published *De tal palo, tal astilla* (A Chip off the Old Block), a novelistic answer first to Galdós's *Gloria* (Glory) and also to his novel *La familia de León Roch* (The Family of León Roch), two works in which tolerance was preached and religious fanaticism was criticized as a prominent ill of Spain. Pereda's insistence that theological orthodoxy and loyalty to the Church were the keystones to all Spanish traditional virtues and necessary guides to a future return to national greatness compelled critics to associate the literary and philosophic qualities of the novel. The reaction, led again by the just, prestigious voice of Clarín, found Pereda's "ContraGloria" (CounterGloria) inferior to the novel of

Galdós and also artistically and thematically disappointing after the promise of *Don Gonzalo González de la Gonzalera.* However, Pereda retained his secure position as the novelistic rallying point for the conservative, rural, traditional parties in Spain.

A change, or perhaps the tactful decision to desist from biting satire against the liberals and social changes in the country for a time, occurred in the subject matter of Pereda's sustained output during the following two years. In 1881 Pereda published *Esbozos y rasguños* (Outlines and Sketches), portraying scenes and characters from the neighborhoods of Santander, reminiscent of his previous books of local-color material; and in 1882 he returned to the novel with *El sabor de la tierruca* (Redolent of the Soil), a story with the prologue by Galdós. Despite their previous confrontation over *De tal palo, tal astilla,* Galdós acknowledged the novel's merit, and Pereda's contribution to the regional, descriptive novel drew from Don Benito a warm, penetrating prologue. Galdós, astutely and correctly, summed up Pereda's compelling personality, in sharp contrast with the expected picture of a cantankerous reactionary as many liberal observers imagined, and thereby the Galdosian interpretation of Pereda enhanced the latter's standing as a sincere, intelligent, and honorable defender of the traditionalist arguments. Also, Galdós accurately grasped that Pereda's claim to literary glory could be better based, not on slashing attacks against liberal and modern tendencies, but on the description of his home region, the province of Santander, emphasizing the regional advantages. Of course, conservative critics praised Pereda heartily, and Menéndez Pelayo (ironically coinciding with Galdós in his insistence upon regionalism, emphasing the Montaña) rejoiced that Pereda had found the path to the development of an authentic Spanish novel: "Blessed be, then, this rustic and highland book, permeated by country odors, and which brings us neither problems, conflicts, tendencies, meanings, nor any other such thing except that which God put in the world to gladden the eyes of mortals: water and air, grass and light, strength and life!"[15]

However, the 1880's were the years of emerging naturalism, that timid (yet bold for Spain) step off the accepted highway of realism and regionalism, recognized as attributes of Pereda's technique. Clarín had previously thrown some sharp darts at Pereda's lack of concern for the less fortunate persons of the *Montaña,* although he had equitably rendered due praise for a rounded portrayal in another novel. Now, however, Emilia Pardo Bazán sarcastically described

Pereda's idyllic vision of Santander as "his beautiful garden, watered and tended well . . . but of limited horizons."[16] Pereda, stung by his neighbors' earlier rebuttals in *Escenas montañesas* and some other sketches, had changed in the direction of idealization, away from negative realism, and thus he faced by 1882 a dilemma: either to continue the idyll or to join the current of naturalism. His name was certainly known and accepted in all literary circles of the peninsula, his previous withdrawals from activity when adversity struck were no longer a characteristic of his reactions, and he undoubtedly felt confident about his talents. Pereda, therefore, published quickly *Pedro Sánchez* in 1883, his only venture into a purely Spanish classical form, the picaresque novel; and his success was conceded by all the critics, including Clarín. Pedro Sánchez, a modern picaresque hero, recalls Pereda's own misadventures in Madrid and subsequent return to the land; but the novel is also a realistic account of the problems of urban politics and life.

Two years had passed between the publication of *El sabor de la tierruca* and *Pedro Sánchez*, works with some fundamental similarities of themes but with a mature progression evident in the technique and conception. In short, Pereda, becoming more than a mere polemicist for rural life and tradition, had conquered the immediate antipathies of urban or liberal audiences by his abilities as a novelist. Until now, Pereda had naturally remained in the *Montaña*, preferring to exchange views with his correspondents, accepting visits willingly, and converting his homes, especially in Polanco, into welcome centers for cultural activities. José Zorrilla, the conservative dean of Spanish romanticism, was received enthusiastically by Pereda during the former's visit to the province of Santander in 1882.

Finally, Pereda in 1884 made a tour of Spain where the receptions were consistently favorable and laudatory. In the same year, the publication of the first volume of his *Obras completas* (Complete Works) with a long critical introduction by Menéndez Pelayo, cemented Pereda's works as a major contribution to nineteenth-century Spanish literature. In this essay, he was ranked with Galdós and Valera, above Clarín and Pardo Bazán, who, however, had still not produced their major novels. Pereda's friendships had widened vastly, and his correspondence (currently coming increasingly to light despite his decline in popularity) opened many doors to him during the triumphal visits throughout the peninsula. Thus, Pereda in 1884 stood on a pinnacle of popular and critical acclaim, although he had certainly not yet produced a novel of the first category. Instead, with all credit due his assiduous workmanship and maturing artistry, he had written a series of good novels utilizing skillfully realism in the first place and regionalism as a secondary element.

X   *The Third, Best Phase*

Despite now occupying the position that he had so long desired, Pereda undertook the composition of a novel that he believed would better satisfy his compatriots in the province of Santander as well as those critics demanding a broader view of Spanish life. By refusing to continue in the successful literary routine of the previous period, Pereda produced his best novel to this date, the outstanding Spanish contribution to sea fiction in the nineteenth century, and the novelistic masterpiece which has earned him a continuing fame. Pereda would be relegated to second rank, and justifiably, without the addition of *Sotileza* (Fine Spun). Immediately upon the novel's publication in 1885, Pereda obtained overwhelming acclamations in Santander and throughout Spain. For the first time, without qualifications, the local and the cosmopolitan readers had no complaint. The municipal government of the capital city of Santander even went so far as to rename a section, *Rampa de Sotileza* ("Ramp of Sotileza"), and a painting, depicting a scene from the novel, was commissioned by friends for a place of honor. The story of the orphan girl, Sotileza — set against the impoverished but honorable lives of the fishermen of Santander, which is realistically and sentimentally described in extensive passages — emerged as the apex of the regional novel. It represents the culmination of a development from Fernán Caballero's books after Pereda's initiation with *costumbrismo*. This local-color quality had been of course exploited by Pereda in his first writings, such as *Escenas montañesas*, and was pursued by him in continuations of this book, before ultimate fusion into the modern novel.

Pereda's friends, content and proud, realized that he had at last met the challenge of the Spanish novel, as he viewed the problem. Menéndez Pelayo had long insisted on this type of novel as Pereda's best vehicle for the combined defense of traditionalism and artistic expression; and Galdós, although obviously no writer of regional books, believed that his long relationship with Pereda had aided both authors. Galdós appreciated more fully the beauties and virtues of the country, and Pereda journeyed more frequently beyond his *patria chica*, thereby tempering his previous attacks upon liberal, modern ideas and ways. Pereda visited Madrid again, in 1885, for a ceremony in memory of Mesonero Romanos, the early *costumbrista* essayist and a probable influence upon the now successful novelist; and the circles of his friendships widened. In addition to literary correspondents such as Narcís Oller, Pereda met Armando Palacio Valdés; and he visited Clarín and Emilia Pardo Bazán, establishing a very personal knowledge of the two naturalist advocates and novelists (against whom he had tilted in the past). These meetings came after a trip to Portugal in that same year, 1885, with Galdós.

Returning to Santander, Pereda consolidated his literary efforts for the next three years, until 1888. He was principally occupied with the publication of his *Obras completas,* although he surprisingly joined an industrial enterprise with his brother and brother-in-law. Undoubtedly, much time was consumed in correspondence, social and personal business, which his recognized position as a writer and leading citizen of Santander demanded. The concentration upon *Sotileza* produced a logical need for a rest from the agonies of composition,and for a period of reflection and decision about the future orientation of his works. Pereda had determined not to retreat into the security of past accolades with present rumors of election to the Real Academia Española.[17]

Naturalism, shortly before 1890, had clearly taken precedence as the dominant movement in the Spanish novel, and even Galdós, the master of the realist school, was veering toward naturalistic themes and characterizations in his continuing productions. Pereda, representing the apex of such tendencies as regionalism and the lingering *costumbrismo*, must have realized that he had arrived at the top precisely when the aesthetic norms of his works were being replaced by vastly different literary forces. In 1888, then, Pereda boldly published *La Montálvez* (The Lady Montálvez), a novel criticized more harshly than any previous work as too naturalistic. Even his loyal supporters through past skirmishes with the critics could not condone this novel, which they felt abandoned all the traditionalist, religious tenets governing portrayal of the "immoral"ideas of the naturalists. Menéndez Pelayo, for the first time, chided Pereda privately in a letter, gently but clearly, and refrained from printing his conclusions. Perhaps portrayal of the negative side of the decadent aristocracy — treated by Clarín, Pardo Bazán, and certainly Galdós — galled the shocked followers of Pereda, who expected despite many trials and adversities "a happy ending," or at least the triumph of rural qualities over those of the city, as Pereda had so repeatedly treated in previous books. In all fairness, however, the author's technique in *La Montálvez* (The Lady Montálvez) revealed what the critics failed to note — a diminishing of artistic powers. Pereda, in short, had actually reached the high point of his novelistic career in *Sotileza*.

Pereda's skill at composition did not deteriorate absolutely, however, and the remainder of his productions oscillated sharply between a few excellent novels and other mediocre books. For example, *La puchera* (The Stew), published in 1889, is accepted by some as one of Pereda's best works, especially by José Montesinos. In 1891 Pereda produced two ineffective, weak novels, *Nubes de estío* (Summer Clouds) and *Al primer vuelo* (On the First Flight). By 1893, if not earlier, Pereda was preparing his final novel, *Peñas arriba* (The Upper Peaks). Strictly speaking, the last novel was *Pachín González* in 1896; but some controversy exists as to whether the latter book was terminated as Pereda wished or whether the narration as is belongs within the *reportaje* ("newspaper reporting") rather than the classification of the novel.

Pereda knew during these years that his reputation was supported by all critics, favorable and unfavorable, and that Clarín, for instance, was advocating (among many other friends and admirers) his admittance into the Real Academia Española. Technically, Pereda did not reside in the capital, which constituted an obstacle to his candidacy for the Royal Spanish Academy, attendance being required. Unfortunately, a polemic with Emilia Pardo Bazán in 1891 about Pereda's two novels, *La Montálvez* and *Nubes de estío* — not his most outstanding books, of course — caused some alienation in literary circles, and attention to the weaknesses of his writings. The exchanges, published in the important newspaper, *El Imparcial* (The Impartial), were begun by Pardo Bazán in an article, "Los resquemores de Pereda" (The Stings of Pereda) and answered by Pereda in "Las comezones de la señora Pardo Bazán" (The Itches of the Lady Pardo Bazan). Pereda recouped lost ground with his opponents by taking part in some celebrations in Barcelona (always a hotbed of separatism) during which he spoke on a topic dear to the people of this province — regionalism and the patria chica. This visit in 1892, where he again saw Narcís Oller, provided Pereda with the occasion to defend his interpretation of the Spanish novel as love of the "little homeland." In 1893 Pereda received Oller in Santander where, at a banquet attended by many old friends and now famous personalities, such as Galdós, Pereda praised Catalonian literature as the most illustrious of Spanish regional writings. Also, Galdós had triumphed in the theater with *La loca de la casa* (The Madwoman of the House); and this congenial setting — another example of the amiable relationships despite literary differences — of the *Montaña* became perhaps one of the last felicitous gatherings for these writers, critics, and intellectuals before the divisive date of 1898.

Meanwhile, Pereda's long agony over the writing of *Peñas arriba*, another indication of his diminishing powers because he had previously worked rapidly, had been compounded by physical decline and family problems after 1890. Again, the following reverses may also explain the uneven quality of his books in the last decade of the nineteenth century. In 1890, deaths in his family and ill health plagued Pereda, psychologically and physically. The loss of a brother, Manuel, and shortly thereafter a brother-in-law (with whom he had previously joined in business), disturbed Pereda greatly; and he now suffered acutely from a series of maladies, such as colitis. Little has been said about Pereda's family life because there were few exceptional events in his happily married years; and he, as one may recall, led a very tranquil, routine existence, without some of the exciting — and bizarre — episodes of the romantics, for example, and even of his contemporaries. Pereda, like his parents, became the father of a very large number of children; and he, like many of the parents of his age, saw them die before reaching maturity. Three offspring, born in the early years of the marriage, between 1871 and 1875, died in childhood. Pereda's strong religious faith, conservatism, and traditionalism accepted these crises sorrowfully but as part of the divine destiny in which he professed so constantly.[18]

In 1893, when he was frustratingly endeavoring to complete *Peñas arriba*, so long delayed, his oldest son, Juan Manuel, shot himself in the garden of Pereda's home on the second of September. The young man, in a mood of deep depression, had evidently become mentally deranged; and Pereda, shocked to see his dead son in the arms of his wife, confronted this serious crisis at a moment when several adversities, those of family and health, had already saddened him. For a Catholic, especially for one so orthodox and staunch as Pereda, suicide signified the loss of heaven and even the denial of burial in consecrated ground (the cemetery plot blessed by a priest before the interment). However, extenuating circumstances, such as insanity (which in the society of Santander must have been a stigma for a member of a prominent family like the Pereda household), can provide the justification for administration of the last rites of the Church. Pereda stifled his grief, sublimating his stunned feelings by a determination to finish *Peñas arriba*. He indicated in the manuscript, at the twenty-first chapter, with a cross and a date the day of Juan Manuel's suicide: and he dedicated the novel "to the holy memory of my son."

Another shock came when Pereda witnessed, two months later, the results of the explosion of the ship *Cabo de Machichaco* in the harbor of Santander, with a loss of six hundred dead and one thousand injured. He used the naval disaster as the topic for *Pachín González*, but he more immediately accepted a divine destiny, according to his fervent religious faith, which allowed not only his personal loss of a son but the universal suffering of so many deaths. Contrary to his youthful reactions, Pereda apparently stood fast in his beliefs and stoically set to work on the last third of *Peñas arriba*.

This novel, published in 1895, became an immediate best-seller and, in fact, ranked first in popularity among all his books. But the effort, representing the force of will against physical and mental distress, exhausted Pereda; and his career as a writer, with the exception of *Pachín González* and some dabbling in the theater, was finished. *Peñas arriba*, accepted as the rival of *Sotileza*, also settled any ideological and technical difficulties about Pereda's acceptance into the Real Academia Española. In the following year, Pereda received the notification of his election to this center of the Spanish establishment, thanks mainly to the persistent petitions of Menéndez Pelayo. Residency in the capital, the convenient but very legal excuse for Pereda's exclusion until 1896, was rationalized by his visit to Madrid, with printed announcements distributed about his decision to spend periods of time in the city, during a longer trip to Andalucía.

XI   *Triumph and Decline*

Pereda, observing all the polished and required forms, went to Madrid on the way to southern Spain with his daughter, María, and paid the ceremonial visits to the members of the Royal Spanish Academy. He also renewed acquaintanceships in the capital, added to his popularity with the attendant publicity, and reduced any lingering opposition among liberal circles by his affability. A just and happy choice of candidates for entrance into the Spanish Academy had been decided: Galdós entered as a member at the beginning of February, and Pereda joined the establishment on the twenty-first of

the same month. Undoubtedly, the ceremony of Pereda's acceptance, in addition to the normal panoply of literary glory, provided a
sparkling swan song of the old Spain, of the realist, regional, and
naturalist doctrines, with traces of the early romantic and *costumbrista* tendencies, on the eve of the twentieth century. Already, the
initial thrusts of the Generation of 1898, with the analyses of Joaquín
Costa, Angel Ganivet, and Miguel de Unamuno, were discarding the
topics of Pereda's speech and Galdós's reply. The brilliant setting of
the Royal Spanish Academy formed an ironic contrast with the approaching Spanish-American War and the revolt of the young
writers and intellectuals against the sway of the Real Academia
Española, including as a main target Pereda.

In the field of the novel, the addresses by Pereda and Galdós, the
two most prominent and successful representatives of the
nineteenth-century Spanish novel, offered a major defense and explanation of this genre, including their own contributions. Pereda
defined the regional novel "as that novel whose material is
developed in a district or place that has its own distinctive life,
characters, and color, all of which enter into the work as the most
principal part of it." At the same time, Pereda attacked foreign influences and imitations in the Spanish novel so that his theory of the
regional novel, and indirectly the Spanish novel in general, resides
around the geographical isolation of the novelistic form in content,
spirit, and description. There is everything "Spanish" in the peninsular novel, which will create a different, recognizable book of prose
fiction. For Pereda, then, the regional novel is the only highway
toward the goal of Spanish contribution to world literature; and this
regional novel must be based in the different provinces, or in short,
centered in the rural or country tradition.

Galdós, replying according to custom, accepted his friend's
defense and love of the regional novel as a distinctive school,
whereby Spain could contribute greatly to the other European
literatures. However, Don Benito, as he was affectionately
recognized in all circles, defended his own choice of locale in the urban centers: "In reality all of us are regionalists, although less
forcefully than Pereda, because all of us labor in some more or less
spacious corner, so to speak, of the Spanish soil. . . . It seems to me
that the metropolis is a region, and one of the most characteristic,
with its varied life, intermingled by elegant foreignisms and the
most Spanish stalenesses, joining native and exotic faults, pure-
blooded cajoleries and freedoms acquired in the open, frank manner

of modern societies." Galdós grasped that the nineteenth-century civilization, in Spain as much as in Europe, revolved around liberty — diversity of opinions and styles — within the hubbub of urban life. Pereda, on the other hand, logically and honestly presented an idyllic return to a past way of life. There is no finer moment in the lives and artistic orientations of these lifelong friends and literary opposites than in the two speeches to the Royal Spanish Academy, summing up their work.[19]

The remaining years of Pereda, overshadowed by the rapid changes in Spanish literature and politics because of the War of 1898, were further darkened by his almost compulsive attempts as a dramatist. The renewed efforts in the theater, reminiscent of youthful illusions about a career as a playwright, only added fuel to the critical and intellectual reaction against the themes and style of his novels, despite their continuing popularity. Failure or a lukewarm reception of some minor theatrical endeavors, and a general disregard of adaptations of his stories, contrasted with the attention given to Galdós as a dramatist. In 1901, Pereda wrote sympathetically to Galdós about *Electra*, Don Benito's scathing play about fanaticism and intolerance. Although Pereda adhered to the conservative, religious views denounced by Galdós, he ironically wrote to his friend that his opposition was rooted in rational discussion and disagreement — as Galdós had described their verbal quarrels many years ago — and not in blind alienation from another's theories. By 1902, Pereda had ceased writing extensively, but he traveled on occasion to see his children in the other provinces, and he remained quite active in the cultural and social life of Santander.

In 1903, the last, great honor came to Pereda and his other lifelong friend, Menéndez Pelayo, when the Spanish government awarded the Grand Cross of Alfonso XII to the two compatriots from Santander. In 1904, Pereda, overtaxing his strength on a trip to Andalucía to see his first grandchild, fell ill. He spent the remaining two years of his life as a semi-invalid in his country home at Polanco. Still a figure of respect, Pereda received visitors, usually from the circles of old friends and supporters; but even "Azorín," one of the young rebels of the Generation of 1898, paid a visit to Polanco in 1905 and published his impressionistic articles about the master of the regional novel in *ABC*, the important Madrid newspaper.

Pereda died on March 1, 1906, at Santander after a steady decline over a long period, and he was buried in the family plot at Polanco.

A memorial service in Madrid on April 23, 1906 — the traditional day and month of the death of Cervantes — was intended to associate the creator of Don Quixote with the *hidalgo montañés* (Highland hidalgo, or "nobleman") whom the man of the North seemed to parallel in his aristocratic, proud, and honorable personal qualities. Lamentably, the reaction against Pereda and his idyll of Spain was inflamed by the national disgrace of 1898, lending a negative, politically motivated tone to the ceremony — a premonition of Pereda's fall from critical favor. But Santander remembered its distinguished son by the dedication of a statue to Pereda on January 11, 1911, with Menéndez Pelayo the official delegate of King Alfonso XIII. Today, the visitor or tourist to Santander, Polanco, and the *Montaña* is still pleasingly reminded of Pereda's vision of the region.

CHAPTER 2

Early Literary Activities

I   *Escritos de juventud*

PEREDA'S early literary activities in the journals of Santander, dating between 1858 and 1879, have more than mere
historical significance as part of his complete writings, because the
promise of the future novelist and the defects of his vision are
equally visible in the *Escritos de juventud* (Youthful Writings).[1] The
bedrock of Pereda's outlook appears throughout the articles in the
rejection of the present age and in the defense of tradition. He sees
no positive features of nineteenth-century civilization: liberty leads
to chaos; religious tolerance results in a proliferation of cults,
destroying thereby the serene unity of Spanish Catholicism;
foreigners unjustly criticize Spain and national ways because the
material conditions in their own countries allow easier travel abroad;
and the political façade of republicanism conceals corruption, inefficiency, and the lack of any true progress. However, Pereda surprisingly concludes that "you will see our homeland when the true
revolution happens, the one that has never as yet appeared, the one
of honorable men against political gangs, the one of those who pay
and produce against those who take and devour" (I, 130).

Pereda's anger was directed principally against the turmoil of the
Revolution of 1868, and he ironically places a great deal of blame on
the press. The press is viewed as the mania of the masses, with conflicting opinions, viewpoints, and reports leading to quarrels and
fratricide. A civil war, the consequence of "la Gloriosa" (the Glorious
Revolution) as the events of 1868 were flamboyantly called, is
Pereda's dire prophecy for Spain, although he expresses hope that
such a tragedy will not occur. Never a middle-of-the-roader, Pereda
ends one article with the thesis: "Liberty and restraint, sovereignty
and tutelage do not fit in the same bag. Either frankly
revolutionaries or frankly conservatives" (I, 113). Apparently, the

thought that such a polarization would force a civil war never occurred to Pereda; or, at least, he did not discuss this possibility. Of course, Pereda had already selected the conservative path, and his dogmatic, emphatic "logic," as he characterizes his conclusion in the same essay, brooked no alterations. Foreigners, especially the French, are criticized sarcastically. In a very biting review of Renan's *Life of Jesus*, Pereda attacks the right to publish and to read without restrictions: "It is not enough that the people read; the people need to know how to choose what is suitable to read" (I, 116). The French author is pernicious in Pereda's opinion because traditional Christianity is undermined by the argument that Christ is a human rather than a divine person, and the historical role of Christianity is vital to Spanish civilization.

Nevertheless, Pereda is correct in many thrusts at the farce of liberal democracy in Spain during the second half of the nineteenth century. He saw clearly the hypocrisy and dishonesty of the politicians and the techniques of his age, and these negative views, so constantly and bitterly discussed, explain Pereda's rejection of his times. There are a few glimpses of his positive traits as a writer in these early writings: the creation of types, or rudimentary character studies, as in "Cosas de don Paco" (Things of Don Paco); the love of Santander, in particular in "Fragmento de una carta" (Fragment of a Letter); the employment of dialect, in "Correspondencia" (Correspondence); and the humorous, warm depiction of local customs, in "Cruzadas" (Crusades). None of the pieces, however, is outstanding in the total canon of Pereda's writings, and all the articles are obviously intended to please the local audiences in Santander. Pereda declares his *costumbrista* intentions and indicates his realistic method: "I should like to have as a painter of customs the necessary colors on my poor palette in order to show you very exactly the pleasant picture that this society represents" (I, 69).

II *Escenas montañesas*

Some earlier foreshadowing of *Escenas montañesas* (Mountain Scenes) does not fully explain the development of Pereda's first book because the scenes of the *Montaña*, or these Highlands, offer a remarkable change from the youthful writings.[2] Perhaps, also, the strong reaction against Pereda's sketches of Santander among his compatriots was due to their expectations created by his earlier ideas, as seen in various articles of the local press. Thus, a familiarity with Pereda's views, style, and subjects in the *Escritos de juventud* provides not only the logical starting point for any analysis of his later writings but also the basis for a better comprehension of the reaction to *Escenas montañesas,* a reaction that affected and influenced decisively the sensitive young author. Pereda mentioned only good in the life and ways of Santander and only evil in the nineteenth century throughout his early journalistic efforts; and he is uncompromising in his entire output for the press, with stress on political rather than literary purposes. Suddenly, then, Pereda's audience received a different and radically opposed negative picture of their province, presented as an equally truthful observation in a very natural language. Middle-class readers (who are omitted as a rule in all the sketches) could not accept this unexpected new facet of their countryman's art. The earlier *cuadros de costumbres,* fashionable prior to 1864, did not limit Pereda's methods, although some precedents may be noted in the very important *costumbrista* work, *Los españoles pintados por sí mismos* (The Spaniards Painted by Themselves).[3]

Local objections coincided with Trueba's conclusion in the prologue to *Escenas montañesas* that "Pereda himself, who is one of its most loving sons [and] who has a special talent to study and to describe its popular customs . . . has had the bad taste to be indifferent to the many good things there are in the *Montaña* and . . . to photograph the many bad things [that] the *Montaña* has, as [do] all regions."[4] The eighteen stories and essays in *Escenas montañesas* vary greatly in style, subjects, and themes so that the only unifying factor is the setting in the province of Santander. The critical consensus has been that Pereda collected his material without any preconceived aesthetic plan; and the author, in a later note to the book in 1885, excused his work thus:

No matter how distracted the reader may be, he will have probably observed that, between the beginning and the end of this book, the author's manner of seeing and sensing country life changes somewhat. The excuse for this inconsistency is that the *Scenes* were not written with a set plan nor at one sitting, nor are they the work of the mature reflection of the philosopher but are the fruit of an impressionable boy's leisure (I, 365).

The various dates of publication for the *Escenas montañesas* and Pereda's arrangement of the articles as a book confirm the haphazard attitude indicated in the 1885 note. The irony lies in the importance accorded *Escenas montañesas* by critics as a *costum-*

brista watershed, an early naturalistic appearance, and a superior endeavor by Pereda.[5] Another ironic feature of this first book is the effect caused on Pereda by the accidental success and scandal of these eighteen scenes from the Montaña.

The best story is usually cited as "La leva" (The Levy), a short narrative foreshadowing several traits of Pereda's aesthetics in the two major novels, *Sotileza* and *Peñas arriba*. Tuerto, a poor, honest, and hardworking fisherman of the port of Santander, is overwhelmed by an adverse fate: the burden of earning a livelihood from the uncertain sea is compounded by an alcoholic wife who neglects their children. Tuerto ("Cross-eyed," the literal translation of his name, conveys the physical bad luck of this unfortunate character) complains about his misfortunes to the old sailor Tremontorio (a nickname in jest for Old Miguel and a play on the word *promontorio,* "promontory"). But Tremontorio merely counsels stoicism against fate and life in general. A storm at sea is only the equivalent of another tempest on land, that of a bad spouse. Nothing redeems Tuerto from his misery, and, on the contrary, an incredible, additional woe befalls him: he is taken in the levy or the draft for service to the country.

The background is authentically depicted with the wharves, the houses, the common folk, and the dialect of Santander. Of course, the tale is a sad history of unfortunate people of the lower classes, cursed by bad luck; but the "unconscious naturalism" of Pereda is the result of memory and observation.[6] The characterization can be readily acceptable, although all the actors are types representing certain values or vices, according to Pereda's moral code. The author intrudes repeatedly in this short story to insist that he is a "poor painter of customs" and not endowed with "the fresh imagination of a poet."[7]

"El fin de una raza" (The End of a Race) is often considered as a sequel to "La leva" because the two characters, Tuerto and Tremontorio, reappear in the second story. The point of view, however, shifts from Tuerto's woes (although he comes back to Santander in search of the miserable life with his alcoholic wife) to the history of Tremontorio, the weather-beaten tar who dies as an indirect consequence of a severe storm at sea, the last of a line of nautical Mohicans.[8] The entire narrative, in fact, changes from a naturalistic short story, as in "La leva," to the description about a type, or rudimentary character study. The true-to-life experiences and vivid dialogue lend authenticity to Pereda's wish to pay tribute to the Santander mariners of a decade before. Already, Pereda has grasped the importance of the sea, the humble but honorable lives of the toilers of the sea, and the effect of "all the noise and ostentation of the new civilization" upon the simple, monotonous ways of these men, who are "facing the marvelous transformation that is being carried out in this city, morally as well as materially" (I, 354). The two stories really exist independently because of Pereda's varied approach to his material, and the ideas in both narratives are echoed in *Sotileza.*

The other contributions to *Escenas montañesas* also anticipate Pereda's later novelistic methodology by his emphasis on the use of detailed descriptions for even minor characters, the whole picture providing the study of a type, as in "El raquero" (The Beachcomber), "La costurera" (The Seamstress), and "Un marino" (A Mariner). These three types represent the poorer classes of Santander, displaced and disoriented by *el espíritu moderno* ("the modern spirit"), the title of Pereda's last article in *Escenas montañesas,* in which he foresees that "within a few years industry will have completely invaded these peaceful lands, and then there will no longer be types" (I, 371). Although Pereda's main purpose is to portray the seamen of Santander and the representatives of other sectors of Santander's humble side, chosen for their picturesque reflection of the province as well as their symbolic challenge to the new age, he also utilized the proud, aristocratic heir to the traditions of the *Montaña,* as in the initial story, "Santander," with its revealing subtitle, "Antaño y hogaño" (Of Old and Nowadays). Don Pelegrín Tarín, serving as the narrator with "his stale memories," is no more than an anachronism and a town character, charming but useless in the present world, according to Pereda's realistic, nostalgic view. Another character, also employed by Pereda later in novels, is the *indiano,* or the Spaniard who has gone to the "Indies" — the New World — to make his fortune and returned to enjoy a comfortable life in Spain. In the story, "A las Indias" (To the Indies), a young man (perhaps like Pereda's older brother Juan Agapito) leaves the saddened family for Cuba, the parting vignette on the wharf contrasting the tearful relatives and the ambitious Andrés. The author's pride in the noble traits of "a pure-blooded man of the *Montaña"* is mixed with regret over the loss to the region of a worthwhile member.

Customs, of course, play a major role in the *Escenas montañesas* with Pereda's description of the religious festivities associated in a close tie to a family reunion in "La noche de Navidad" (Christmas

Night); with the love of traditional dancing in "Los bailes campestres" (Country Dances); and with a hearty feast on a saint's day in "Arroz y gallo muerto" (Rice and a Dead Rooster). But the descriptions offer a less innocent side of the province as in "La buena gloria" (The Good Glory), where a wake for a deceased husband leads to violent accusations against the widow after heavy drinking by the gatherers; in "La robla" (The Treat), where humorous comments may lead to a felicitous (in this instance) or an angry conclusion to the drinking after some business deal; and in "El día 4 de octubre" (The Fourth Day of October), where peasant wisdom can bring justice after a potentially dangerous argument. One recurring theme in the *Escenas montañesas* is the problem of alcoholism, common among the wives of the poor classes, and the accusation of drunkenness (in acceptable and more vulgar forms) is frequently hurled at the women in these eighteen scenes. Here may be a sensitive point for the middle-class readers of Pereda's first book, resenting this overt depiction of a provincial vice; and here is also a tantalizing example of Pereda's penetrating observation and psychological understanding of the miserable lot of his beloved "noble race."[9]

The singular exception to Pereda's general defense of regional life is "Suum cuique" (To Each His Own), the longest contribution in the series. If counted as a short novel, it is the forerunner to the three novelettes in *Bocetos al temple*. "Suum cuique" has also won recognition as the sole major expression of Pereda's antibucolic attitude that soon led to "the conception of a new bucolic spirit."[10] Although some characters and situations in the other stories, coupled with the innovative use of the rough dialect of the humble Santander people, irked Pereda's audience, no one story is so devastating an attack upon provincial life as is "Suum cuique."

The portrayal of Silvestre Seturas, the heir to an aristocratic but impoverished estate in the *Montaña*, is in fact a caricature of the hero; and the resemblances to Don Quixote are stressed to the detriment of any defenders of the social system. The quest of Pereda's main character is the continuation of a lawsuit, transferred from father to son in the family, with no end in sight for the litigation and a diminished inheritance the inevitable consequence of legal expenses. By chance, the dejected Seturas sees one day in the "Gaceta" (gazette where government decrees are published and which he and his companions of the outmoded landed gentry read devotedly) the name of a former schoolmate. Seturas writes to Fulano de Tal (John

Doe) in the hope that his vaguely remembered acquaintance will be able to help bring the unending lawsuit to a victorious conclusion. Invited to Madrid, Seturas is soon disillusioned by the political, social, and general activity of the city (perhaps like Pereda in his youthful sally to the capital); but Fulano de Tal surprises his country visitor by expressing his wish to reside in the rural isolation, recently abandoned by Seturas. The two friends return to the *Montaña*, where Fulano de Tal's ecstatic reaction to the provincial mannerisms is unappreciated by Seturas, who sees realistically the difficulties — mainly the lawsuit — besetting the financially embarrassed hidalgo, or member of the minor nobility.

The end of the pleasant summer weather, however, brings a changed mood because of the approaching winter hardships and isolation; and Fulano de Tal is shocked and victimized by some rural customs, resulting in injuries. His melancholy increases as the monotony of daily existence in the *Montaña* becomes more pronounced; and he no longer sees "noble savages" in the rough behavior and unrefined speech of the natives. Finally, Fulano de Tal is prosecuted because of an incident during a hunting trip; and the trial, where his lying accuser, Merlín, is believed because he is an old resident of the area, ends with the stranger's guilt determined by the prejudiced magistrate. Fulano de Tal, bidding farewell to his host, moralizes to Seturas that "each person, in order to live, needs the element which has formed him: the cultured man, civilization; the savage, nature" (I, 309). "To each his own," concludes Fulano de Tal; and the two men part, still friends, and with the later news that Seturas has at last won his lawsuit, thanks to the former's help.

The solution to "Suum cuique" is the opposite of Pereda's thesis in his novel, *Peñas arriba*. Rather, the woes of Fulano de Tal are reminiscent of Pepe Rey's harassments in *Doña Perfecta* by a countryside hostile to urban fashions, or to anything new and different. The narrative is humorously related, with an undercurrent of sarcasm always present and always in favor of Fulano de Tal. Although Silvestre Seturas, "the most notable offspring of the renowned Highland family of the Seturas" (as Pereda comically concludes his story), is pictured sympathetically, the view is nonetheless that of a charming but pathetic anachronism. Few or no favorable aspects of the *Montaña* way of life are mentioned or advocated in "Suum cuique"; and, ironically, this story is one of the most effective in *Escenas montañesas*, providing needed variety and contrast with the most recognized contribution, "La leva."[11]

The historical interest of *Escenas montañesas* resides in "the first explicit manifestations, favorable or hostile, before the promise of a new Spanish realism."[12] Pereda insisted that his primary aim was to record the truth,[13] while Menéndez Pelayo emphasizes that his compatriot from the *Montaña* cannot be logically assigned to any literary school and is "an unintentional realist" who "reduces all his aesthetics to the common-sense proposition that *art is truth.*"[14] The local-color background in all the sketches — and some of the articles are only *cuadros de costumbres* — follows the securely established formulas of the *costumbristas*, with novelty residing in the reflection of a hitherto unexploited region, the mountains, seas, and towns of Santander. Pereda admits that his intention is to show his home region truthfully in the "prologue, foreword, prelude . . . or whatever you want" that serves as the defensive introduction to the second series of *Escenas montañesas*, published as *Tipos y paisajes* (Types and Landscapes) in 1871.

The two books, nevertheless, offer many differences in their contents; and the introductory words of the author serve to illustrate his evolving philosophy of literary presentation of Highland scenes. Although Pereda may not have consciously followed or adhered to any aesthetic school, as Menéndez Pelayo insists in his prologue to his friend's complete works, the foundations of a correct understanding of certain basic principles of realism are apparent in the opening pages. Defensively as usual, Pereda denies with a note of bitterness the gossip about his disloyalties to Santander. He ironically expresses his "profound gratitude to my dear friend Antonio de Trueba, whose sole name, placed at the front of my book, embellished its innumerable defects, upon being admitted not unwillingly to the Spanish literary republic" (I, 376), and whose criticisms are answered deliberately or accidentally in these first few pages. Pereda's definition of realism (for him at least) is set forth at the beginning: "One can represent men in two ways: as they are or as they should be. For the first, the portrait painter suffices; for the second, the painter of genius, of creative inspiration. I freely concede that the latter's merit is absolutely superior to the former's; but that, by trying to make known an individual, one is to represent him as he should be and not as he is, I do not concede that point, although they may crucify me" (I, 373).

This argument, truthfulness versus invention, common observation against artistic creation, has the familiar ring of Fernán Caballero's allegation of faithfulness to the exact, accurate presentation of customs and characters; and, indeed, Pereda's debt to Doña Cecilia is acknowledged in this definition of his realism, an influence also indicated by Menéndez Pelayo.[15] Pereda, however, has already advanced beyond the limitations of Fernán Caballero's art, and he has significantly carried the observation of the truth — two key words for all the realists — to the edge of naturalism, according to bolder critics.[16] Pereda insists in his continuing explanation of realism in *Tipos y paisajes* (Types and Landscapes) that "although I am a portrait painter when I depict the customs of the Montaña, being still unworthy and a slave to the truth, I copied them from life, and as life is not perfect, their imperfections came out in the copy" (I, 374). Pereda, then, rejects romanticism (against which Fernán Caballero also fought consistently in her works) as well as the pioneering, imperfect realism of his influential mentor in her repetitive didacticism and moralizing, which he astutely comprehends herein as a literary defect. Pereda's main objection, however, to "a book of poetic and edifying legends" is the reaction of his own compatriots who, not recognizing themselves, would object to a falsified rendition of the *Montaña* — a skillful inversion of Santander's vociferous opposition to *Escenas montañesas*. Pereda censures his local readers for their reluctance to admit faults and vices in their neighbors, and failing to recognize the noble virtues of the inhabitants. The essence, therefore, of Pereda's realism is a panorama of Santander, rounded by scenes and types embracing all facets of the regional way of life, neither idealized nor denigrated, neither within romanticism nor within naturalism (as critics might try to classify his writings).

III   *Tipos y paisajes*

The twelve stories in Pereda's second book, categorized as a second *Escenas montañesas*, repeat many innovative ideas of the first work and thus lack some historical as well as aesthetic merits of the initial collection. However, certain changes can be detected in *Tipos y paisajes*, although the local-color and stylistic traits — Pereda's positive contributions — remain constant. There appears to emerge a nebulous endeavor to wed the *costumbrista* sketch to the narrative inspiration. But the attempt is largely unsuccessful, with the separation between description and story too apparent. The lack of action is unfortunately compounded by the descriptions, frequent and detailed, with only a limited reader interest because of Pereda's failure to blend all the elements into a compelling, original formula.

The first two stories offer essentially the same psychological problem and attendant conclusion: "Dos sistemas" (Two Systems) contrasts the avaricious but practical instincts of a father with the generous but impractical ideas of a son, resulting in financial ruin for the family business; and "Para ser buen arriero . . ." (To Be a Good Muleteer . . .) shows the unhappy existence of a husband and wife whose sudden inheritance arouses jealousy in their neighbors, in addition to their own inability to adjust to a different social status. The moral in both stories, evident and also stated at the end, destroys the timid efforts of Pereda to develop some interesting characterizations; and the characters themselves seem trapped in the author's predetermined judgments.

In "Blasones y talegas" (Coats of Arms and Bags of Money), the story — the longest in *Tipos y paisajes* — lacks originality. It offers no more than a charming, whimsical plot in the aristocratic father's stubborn refusal to allow the illustrious but impoverished family title, despite his daughter's enthusiasm, to be joined in marriage to the humble but wealthy name of a sincere suitor. The conclusion is equally unimaginative: the respective fathers of the young couple, as opposed in their outlooks as their children are compatible with each other, finally rejoice in later years, seeing their offspring so happy. The four characters are not even types, as desired by Pereda in his characterizations, and these personages certainly do not depict residents only of the *Montaña*, despite the regional setting.

Some stories, nevertheless, do provide the flavor or the local color of Santander. "La Romería del Carmen" (The Pilgrimage of Our Lady of Mount Carmel) depicts humorous and religious associations of a Highland tradition, with a concluding regret about the railroad's supplanting of the custom by a more rapid and less human means. "Las brujas" (The Witches) offers a curious mingling of romantic and Gothic beliefs with the traditional, religious faith of the *Montaña*, ending in a realistic, moralizing explanation of the power of good works. "Los chicos de la calle" (The Children on the Street), is probably a semiautobiographical recollection of the simple amusements and language of youngsters before they are forced to learn a trade or prepare for serious studies. "Al amor de los tizones" (Around the Glow of the Flames) reproduces the innocent chatter and gossip of the *tertulias* ("evening parties") in the warmth and light of burning embers; and "Pasacalle" (Quickstep) gives the reader a tour of Santander's main streets and sights, in addition to the innocuous generalities of daily conversations. These examples resemble the usual local-color sketches. Although Pereda tries at times to add a complication or problem for narrative interest, he achieves only minor success. By now, however, the formula shows how Pereda has abandoned his first, more effective pictures of Santander, with types drawn from the poorer residents, in favor of the middle class and, at times, upper or noble classes of the region. And the results demonstrate no originality, unfortunately, with a surprisingly weak portrayal of regional uniqueness.

In addition, Pereda is slowly revealing certain lines of an approach to the problems of the century that will cause critical disfavor and no aesthetic durability. Thus, in "Ir por lana . . ." (To Go for Wool) the city is indicated as the cause of the moral downfall and eventual death of a simple girl of the *Montaña,* unable to resist the lure of the materialistic society; and in "Un tipo más" (One More Type) the demanding, unscrupulous politician, Hermenegildo Trapisonda, is generalized in his conversation with the narrator, undoubtedly representing Pereda, as "typical" of the political scene. The city and politics, then, symbolize two facets of the present age to which Pereda is opposed, overtly in these two stories, and persistently, though as an undercurrent, in other selections of *Tipos y paisajes.* The *Montaña* is being converted into a symbol of the past, vanishing slowly in the changes of the nineteenth century; changes are destroying the "good" and superimposing the "bad" within Pereda's simplistic interpretation, usually rendered as a moral conclusion.[17]

IV *Bocetos al temple*

With *Bocetos al temple* (Sketches in Distemper) Pereda definitively entered the arena of the novel, but the three novelettes do not form a trilogy and, in fact, share no common idea or unifying theme. Of course, common strands of Pereda's emerging ideology appear throughout *Bocetos al temple,* and the longer narrative form had characterized some of the previous sketches and stories. In short, the three novelettes are really not so different from the pioneering *Escenas montañesas* and its sequel *Tipos y paisajes.* The effort, however, is revealing and significant for the attempt to unite description, narration, and types (as Pereda understood characterization) in the decade of the 1870s, when the realistic novel began to come into prominence and perfection.

Perhaps the "sketches in distemper" are aptly named because Pereda shows in the title his displeasure at certain aspects of present-day life, and the humor with which he penned his barbs, creating a satirical effect. The common point of the short novels is the picture of the calamities besetting simple country people, of limited background and education, who are overwhelmed by the temptations of the urban nineteenth-century society. A polarization, lacking any evidence of a possible compromise, is very apparent in Pereda's vision; and the conclusions are totally negative as to the direction of Spanish civilization.

   La mujer de César (Caesar's Wife) is the only story with a happy ending. Isabel, the innocent but foolish wife, flattered by noble, hypocritical circles in the city, is saved from moral and social ruin by the bold actions of Ramón, her husband's brother, who perceived a plot by enemies to destroy the status and career of his relatives. The novel resembles the structure of a drawing-room comedy, and the dialogue, especially, is closer to theatrical conversations. The plot, again, is very thin for the obvious intention of the author, and the satire, while humorous, is too blunt in its one-sided attack on Madrid society. The husband and wife are so uncomplicated and unsuspecting that they fail to provide any opposition to the developing conspiracy.

   Oros son triunfos (Diamonds Are Trump) offers further theatrical elements, with a melodramatic ending relying too heavily upon coincidence and a bitterly sarcastic conclusion. César, too poor to marry Enriqueta, goes overseas (once more the *indiano*), hoping to return with enough money for the future wedding; but he has been defrauded by a stranger and comes back to Santander one day too late: Enriqueta has just gone through the marriage ceremony with another man. Romualdo, Enriqueta's husband, had arrived in Santander at the advantageous time when he could financially rescue Serapio, the girl's father, from bankruptcy; and Sabina, the bride's mother, had eagerly looked to the marriage to improve the familial social status, especially her own situation in the city. César recognizes in Romualdo the man who absconded with his money; and the latter, alone with the former, returns the stolen sum. César leaves the city without revealing the truth; but Romualdo lies to Sabina that he had paid the rejected suitor to depart in peace, and the girl's mother, not unhappily, repeats the lie to all listeners. Again, ambition and money have corrupted society, in Pereda's view, although it is difficult to argue that such a story (with the improbable climax) is restricted to any century or place.

   Los hombres de pro (Men of Worth) traces the rise and fall of Simón Cerojo, who becomes politically ambitious after he acquires a considerable sum of money. Politics and money, once more, cause tragedy, fomenting ambition in a simple man. Pereda's growing conservatism can be noted by now in this combination that compels a person to leave his established place in the local society. If, as Pereda is obviously stressing, an individual who is unprepared morally and by training departs from the traditional hierarchy of values and social order, a catastrophe is the sad result. Simón Cerojo's initial undertakings are very successful, and his ambition increases with each new step up the ladder of power and prestige. Along this apparently glittering highway, the moral decline of Simón, his wife, and his daughter slowly but surely continues. They are increasingly tempted by the reward of nineteenth-century urban life — money, power, and material comforts. The collapse comes almost simultaneously for the three characters: Simón is ruined financially and politically by machinations beyond his limited understanding; the wife is devastated by the fall from grace; and the daughter marries a man, disliked by her parents and ridiculed by their new acquaintances in Madrid, who, however, proves himself a respectable son-in-law by working to restore the family fortune after the four have returned to their small town.

Pereda reinforces his clear moral and explains the satirical intention of the novelette's title by defining in the last paragraph "men of worth": "The evil is not that, by chance, a good minister, mayor, or a perfect model of a man of society may come from a bad tavernkeeper; the misfortune of Spain, that of the present world, consists in all tavernkeepers wanting to be ministers . . ." (I, 725). Grudgingly, Pereda grants that, perhaps accidentally, a humble citizen may become an exemplary governor; but the chances of the masses succeeding as politicians and statesmen are very small. The efforts of Simón Cerojo, like the sallies of Don Quixote and the experiences of Sancho Panza as governor of Barataria, fail to achieve any permanent improvements, lead to disillusionment and defeat, bring scorn from onlookers, and finally terminate in a tragic manner. Pereda has skillfully updated the misadventures of his hero by utilizing the background of national politics, based undoubtedly on his own bitter experiences with parliamentary elections and maneuvers. Simón Cerojo's visits to his constituents, where he is required to sacrifice any lingering ideals in exchange for votes, and his frantic scrambles in the meetings of the Cortes, where he saves himself from defeat by changing parties in the nick of time, demonstrate Pereda's astute observation of the political corruption in Spain.

More generally, the scenes and analyses of the participants'

behavior, compromises, and shallowness provide an excellent portrait of the defects and ills of any political process, given the frailties
and temptations of representatives seeking money and power. All
these vignettes, more effective and impressive as separate units, are
unfortunately marred by the heavy hand of caricature and complete
partiality for the aristocratic heritage on the part of Pereda. A
balanced presentation is lacking in this admittedly correct and useful
rendition of the problems of republican government and democratic
aspirations.

The promise of a winning novel, nevertheless, emerges in this best
publication heretofore by Pereda; and foreshadowings of Don Celso
of *Peñas arriba* appear in the hidalgo Don Recaredo, providing an
antithesis to the ambitious urges of Simón Cerojo. More immediately, *Los hombres de pro*, while an extravagant outpouring of
Pereda's fears at the approaching crisis of Isabel II's reign, brought
public attention (a great deal of it equally fearful about the author's
exaggerations) and constitutes the inspiration of a better publication,
the "prelude of *Don Gonzalo González de la Gonzalera*."[18] The transition from essays and local-color sketches to more sustained pieces
could now be made.

V   *Tipos trashumantes* and *Esbozos y rasguños*

One more return to a collection of short stories and sketches
remained for Pereda to publish in 1877 before he launched his first
long novel. In *Tipos trashumantes* (Nomadic Types) Pereda offers
caricatures of summer tourists and city dwellers swarming to the sea
and mountains during vacations. These "nomadic types" are consistently portrayed in a satirical, scornful fashion; and possibly the
author's neighbors felt that he had made amends for the sketches in
Escenas montañesas. The articles are very ineffective, however, both
as literary creations and as a faithful record of visitors to Santander:
the exaggerated types are so distorted that the author's intention is
too evident, too burlesque. There is no variety in this one-sided attack on middle-class and aristocratic vacationers coming to the
North of Spain, and a monotonous repetition permeates this entire
"summer physiognomy of Santander," making the reader doubt
Pereda's conclusion about making "sketches" and not "autopsies,"
only "copying" the public as "the public has forged itself" (I,
778,781).

Some redeeming features save *Nomadic Types* from total
mediocrity, although the suspicion must linger that the book

represents a sop to Santander after *Escenas montañesas.* The abundant details reflecting the physical mannerisms and habits of the tourists show again Pereda's ability to draw strikingly realistic characters. Many of the criticisms of the strangers, who care little about the province and the natives' way of life, ring true as the ostentatious result of money and urban snobbishness.

The most interesting article is "Un sabio" (A Scholar) in which Pereda, through his portrait of the Madrid professor on vacation in the *Montaña,* expresses his scorn at the European philosophies current in the capital and in university circles, especially the influence of the Krausist movement. Pereda's comprehension of the Krausist philosophy and pedagogy shows an accurate reading of the texts, and he summarizes with impressive acumen the main tenets of this influential school in its early ascendancy. But his immediate rejection of the Krausists, pungent comments about "the nineteenth century, legitimate child of the glacial philosophy of the eighteenth," and the familiar misrepresentations of Darwin as an advocate of man's development from monkeys demonstrate Pereda's prejudices, narrowness, and mental rigidity. His main objection to Krausism and other philosophies, such as that of Hegel, is stated as their attack upon Catholicism; Pereda emphasizes that the intellectuals of the nineteenth century have rejected orthodox faith and, in place of the Church, are creating a secular religion based on the doctrines of Krause and the authority of other foreign ideologies (I, 739 - 43).

Chronologically, *Esbozos y rasguños* (Outlines and Sketches) falls within the same period as the five novels with which Pereda successfully established himself in the field of longer prose fiction. This additional series of scenes and types from the neighborhood of Santander is flawed as markedly as its immediate predecessor, *Nomadic Types.* Once more, Pereda has recoiled from his success in *Escenas montañesas,* preferring to depict rather innocuously boring and gossipy social visits, the ceremonies of the local dance, the glove shop as a gathering place, and the confusing, expensive legalistic jargon exploiting poor citizens in the maze of governmental bureaucracy installed by the experiments of democracy.

The articles have some autobiographical value in Pereda's reminiscences about growing up in Santander, and a certain amount of the information available in biographical outlines is due to these charming, nostalgic, and credible views of the author's past. All in all, these remembrances, like the pleasant tone of the author's essays

about the provincial customs, are broad impressions like those of any
typical youth of his age. They do not offer pertinent references to
Pereda's own problems and thoughts. Most of the content is of a
generalized nature, as in the essays "Los buenos muchachos" (The
Good Boys) and "El primer sombrero" (The First Hat), which
provide familiar humor in reactions to the age-old dictum that boys
should be always good and to the first wearing in public of a hat, in-
dicating manhood.

Whatever the precise explanation of Pereda's failure to pursue the
artistic promise of *Escenas montañesas* may be,[19] his suppression of
the unhappy but more realistic and contemporary traits of his surroundings is fortunately not absolute. "Más reminiscencias" (More
Reminiscences) gives an excellent commentary upon his education
in Santander: the boring recitations of memorized lessons, the
agonies of dull translations, the teacher's usual harshness with occasional kindness, and the overall failure of the classroom. Curiously,
in the same volume in which Pereda rejected the Krausist
methodology (the advocacy of an educational system opposed to the
traits described by the author is a cornerstone of Krause's followers
in Spain), the strong conclusion is made that "if living under the empire of its barbarism distressed me then, today, when I have
children, the thought that some of it still remains in the centers of in-
struction frightens me" (I, 1322). A sound plea in "La intolerancia"
(Intolerance) is expressed for the right to disagree, vociferously if
need be, rather than to acquiesce silently when opposing viewpoints
are spoken or printed. Pereda also reveals his youthful writing ambitions and his adolescent love for the theater, commenting acidly
but winningly on the problems of achieving publication and warding
off opponents, both in print and in conversation.

The by now familiar attack on the nineteenth century is quite
muted in these items, and the last essay, "El cervantismo" (Cervan-
tism), defined by Pereda as "the mania of the Cervantists," advocates the reading of *Don Quixote* for pleasure instead of interpretation, especially the effort to force current ideas within the
framework of the text. The thesis, of course, is conservative and
traditional, adhering to Pereda's philosophy, that Cervantes's
masterpiece has been accepted by past generations and that there is
consequently the need to return to the past, to the original text and
initial impressions of the seventeenth century. Nevertheless,
Pereda's arguments against the mania — a favorite word throughout
Outlines and Sketches for his criticism of present defects and vices

— of the Cervantists are cogent on several points: too much emphasis on the man rather than the book, with exorbitant claims about the author's brilliance and intentions; the pedantic correction of the first edition changing too greatly the words read by the first audiences of 1605 and 1615; and the tendency to employ historical backgrounds, in addition to the cultural ambiance, as the frame of reference for *Don Quixote.* In short, Pereda is urging his contemporaries: Down with the Cervantists! Up with Don Quixote! Let us alone to enjoy the book as our forefathers did!

Pereda is very close, ironically, to some of the outcries of the men of the Generation of 1898, such as Unamuno, in his desire to concentrate on the reading of the chapters rather than the commentaries of erudite critics; and Pereda's admiration and advocacy of *Don Quixote* certainly place him in some small degree within the characteristics of this following literary generation.

Nonetheless, the judgment about Pereda's early literary activities is unhappily a negative and sad verdict. Only in *Escenas montañesas* did he produce a valuable book in terms of aesthetics and literary history; two or possibly three short stories (with "La leva" in first place) definitely stand out as superior pieces of short fiction. Paradoxically, he retreats from the very realistic and even naturalistic "slices of life" in the scenes from the *Montaña* in his first book of 1864, to the more placid *costumbrismo* of before 1850, at precisely the time when realism and naturalism were beginning to emerge significantly in Spain. But the future promise still emerges in Pereda's observations of his province and his reproduction of the authentic language of the people. Now, wedded to the genre of the novel, explored in the three short works of *Bocetos al temple* and some longer stories, the artistry of Pereda could embark on a defense of his philosophy and ideology, already perceptible within the published material to date. Similarly, he would challenge the nineteenth century in all its encroaching facets, materistically and morally.

CHAPTER 3

The Novel as a
Defense and Challenge

THE very productive period from 1878 until 1884, when in that latter year Pereda began the publication of his *Obras completas,* brought the author recognition based on five novels written in rapid succession. Unlike the generally ignored reception of the preceding books, these five works brought Pereda into the public and critical limelight, establishing him as a competent novelist with the artistic stamina to complete long, serious novels. If hypothetically Pereda had written no novels after this first edition of the complete works (often the sign not only of the acceptance of a writer to literary immortality but also, sadly, the apogee of his creative trajectory), the inclusion of his name within literary histories would have been still assured. His merits would have been recognized as those of a fervent polemicist, bolstered by keen observation of details and types and possessing a very effective style to serve his causes. It is, however, somewhat dubious if Pereda would have been judged a first-rank novelist, aesthetically and on the basis of originality; and this judgment is essentially the thrust of Menéndez Pelayo's critical introduction to Pereda's complete works and the persistent theme of his advice to his compatriot from the *Montaña.*[1]

I *El buey suelto*

The first novel, however, has been often criticized and classified as not a novel at all, properly speaking, because Pereda has sacrificed so many qualities of the novelistic art to serve his didactic and moralizing aims. The intention to answer Balzac's *Petites misères de la vie conjugale* (Minor Miseries of Married Life) and, less directly, the same author's *Physiologie du mariage* (Physiology of Marriage) led Pereda to produce this bold, strong, but artistically defective book. With constant sermons and moral asides he recounts the "edifying pictures of the life of a bachelor," as Pereda sarcastically subtitled *El buey suelto (The Bachelor);* and he further qualified this book, in the dedication to Menéndez Pelayo, as "this poor essay of celibate physiology," calling attention also to the work's style.[2] It is primarily a rebuttal of Balzacian ideas, and also to liberal ideas of his age, rather than an imaginative effort as a novel.

The plot, consequently, exists for the expression of the thesis; and the characterization is limited primarily to the one main personage, Gedeón. This character is a type, or "physiology," of the bachelor who acts from selfishness, egoism, and the rejection of traditional, religious standards. Pereda immediately and repeatedly associates all these issues in the presentation of his type; and it is no accident that Gedeón lives in Madrid, although references to the city are not particularized. Gedeón, in short, is a product of urban nineteenth-century civilization, a type appearing as a distinctly unhappy, reprehensible example of the new society and mores. Pereda's heavy-handed ideology weighs down the action, fails to instill much interest in the audience, and turns aside the readers from any convincing aspects of the author's sincerely held arguments.

Gedeón's life is traced from the time when, as a young man, he made his arrogant decision not to marry for the sake of enjoying himself more fully. He is seen as a middle-aged bachelor, beginning to be plagued by the follies of his youth and the onset of physical maladies; and as a dying recluse, despised by his cast-aside mistress with two illegitimate children and his housekeeper with no hope of a substantial inheritance. A few types are drawn somewhat convincingly: his mistress Solita, the poor servant girl who submits to Gedeón, loves him at first, bears him two children, and ends by hating him for his refusal to accept marriage until the final moments of his life; Regla, the widow with her obstreperous son who tries to break down Gedeón's resistance to marriage for security; and Judás Cerote, the devious father of Solita, who wants to blackmail Gedeón into marriage with the girl. At times, the portrayal and dialogue of these minor characters show realistic, credible persons; but the overall presentation is weak because of Gedeón's consistent appearance as the principal actor and his rendition as a completely negative individual.

Other characters are even more in the vein of symbols or spokesmen for Pereda's one-sided attitude toward celibacy and marriage: the doctor, who is obviously the spokesman for Pereda's thesis; the priest, who symbolizes the Church's teachings about the values of the wedded life; and Merto, who personifies the problem of children and, ironically for Gedeón, the agony of dealing with youngsters not of one's own blood and therefore lacking in unbreakable ties of love. The final year of Gedeón's life, when he contritely admits the error of his ways, is sketched so totally against the choice of bachelorhood that this last part lacks verisimilitude. There is a tedious and dreary reaction to the expected and easily anticipated events occurring in these concluding pages. The use of confrontation, with heightened conflict and possible suspense, found no place in Pereda's well-planned attack on bachelorhood. Structure, however, is not lacking in this first *novela de tesis*, and the logical progression of Gedeón's mistaken views is charted convincingly within the lines of the admittedly prejudiced thesis.

The failure of *El buey suelto* was perhaps a blessing in disguise for Pereda because he, in view of the deeply motivated convictions about the nineteenth century (recognized so quickly by Galdós from the start of their long friendship), would have probably continued to compose the same kind of thesis novels. There appeared not one favorable review or commentary of Pereda's initial *novela de tesis*, and even Menéndez Pelayo was forced to concede that *El buey suelto* "may be the weakest" of Pereda's publications despite the portrait of Gedeón as "the incarnation of bourgeois egoism."[3] Clarín's attack proved the most devastating for the book's survival and for Pereda's own ego; and later criticism has sustained the unfavorable reaction as, for example, in this verdict of Montesinos: "*El buey suelto* is a novel frustrated by the intention, by unskillfullness, by the moralizing pounding," and "the defense that Pereda sought to make of Catholic marriage does not succeed either, because the examples that he alleges are the least convincing."[4]

II   Don Gonzalo González de la Gonzalera

Montesinos also stresses the invaluable lesson for Pereda in that the author rejected *costumbrismo*, practiced and accepted by himself and other writers, in favor of a realistic local color: "Soon the peculiar genius of Pereda balks at these unacceptable yokes, breaks them, and continues in an unexpected direction, the one that his natural disposition as a realist imposes upon him, as a reproducer of concrete realities that are picturesque or seem so to him."[5] The artistic crisis caused by the dismal reception of *El buey suelto* resulted in a second thesis novel, so different and so greatly improved in comparison with the first *novela de tesis*, that Pereda must have made a complete reappraisal of his intentions. At least, he complained about the composition in letters to Menéndez Pelayo and Galdós.[6] Indeed, a comparison and contrast of *El buey suelto* and *Don Gonzalo González de la Gonzalera*, written within a very short time of each other, show important differences, although the basis of Pereda's ideology is consistent at the heart of both endeavors.

One explanation for Pereda's success in *Don Gonzalo* and a clue to the subsequent triumphs of *Sotileza* and *Peñas arriba*, is the use of his home territory, the *Montaña*, setting of *Escenas montañesas*, which he could describe with more firsthand knowledge and with a loving concentration not associated with any writings about the city, especially the capital. Another explanation is the time, "the beginning of the memorable year, 1868," as the author states immediately. That catastrophic decade, especially for traditionalists like Pereda, remains engraved as a climax of nineteenth-century Spanish history, a political stimulus for a novelistic interpretation. The first chapters, slow in establishing the conflict, nevertheless serve to create the mood of the rural idyll, the placid, happy, unambitious mood of the Highlands, where the *romerías*, (the festive gatherings on a saint's day) and the familial histories, pleasant and not so pleasant, occupy the inhabitants' lives and conversations. The dialogues are frequently the daily gossip, with no immediate reference to the plot but with a pattern of psychological realism about the minor types. The setting, the speech, and the actors are, for the first successful time in the Peredian novels, a fusion of realism and regionalism, at the service of a political purpose.

The thesis of *Don Gonzalo* is contemporary and personal: the events, rendered in a literary garb, refer very specifically to the author's own time and his *patria chica*. The story, although the plan is imaginary and inventive, corresponds to the broad picture of what had happened in Santander and other parts of Spain during the Revolution of 1868. There are several facets to the political thesis of *Don Gonzalo:* the destruction of a traditional way of life with no betterment, and only regret and suffering as the bitter aftermath of any revolutionary attempts; the farcical outlines of liberal democracy and social idealism; the inability and unwillingness of simple, uneducated commonfolk to be rulers; and the danger of demagogues and ambitious politicians manipulating the contented people of a rural area. No one can argue against any of Pereda's postulates completely because he is clearly defining the defects and evils of the new political system, and the history of Spain during the nineteenth and twentieth centuries reveals the disastrous consequences of these weaknesses in theory and practice as well as in human nature.

At the same time, few readers would accept wholeheartedly Pereda's thesis; and the key word is this term, thesis, because art has been placed at the service of a political or social attitude. Only if one grants momentarily, or at least during the reading of *Don Gonzalo*, a "willing suspension of disbelief" by not opposing at once the Peredian ideas can the artistry of the book be enjoyed and appreciated. Later, of course, the ramifications of this thesis must, in all fairness, appear for judgment before the bar of criticism. The polarization in Spain between liberal and traditionalist opinions prevented this initial objectivity; and reactions to *Don Gonzalo* floundered on the problem of art and ideology. However, Pereda had skillfully utilized style, technique, and structure to write a very readable novel, a book worthy of respect, aesthetically.

The title is misleading but very symbolic because Don Gonzalo González de la Gonzalera, rather than the leading actor in this drama of the Highlands during 1868, emerges as the embodiment of the rebellion against past standards. He is, within the framework of the Peredian thesis, an upstart who, by rejecting his given name of Colás Bragas for the noble pseudonym of Don Gonzalo González de la Gonzalera, has refused to remain in his social class (a very humiliating and poor position); and who, by returning to the Highlands as an indiano with the money earned abroad, has now sought to enter a higher circle of power and prestige. These ideas, of course, exist as problems in the nineteenth-century novel, especially for Balzac and Stendhal; but Pereda has sketched the former Colás Bragas, even as a young man ambitious and dissatisfied with his lot in life, as the present Don Gonzalo González de la Gonzalera who is determined to climb to the top of the Santander ladder socially and politically, and indeed in all aspects of the provincial world, by the new means at hand, the trappings of change and revolution. Don Gonzalo has no sympathetic traits, however, so that the reader reacts against him from his first appearance; this protagonist is lacking in both natural aristocracy and nobility of birth. He appears in the sixth chapter for the first time, after one-fourth of the novel, and never fully dominates or controls the action; he is either subservient to his equally ambitious cronies or overshadowed by the hidalgo types when he finds himself in their company. Nevertheless, Don Gonzalo's money acts like honey to his eager accomplices and shields him from the consequences of his cowardice and stupidity. Pereda has certainly created a type who, with the familiar nineteenth-century vices of money and ambition, can succeed in fomenting strife and suffering.

Don Gonzalo, determined to become the major link in the chain of Santander society, unites other rebellious and dissident elements, such as Patricio Rigüelta, who undertakes the organization of his master's ambition by exploitation of the people and politics. The evil talent in this novel is Patricio Rigüelta, and Pereda was apparently obsessed by this type of political boss, or *cacique,* within the Spanish frame of reference, who was spawned by the governmental process of the modern age.[7] Gildo Rigüelta, Patricio's son, Lucas, Polinar, Gorión, and Carpio, in approximately descending order of importance and wickedness, promote the conspiracy, inspired principally by Don Gonzalo's funds and Patricio's wily schemes:

> Four rascals exploiting four hundred ignorant people; this is seen everywhere and will be seen until the end of time because it is the natural product of the human condition. Does my concern arise from the fact that this crime is the greatest that I have witnessed in my life? Indeed it does: the unjustness of the situation in itself; the quality, the conditions of the insulted person; the place, the occasion so solemn for this person; so many rights, so many hopes, so many feelings trampled upon, mocked in a single instant; so many joys drowned in tears by the treacherous blow of half a dozen scoundrels, lawless and godless, cry to heaven for swift and terrible vengeance. (I, 1022 - 23)

This quotation summarizes the essence of the thesis and the plot of *Don Gonzalo* because the conspirators, realizing that the swiftly moving national events can be the justification for their rise to power, also play upon the base emotions and suppressed feelings of the poor people of the *Montaña.* Don Gonzalo and his party can come to political control legally, if not honestly, within the rules of this new game; and, in fact, they are more cognizant of the changed possibilities than Pereda's heroes, their opponents — an interpretation that the author obviously never intended. First, the elections supply the opportunity to install Don Gonzalo as the mayor, with the realization that the general concept of one man, one vote will overwhelm the ruling minority; and in the second place, a direct attack upon latent resentment against the Church and the local establishment, in the persons of the hidalgos, will topple the whole prevailing structure of their society. Again, Pereda has analyzed, perhaps unconsciously and without doubt unintentionally, this shrewd, correct advice to his foes.

Pereda, of course, opposes the whole façade of democracy, such as

the elections planned for the town of Coteruco; but his audience is
not aroused against Don Gonzalo, the Rigüeltas, and the others until
their boldness leads to a frontal attack upon the village church and
the parish priest, Don Frutos. This anticlerical outburst, coupled
with increasing anger over the electoral campaign, is the forerunner
to the kidnapping of Don Román Pérez de la Llosía, the most prominent hidalgo opposing Don Gonzalo. Don Román's daughter,
Magdalena, has also rejected Don Gonzalo as a suitor; and he, joining political and personal enmities, takes this dishonest, violent
measure. The struggle is now joined between the aroused, previously
complacent aristocrats, the shocked devout Catholics, and their loyal
followers on the one side; and on the other hand, the majority of
credulous citizens spurred by the rabble-rousers, especially Patricio
Rigüelta.

   This sharply divided cast, deliberately polarized by Pereda, faces
the inevitable and logical result of the whole series of actions —
violence. The tangled strands of the plot are unwound by the author
with the assistance of romantic melodrama: Don Lope del Robledal,
another noble son of the Highlands, appears to wield a forceful hand
against the plotters, who cannot face honorably a direct account of
their misdeeds and crimes. An additional moral feature is contributed with not only the release of the captive, Don Román, and
the marriage of Magdalena to a young man whom she loves; but also
with Don Gonzalo's wedding to Osmunda, a shrew who will
probably subject him to many long years of humiliation for all of
Coteruco to observe with pleasure. Other small threads of the story
lead equally to a justifiable end: Patricio Rigüelta is killed, appropriately, in a brawl with Polinar over stuffing the ballot boxes;
and the latter, after wounding Don Frutos in the same scuffle, is ap-
prehended for punishment. With the physical assault on the priest,
Pereda draws the charge of sacrilege on the heads of these rebels
against the established order.

   Understanding popular psychology, especially that of the
Highlanders, Pereda has described types on both sides of the widen-
ing chasm between traditionalists and liberals. The inhabitants of
Coteruco, a small, unimportant place in the province of Santander,
itself an area of Spain without the primary status of Castile and
Catalonia, will never recover fully from the effects of the polarization and violence. Pereda is not so obtuse, nor is he so stubborn, that
the effects of the new age can be magically removed by the writer's
sentiments and beliefs. The railroad, that constant symbol in

Pereda's works for the nineteenth century, will affect provincial life; the ease of travel will result in different homes for the young generation; and the hidalgos can only look with longing upon their past traditions. Their winning of a battle is recognized as the loss of a war; and Pereda sadly accepts this present and future consequence of the events of 1868 in the final chapter of *Don Gonzalo*. More pessimistically, and more tragically for the Spanish nation and people, Pereda foresees a civil war, as Don Román melancholically looks down from the heights above Coteruco to the *aldea perdida* ("lost village") in the distance:

> Don Román could not pass from there without turning his eyes to that beloved land. There, below, almost at his feet, was Coteruco, spread upon the lap of the hill and the mountain like a drunken person who has slept it off in the open air. It seemed to him that those little houses, still white, a remnant of lost virtues, with their windows open halfway and their eaves hanging over the front were ashamed of the sun which struck them fully because it illuminated the vices that they concealed. Coteruco! The deleterious quagmire from which it was necessary to flee in order not to become poisoned in its atmosphere! Coteruco! Formerly a nursery for virtues, then a center of the pestilence that was carrying death, from town to town, to the whole valley!
>
> With these and other suspicions, allowing his imagination to wander in a sea of conjectures and hypotheses, his ideas came to acquire reality and forms before his eyes; and there was a moment in which he saw the hamlets burning, the love for work lost, the faith corrupted and discord rampant, and ultimately, the towns destroying one another, upon those green meadows converted into a bloody battlefield. "You are already going," he thought then, "you are going, misguided people, toward the concert of free peoples; but you are really going, like the stone dragged by the torrent, among the slime at the bottom, blocking the river bed and, blocking ceaselessly the waters running over you, to the sea of all ambitions. Yesterday you had your homes full of bread and abundance; today you live hungry, naked, despairing, and with envy and hatred in your hearts. This is what the apostles who have redeemed you from slavery, from faith, and from honest labor have given you! (I, 1063)

There is the glimpse of the future agony of Spain in this forceful, yet poetic passage; and Pereda is certainly an accurate prophet of the possible pitfalls of the liberal, democratic ideas emerging in his homeland. This bloodshed, for him, will be the logical consequence of the selfish ambitions of ruthless leaders and the unthinking reactions of the masses. Pereda's novel survives very well, then, as a textbook revealing the political dangers of the century; and, indeed, his penetrating types, with realistic psychological characterizations, can be applied to the contemporary scene, unfortunately. But *Don Gonzalo* must be judged also in the light of the Peredian theses; and these ideological ideals are what prevent the novel, a good novel admired at the time and still today, from entering the ranks of the Galdosian creations, even possibly of outstanding European productions, as a flawless political novel.

Pereda, sincerely and intentionally, has failed to develop his characters impartially; and all his personages, major and minor, while reflecting carefully and accurately the *Montaña*, lack the verisimilitude required for easy acceptance. The two parties of the village, meaning of course the entire nation, are divided into two groups — the "good guys" and the "bad guys." Without any relief from this ideologically and politically convenient formula, Pereda has compelled a one-sided but unconvincing reaction. There are dupes on the side of the dissidents, mainly the simple-hearted peasants and workers, who should have remained loyal to the *hidalgos* and the Church from gratitude and respect; but no single individual adhering to Don Gonzalo's shabby cause is pictured favorably. Likewise, everyone of the adherents to the traditionalist, clerical party is unrelievedly a noble, dedicated servant of the patria chica. The characters and types, therefore, are not rounded in the sense of believable persons because there is no variety in the total psychology of these figures. Also, these people must react in a certain manner, representing the expression of the Peredian point of view, *pro* or *con* the particular attitude desired in each scene.

This flaw in Pereda's historical novel (the political thesis is clearly attuned to the events of 1868 within the microcosm of Coteruco) has produced a whole series of persons without separate qualities, without existence as individuals. Their roles in this drama are submitted to a larger context, and Pereda has failed to follow correctly the lessons of Galdós, Balzac, and even the romantics, Scott and Cooper, in their character representations. *Don Gonzalo* is reminiscent of Gironella's successful novel, *Los cipreses creen en Dios* (The Cypresses Believe in God) with the attempt to weave back and forth between the various sides, except that Pereda has omitted any appearance of impartiality about his feelings. The two novels complement each other curiously in their interpretations of the causes and effects of the centrifugal situation; and the two books offer ably and successfully the nineteenth- and twentieth-century political backgrounds, respectively. And, indeed, a general objection to Gironella from some critics has been the intrinsic lack of an impartial stance despite the author's claim to this attitude.[8] Nonetheless, *Don Gonzalo* still retains an importance for comprehending the background in all the novels, domestic and foreign, dealing with the Spanish civil war. More directly, for Pereda, the terrible example of the French Revolution, which he always saw as a fatal step against traditionalism, may be an influence upon the nascent revolutionaries and disturbing events of Coteruco; and the pattern and mood of *Don Gonzalo* recall interpretations by Dickens, Carlyle, and especially Balzac, of the upheavals before and after 1789.

At the moment of publication, *Don Gonzalo* was acclaimed by the critics on all sides: Menéndez Pelayo, naturally, led the chorus in praise of his compatriot's novelistic artistry but insisted that the political theses were minor features; Clarín stressed, very astutely, that Pereda had advanced enormously in a short period of time as a writer over his previous failure in *El buey suelto,* with authentic settings and realistic characters; and other commentators, forgotten today, indicated their feelings about the author's ideology, depending on their own orientations. Thus, the victory of Pereda, signaling his arrival as an important novelist, was based upon the major critical reviews of *Don Gonzalo* as a work of art and not as a thesis novel. Later, after Pereda's continued employment of this winning methodology, criticism, both ideological and impartial, observed that art was essentially in control of a novelist with very determined ideas. "Upon writing *Don Gonzalo González de la Gonzalera,*" concludes Montesinos, "the novelist creates the type of narration that, essentially, he will faithfully cultivate to the end of his life and that, under these same forms, will be characteristic of his first manner. In it he tries to subordinate his instinctive realism — love of the picturesque, of what he believes typical, of what he feels as pure and peculiar, and a faithful reproduction of all of it — to a feeling of life uplifted in contemplation of these oases, which are the rural paradises he imagines, and which wild nature guards against the snares of agitated, violent modern life."[9]

III   De tal palo, tal astilla

Obviously, then, the literary die is cast for Pereda to pursue and to exploit more fully other features of "these oases" or "rural paradises," creating thereby a complete picture of the *Montaña,* before the nineteenth-century erosion carries away all signs of the past. In *Don Gonzalo,* Pereda had defended the heritage of the *hidalgos* against the democracy of popular rule; and in *De tal palo, tal astilla* (A Chip off the Old Block), he undertook a challenge to the ideal of tolerance, at heart a concomitant part of the whole liberal process. There are in *Don Gonzalo* the indications of some of Pereda's objections and replies to tolerance as a trait of religion, in particular, of course, referring to Catholicism: Don Frutos is the exemplary village priest, against whom latent anticlericalism is exploited by the unscrupulous agitators (the author never probes into possible abuses by ecclesiastical figures or the system as causes for the lower class's resentment); Don Román and Don Lope consider the Church as a bulwark for their own survival, treating this age-old alliance in Spain between cross and crown as necessary forever; and the explanation for the popular revolt is naively generalized at the end as the neglect of religious practices, such as attendance at Mass and the decline of morality, maintained by Catholic doctrine and teachings.

Other reasons may be suggested for this new *novela de tesis* being a challenge to the advocates of tolerance: a cogent argument, omitted by commentators interested in the literary background, resides in the general situation of the Church in 1880; and the previously analyzed problem of the Galdosian novels, linked to the personal friendship between the two authors. The death of Pius IX in 1878 had seemed to many European observers as the end not only of the longest recorded pontificate but of the papacy as a potent force, and indeed of the Church as a whole; and the conservatives saw the loss of a pope who, in the thundering *Syllabus of Errors* in 1864, had challenged all the trends of the nineteenth century, failing to make any effort to accept or to compromise with the new movements. Pereda, a devout Catholic, perhaps even "más papista que el papa" ("more papal than the pope") according to the accepted expression, certainly agreed with all the rigid directions of this pontiff; and Pereda, in some articles and scattered remarks, makes reference to his wholehearted adherence to Pius IX's leadership. When, in 1878, Leo XIII was elected pope, a very different spirit pervaded ecclesiastical circles; and this new pontiff, correctly in the light of history, embarked upon a more liberal, open, and tolerant policy. Pereda, with all other traditionalists, could not feel completely happy — though he remained loyal and obedient to Rome — at this emerging reconciliation with the nineteenth century; and this conflict, for the novelist and for other conservatives, was certainly revealed in the second half of his novel, with particular clarity and emphasis in the concluding chapters.[10]

De tal palo has been more familiarly interpreted as Pereda's literary answer to the two Galdosian novels, *Gloria* (Gloria) in 1877 and *La familia de León Roch* (The Family of León Roch) in 1879; but a broader conclusion is that the Peredian novel offers the ideological attack against the ideas and themes of Galdós not only in the two mentioned books but also in the growing opus of Don Benito. The complete correspondence, only available very recently, discloses the interesting fact that Pereda's first drafts of letters to Galdós were full of fire and brimstone, the first reaction of his granite beliefs; but that the letters as revised and actually sent are courteous and less dogmatic.[11] In short, the chivalric temperament and training of Pereda, which Galdós acknowledged in his reply to the former's acceptance speech for the Royal Spanish Academy in 1897, illustrate that the Peredian ideology sincerely and honestly reflected the man; or, perhaps conversely, that he practiced what he preached. No hypocrisy characterized Pereda as a writer; his views were overtly stated and stressed — a common conclusion (and complaint) about his work. Pereda preached without fear of the consequences for his own literary immortality and for his friendships; and *A Chip off the Old Block*, more than any other novel, undoubtedly froze liberal opinion against his entrance to the Real Academia Española, until a late date and also produced a direct collision with Galdós.

Actually, there are no structural and thematic similarities between the two novels of Galdós and *A Chip off the Old Block*, so that the basis for comparing the works involves the novelists' respective approaches to the role of religion, specifically Catholicism, in Spanish life, and for the individual person, in the present age; but the problem is also faced as to the possible irrelevancy of adherence to any formal doctrines and the sect, with the hypothesis carried to the point that orthodoxy may be indeed destructive of human happiness. Galdós, of course, touches upon this latter issue in *Gloria* and *La familia*; and Pereda concentrates upon the former questions of Catholic beliefs and practices. It is pertinent to keep in mind that Pereda, unlike Galdós, narrows his sights to Catholicism and not to the broader area of Christianity, in general, a topic that became increasingly vital to Galdosian thought and literary expression.[12]

In *Gloria*, Galdós has established an exceptional situation, adding to this unusual plot two main characters completely opposed on all

grounds. Daniel Morton is an intelligent, cosmopolitan young
Englishman who is Jewish and a stranger in Spain; Gloria is a provincial girl with limited education who has lived in a strict Catholic ambiance. The love between these two youthful characters is obviously
doomed from the start; yet the reader is immediately compelled,
against his logical reactions, to hope for a happy outcome. The
Galdosian thesis is that Daniel and Gloria might have found happiness without the interference of family and church, not only in the
case of the weak Gloria, but also of her lover, whose mother is as
fanatical as her Catholic counterparts. The result is tragic: Gloria
goes insane and dies and Daniel flees, probably to England, with
their illegitimate child.

In *La familia*, the plot is described as, perhaps, one step beyond
what might have been a felicitous ending in *Gloria:* the domestic
complications of a family, namely the husband and wife, when the
former is a man of science and a freethinker (the two are always synonymous in the nineteenth-century Spanish novel) and the latter is a
practicing Catholic; and the influence of outside forces, primarily
the confessor or religious adviser, upon the woman in the household.
Galdós is in some measure commenting upon the old Spanish adage
(applicable probably to any strongly Catholic area) that, if the wife
controls the husband, then the local priest dominates the thinking
and decisions of the woman, through the confessional and other
religious ceremonies and counsels. Galdós is portraying the disastrous results of clerical, orthodox influences upon the lives of individuals who, personally and lovingly, could solve their own
problems with success and happiness. The Church, as distinct from
religion as tolerant, liberal, understanding belief and practice, in accord with the Galdosian concept of *caritas* ("charity"), or love, is the
obvious chasm, dividing fatally the compatible couple who are introduced in *La familia*. The ending, then, is tragic with the destruction of familial unity, indeed, with the collapse of the marriage — an
intentional irony vis-a-vis the opposite aim of Church policy to foster
and to strengthen the marital state. Aesthetically, *La familia* has not
attained a position among the most respected of Galdós's *novelas
contemporáneas* ("contemporary novels"). Galdós has succumbed to
some of the same shortcomings as characterize his friend's novels.

The touchstone of the two opposite viewpoints, especially in the
two Galdosian novels and in *A Chip off the Old Block* resides in this
one word — tolerance. The lesson of the Galdosian works, before
1880, is tolerance, and the word is frequently used also in the novels

of Pereda. But for the latter writer, there can be no tolerance regarding error; error, in fact, has no rights; and Catholicism is the truth — an argument contained in the *Syllabus of Errors*, which Pereda follows to the hilt in *A Chip off the Old Block*.

This novel, as a work of art and within the artistic course of Pereda's work, also demonstrates his surer grasp of the genre, structurally, and provides evidence of his theories about his contributions. In the prologue he draws the line between realism and naturalism:

> Upon God and upon my soul I swear to you that I no longer know what is realism in the works of the creative faculty since the word is so worn out by the pens of criticism. If by realism one understands the fondness for presenting in the book human passions and characters and scenes of nature, within the decorum of art, I am a realist, and I am very honored to be one; but if one wants to label me with such a term, as has been done, and even under the guise of praise, under the banners, triumphant today over the mountains, of an obscene naturalism nakedly painting the havoc of alcoholism, the filth of laundries, and the obscenities of brothels, I protest against the injury that in such a way is inflicted upon me. There is, nevertheless, the person who has seen poetry and beauty in the bottom of those latrines of literature. What may not certain lynxes of criticism be capable of seeing?[13]

The techniques used by Pereda are a step backward from the path of realism; but it is difficult to accept Montesinos's statement that "what removes realism from *A Chip off the Old Block*, in this author's judgment, is that it is a novel of thesis."[14] Pereda returned to the romantic, and even Gothic, elements of before 1850 to construct his plot, admittedly giving a readable, interesting story; and he is immediately concerned, at the novel's outset, to defend his status as a novelist. There is no reiteration of his previous insistence that he is a painter of the local-color scenes in the Highlands. The novel begins with two very different characters, Doctor Peñarrubia and Macabeo, traveling on an unusual mission during a storm, contributing thereby an exotic, mysterious flavor in the first chapter. Doña Marta, the mother of Agueda, is dying; and Doctor Peñarrubia is very uneasy about coming into the house of this family. His humanitarian idealism and his medical oath, of course, determine him to render any possible services; but he is sad and bitter about his son's experience with this family. Doctor Peñarrubia, scorned as the symbol of science and as a freethinker, has raised his son with the same attitudes; and Fernando has matured into an atheist, for which reason the young man was refused permission by Doña Marta to court her daughter. Agueda, determinedly but sadly, likewise rejected Fernando's sincere interest in her as a wife, although she is still in love with him.

After Doña Marta's death, the plot is divided between Fernando's renewed hope of marrying Agueda because of the elimination of her mother's opposition; and the arrival of Sotero Barredera, who has wangled his way into Doña Marta's confidence as her majordomo and now seizes upon the chance to gain control of the whole estate. Sotero divides the story interest with Fernando. Not only are these two characters rivals for Agueda's love and money, but, fearing and hating each other, they begin to symbolize the very sins to which Pereda's religious *novela de tesis* is opposed. Sotero is the repulsive symbol of hypocrisy in general and religious insincerity in particular. He resembles noticeably in appearance, actions, and unscrupulous deviousness Molière's Tartuffe; and Pereda refers in his works on several occasions to the French dramatist. Sotero is also a stock character from the romantic and Gothic tradition, representing the complete villain, without any redeeming features.

Exploiting and coercing his unappealing and lazy nephew, Bastián, Sotero conspires to have Agueda and her younger sister, Pilar, live in his home for protection. Sotero then arranges for the supposedly intoxicated Bastián (during the local festivities for the feast of San Juan, that recurring date in so many Spanish works) to attempt a seduction of Agueda, thus making her decide to marry the nephew for a maintenance of her honor. The melodramatic and rather hackneyed conspiracy fails due to Bastián's limited will and intelligence as well as to the timely entrance of Macabeo, sent by Agueda to bring the girls' uncle, Plácido Quincevillas, who arrives with the loyal servant. Stunned by the accusations of his nephew and unmasked by his intended victims, Sotero likewise envisions all his schemes undone by Fernando's conversion and consequent marriage to Agueda; and the hypocrite suffers a stroke, dying alone and scorned by everyone, including the curate of Valdecines, who was never deceived by the unctuous religiosity of the majordomo. This part of the plot, with dynamic scenes, suspense, and much melodrama, nevertheless lacks any realistic originality, although Pereda has learned the technique of constructing an exciting argument.

The events constituting Fernando's dilemma are more restrained and concern, primarily, the thesis that Pereda developed in *A Chip off the Old Block.* Fernando, renewing his suit for Agueda's consent to marriage, realizes he cannot convince her that, after all, the two of them could be happy: he as an atheist and she as a devout Catholic — the liberal viewpoint, as Pereda defines the issue. As a desperate gesture, Fernando decides to consult the village priest and also to embark upon the study of Christianity on his own, to the dismay of his father. Fernando's visit to the priest, which is reported to Sotero, decides the latter to destroy his rival by spreading gossip about the young man's errors in the past. Fernando, undergoing the crisis caused by Agueda's love and his inability to accept conversion, is destroyed psychologically by all the accumulating obstacles; and he shoots himself as an act of escape from too many problems with no solutions. This suicide shatters Doctor Peñarrubia, who failed to direct his son in the youth's agony; Agueda, who suffers torments of doubt about her obstinacy in accepting Fernando on her terms; and the entire town, because of their persecution by hearsay of the victim's past conduct. Plácido, however, arrives to save his niece emotionally as he has just rescued Agueda physically from Sotero's scheme; and the uncle's counsel (or sermon), containing the novel's title, summarizes the entire thesis of *De tal palo:*

"Come now, my child," he said to her affectionately. "Courage, and courage always, because, after all, you are not alone in the world! Having considered well this event, it was to be expected sooner or later, and, frankly, it is preferable that it has occurred now. I mean that it was to be expected because good works have no place where there is no fear of God; and you well know how religion goes with that breed. It is true that his father, though a heretic, is now dragging through his life calmly; but this may be due to the isolation in which he lives, sheltering him from the annoyances through which the temper of souls is tested. Besides, according to my reports, the father's heresies are not so bad compared to the lack of any belief about which the son boasted. And that had to happen because of the very force of circumstances: 'A chip off the old block.' From a lukewarm and negligent person in the matter of faith, like Doctor Peñarrubia, is born a Voltairean, an atheist who loses his head at the smallest disappointment; and who goes crazy, or takes his life, for it's all the same. And in their logic, they act very rationally: the dog is dead, the rabies is ended, therefore I kill the dog. As for the fools whom such wise men leave in the world, weeping over their criminal madness, is that worth while? He who does not succeed in knowing God in his whole life, how is he going to pay attention to similar trifles at the moment of committing the heroic deed? There are unfortunate people who will applaud it, and even imitate it, you can depend upon that.

An admirable breed to regenerate the old world! An admirable intelligence of men who are eager to throw toward that trough the currents of ideas! (I, 1213)

Agueda, bolstered by this fanatical and strident analysis of her uncle, faces Doctor Peñarrubia, coming as a last request from his son. The interview is theatrical in the obvious confrontation and very melodramatic in the presentations of the two arguments. Doctor Peñarrubia claims that "the tenacity of an unmerciful fanaticism" killed his son, meaning of course the girl's obstinate beliefs; but Agueda replies very confidently that Fernando's "rebellion against the decrees of God" killed him (I, 1215). Love, invoked by the doctor, as his son had likewise urged upon Agueda as the bridge over their religious differences, can never supersede the necessity to believe in God and to practice the Catholic faith. Too easily, and too unconvincingly, Agueda triumphs over the father's reasons and pleas, and she is merciless in her verdict about Fernando, even the fact that parent and child cannot be buried in the same cemetery: "What a frightful misfortune! Separated from him in the earth, and eternally separated afterwards! . . . He died rebellious, impenitent. . . . The only crime that is not possible for divine mercy!" (I, 1216 - 17).

This interpretation of Catholic doctrine, through Plácido's and Agueda's arguments in the last chapter, failed to win any support, even from strongly Catholic circles, where Pereda's novel was ignored or mentioned very briefly. Menéndez Pelayo followed Clarín's attempt to find some merit in the types, such as Macabeo and the visitors to the apothecary's shop, and, of course, the setting in the Montaña. This novel stirred up more controversy than any other novel of Pereda, lending support to the obdurate traditionalists and, more unhappily, to religious fanatics; and liberal Catholics, politely ignoring Pereda's rigid theology, were set back in any attempts to modify church teachings dating from the Council of Trent in the sixteenth century and the more recently terminated Vatican Council I. The opposition, of course, was overjoyed at Pereda's dubious presentation, with the religious problem tilted so extremely on one side. Combining romantic and Gothic features with realistic dialogue and regional scenes, Pereda failed, as in El buey suelto and Don Gonzalo, to present two sides of any issue, and this defect, dangerous and perhaps fatal for any first-rank novelist, lowered his reputation in the eyes of friend and foe alike. His stock, on the climb after Don Gon-

zalo, plummeted upon the offering of *A Chip off the Old Block*, and his critics were made more acutely aware of these same biased, crudely introduced obsessions and extremisms in Pereda's prior writings. All in all, this novel represents the nadir of Pereda's career as a novelist and as a respected spokesman for a certain point of view.[15]

This point of view, in the hindsight of almost a century and with the sweeping changes in theological thought, is totally discredited; and, if readers of 1880 — both practicing and nonpracticing Catholics — were embarrassed by the Peredian dogmatism, then the audiences of today, without exception in all probability, would find little to approve. At best the recitative speeches of Agueda and Plácido would be considered possible, but, at the same time, certainly ironical and paradoxical. Most of the theological positions espoused by Pereda, although in strict alignment with nineteenth-century orthodoxy, have been swept aside by more mature literary treatments in the novels of Graham Greene and François Mauriac. Another irony of this twentieth-century progressive spirit is that the modern Catholic novelists oppose precisely the self-assured, middle-class stance (found respectively in the same examples, Greene and Mauriac) of Plácido and Agueda. Both Galdós and Pereda floundered in the quicksand of the religious issues of their age, especially in *Gloria, La familia,* and *A Chip off the Old Block;* but the Peredian reply to his friend's efforts is the more disastrous because, at least, the Galdosian struggle merits contemporary respect, despite the weighted arguments.

The paradox in any present analysis of *A Chip off the Old Block* can be gleaned from the documents of Vatican Council II, when Pereda's church stressed the regard for tolerance, the right of conscience, the mystery of salvation and damnation, and a love for the sinner. Thus, Fernando and Doctor Peñarrubia, while their agnosticism and atheism (Pereda's apparent description of their respective philosophies) do not find acceptance or admittance as valid attitudes toward life, would not be so harshly and bitterly condemned. And, of more importance, the men themselves would be treated humanely, in a Christian manner. The main objection, then, to Pereda's depiction, with particular reference to the concluding chapters, is this self-contradictory mentality of the two Peredian spokesmen, Plácido and Agueda, joined in the same heartless, uncomprehending obduracy by the townspeople. These characters profess the Christian faith, with especial claim to total adherence to

Catholicism, and yet they neglect some of the essential tenets of that religion, in addition to lacking any sense of brotherhood and humanity. The rhetorical question can be posed of whether these two accusers, uncle and niece, of the Peñarrubias could be any more cruel, inhuman, and tactless without their theological doctrines.

However, Pereda has tried to portray the other extreme of condemnation with the example of Sotero. In fact, Fernando and Sotero illustrate for the author the two opposing pitfalls of religion: the former has renounced completely any faith, openly and honestly, despite his later attempt to overcome the "obstacle" (Pereda's repeated term for the young man's inability to accept conversion); and the latter projects with ostentatious appearances his supposed faith. Both men live in sin; and the two individuals die in the state of mortal sin. This fact bears considerable importance for Pereda's whole outlook because these two sinners are equally condemned to hell for eternity, according to Catholic theology. Plácido is indeed "placid," for he best expresses the Peredian religious thesis; and he is the character who also solves the twin complications of the plot revolving around Fernando and Sotero.

But again, the contemporary audience cannot fail to agree with Fernando on other points: the young man's views are attuned to the present day with his plea to Agueda about the primacy of love in marriage and also about the possible, feasible omission of any wedding ceremony, indeed of any formal rites within a society, to give place to the will and freedom of individuals; and, perhaps cruelly and certainly very hypothetically, he was rather lucky not to have won Agueda as a wife — an argument raised by Doctor Peñarrubia when he suggested that his son forget her and look for a more compatible mate elsewhere. Pereda's heroine is certainly an appealing, attractive, and kind woman; and Agueda would have undoubtedly been a dutiful wife and mother, as indicated by her devotion to Doña Marta and Pilar. Nevertheless, Agueda's stubborn reliance upon all the tenets of her religion and her unwillingness to compromise, or at least to listen to opposing ideas, with an attendant effort to understand, as in the scenes with Fernando and Doctor Peñarrubia, would seem to foreshadow a very difficult relationship in marriage. Again, with this hindsight of a century one may conclude that Pereda's intentions have been further upset by changing times because Fernando emerges as a more rational, intelligent, and sympathetic character than Agueda; and his ideas have survived — and have triumphed — against those of Agueda.

Pereda, to his credit, has inserted a positive dimension to Fernando when he obviously draws a parallel between his hero's sufferings and those of Christ during the events of Holy Week. In fact, Fernando is very effectively described as a Christ figure during his persecution by the townspeople, goaded by Sotero's plan to discredit Agueda's suitor completely. The references to the Passion of Christ are direct and credible. Fernando in the garden, like Gethsemane, undergoes mental and spiritual suffering and uses words similar to those of Jesus in the New Testament. The chapter headings likewise refer to Christian symbolism, for example, "the drop of water" and "the dregs of the chalice." Finally, there is the intimate, beseeching plea of Fernando, when close to suicide, about the divine forsaking of his sacrificial life. Of course, Pereda repeatedly indicates Fernando's grave errors; but the symbolism provides a more balanced, mature technique with some regret and some comprehension on the author's part during the last few dramatic moments of the protagonist's agony. This redeeming quality of the usually one-sided thesis, contributes poignancy and psychological versimilitude to the hero; and two chapters, 26 and 27, stand out as a superior presentation.

Pereda is unknowingly sketching in quite close detail and with eerie coincidence the background of his own son's suicide about thirteen years later, in 1893, during the father's writing of *Peñas arriba*. Juan Manuel's suicide affected Pereda very severely, and one wonders if the author's harsh judgment about Fernando's sin and damnation came back to distress the sorrowful father. There are, apparently, no resemblances between the religious crisis of Fernando and the nervous anguish of Pereda's oldest son; but the literary description in *A Chip off the Old Block* about the wavering between life and death of a person with suicidal tendencies, the use of a pistol as the choice for a weapon, and the setting of a garden for the action certainly coincided with the real-life event. The piercing effect on Pereda of the denial of burial in consecrated ground of a person who has committed suicide, a theological tenet in Catholicism symbolizing eternal damnation, may have turned his mind to his fictional hero of 1880; and one wonders if the author's faith then might have admitted a more open-minded attitude. Pereda, with all charity, was later placed sadly in the true-to-life shoes of Doctor Peñarrubia, hoping that some mercy might be due to his son despite the stubborn sermon of Agueda, learning her lines from Plácido, the two mouthpieces of Pereda in 1880.[16]

IV   El sabor de la tierruca

The negative reception of *A Chip off the Old Block* plunged Pereda into another depression; and he again returned to the surface with concentration upon the region of the *Montaña*. In 1882, Pereda published *El sabor de la tierruca* (Redolent of the Soil), considered by some critics as the best novel of his five books of this period; at very least, the work is conceded to be a meritorious effort by Pereda.[17] He had abandoned the obvious category of the thesis novel without omitting his firm conceptions and ideals. The endeavor, though necessary for aesthetic and critical reasons, went against the grain of Pereda's frankness and desires: "My novel is going forward very slowly since I am encountering difficulties in moving so many people without a transcendental subject"; and later, "I shall not be able to go to Polanco this year until the month of August, nor consequently to work until then with good results on the novel, if a series of pictures stitched together with a threading needle merits such a name."[18]

Nevertheless, Pereda was pleased with his return to the soil of Santander, with his abandonment of overt political, religious, or marital theses, and he could finally explain near the end of the book's composition: "There is neither religion nor politics in it. Everything is nature, types, and customs; something in short that may give an idea of *El sabor de la tierruca*, as I am thinking of calling it, if I do not baptize it with the name of *La epopeya de Cumbrales* [The Epic of Cumbrales] between which titles I am vacillating, although neither of the two satisfies me."[19] Thus, close to the start of *Sotileza*, Pereda had turned his back on the previous three novels, bringing storms of controversy and doubtful immortality upon his sensitive spirit; and he has in a sense come home to the artistry of *Escenas montañesas*. He likewise seized upon the notion of an *epopeya* ("epic poem") about the *Montaña,* and the *cuadros de costumbres* of the *Escenas montañesas* were merged and broadened into a whole story, or epic, around the life of this region, the province of Santander.

At the same time, the idyllic features of the Highlands characterized predominantly the approach of Pereda toward his vaster subject, his reaction to criticism of him as a naturalist, or even as a disloyal son of Santander. The faithful Menéndez Pelayo, exaggeratedly praising this book as one he felt rather than read, also compared *Redolent of the Soil* favorably with the best "idyllic poems" (the phrase gives a significant clue to the Peredian philosophy); but Don Marcelino likewise admits that, concomitantly, the action is limited, or, in later interpretations, the novel has yielded to the idyll, to the description, and to the style. *Don Gonzalo* and *A Chip off the Old Block*, to their credit, provided swift-moving action, which kept alive audience interest with admittedly romantic, Gothic, and some melodramatic scaffolding. The problem for Pereda, as he expectedly veered back to home territory, was to achieve the balance between an idyll and a novel.[20] Galdós, characteristically showing his liberalism by writing the prologue to *Redolent of the Soil* shortly after the controversy over *A Chip off the Old Block*, analyzed the dilemma — and the failure — of his friend in a lengthy, laudatory, and too-flattering introduction. Galdós praises Pereda, for example, for "his very fortunate boldness in the painting of the natural," for which "it is necessary to declare him the standard-bearer of literary realism in Spain"; "the great reform he has made by introducing popular language into literary language"; "this country book, essentially of the Highlands, *El sabor de la tierruca* . . . [is] the sure highway of natural observation" (I, 1353 - 58). Unconsciously, Don Benito is describing his own contributions to the Spanish novel, more critically recognized in his favor than Pereda's, although this was probably not the intention of the generous Galdós.

Galdós lifts the curtain on the personal background of Pereda at the time of *A Chip off the Old Block*, in addition to remarking on the "caustic intolerance" of Pereda and stating that "the intolerance that encourages and invigorates so much the powerful creative faculty of Pereda is usually poured out in the intimacy of friendship" (I, 1356 - 57), a very applicable commentary to the recently published Peredian novel of religious thesis. With the same honest, blunt intimacy, Galdós describes this episode, revealing a glimpse of Pereda's psychological problems:

If it is a question of nervous temperaments, one must pass over all of them in order to give a diploma of honor to that of my friend, whom it is necessary to scold, as one scolds children, so that he may get out of his head a thousand apprehensions and manias. There is a person who tells him that all these destructive notions are a pretext for laziness, and a medicine extremely profitable to the doctor is prescribed for him to be cured, that is to say, for him to take five hundred sheets of paper and make us a novel. I remember one spell when he hit upon the idea that he was going to fall down in the middle of the street, and he used to go out taking a thousand precautions and with very strange fears. His friends prescribed that he should put himself to work. He did not want to do so, not even by fits and starts; but

there was so much argument about it that the happy ending of that whole
nervous disorder was the delightful novel *De tal palo, tal astilla*. (I, 1357)

Both Menéndez Pelayo and Galdós, coinciding accurately in their
prophetic critiques of Pereda's talent, stressed that his permanent
place in the nineteenth-century novel would be as a regionalist,
where he could bring to bear on the *Montaña* all his strength as an
observer and as a poet. Description and style, as noted by both sympathetic critics in their long reactions, stand out in *El sabor de la
tierruca* as excellent proofs of the merits of the regional novel; and
these same two traits become the ideals of a possible first-rate novel
by Pereda, exemplified in *Sotileza*, only three years later.[21]
    The description applies to the scenery as Pereda paints slowly and
with abundant detail the town of Cumbrales, adding an equivalent
sketch of the rival village, Rinconeda, with the meadows, trees, and
hills. Then, the author's focus brings close to hand the houses of the
two towns, with primary emphasis on the main place of action, Cumbrales, especially the church. The physical setting for the coming
events and the tranquil existence of the inhabitants seem eternal; as
in the next novel, *Fine Spun*, Pereda would like to stop time, to show
the *Montaña* before 1868, and even earlier, before any ominous hints
of nineteenth-century changes. In 1882, Pereda sums up his firm
regionalism in the final paragraph of the novel: "How lucky I would
be if, with this poor book, since I have not succeeded in so many
others made with the same feeling, I could manage to give you even
an idea, but exact, of the people, of the customs, of the things, of the
land, and of the skylight, in short, of *El sabor de la tierruca!*" (I,
1498).
    Here, coinciding with the emergence of naturalism, is the most
successful amalgam by Pereda of regionalism and realism; and here,
also, is the opportunity for the rather eclectic standard-bearer of the
naturalist cause, Emilia Pardo Bazán, to launch a probing, convincing argument, very pertinent in reference to *El sabor de la tierruca:*

One can compare Pereda's talent to a beautiful garden, watered and
tended well, aired by fragrant and healthful country breezes, but of limited
horizons. . . . I do not know if, with deliberate purpose or because living
where he lives forces him, Pereda confines himself to describe and to narrate
types and customs of Santander, thus enclosing himself in a small circle of
subjects and characters. He excels as a painter of a definite country, as a
bucolic poet of a countryside always the same; and he never tried to study

thoroughly civilized means, modern life in the large capitals, a life which is antipathetic to him and which he hates; therefore I characterized Pereda's horizon as limited, and therefore it is important to declare that if, from Pereda's garden, an extensive panorama is not revealed, on the other hand the place is the most pleasant, fertile, and delightful that is known.[22]

The characters in *El sabor de la tierruca* show realistic and naturalistic qualities; the lower classes are portrayed in a less exemplary manner than representatives of the upper stratum, the *hidalgos*, a feature not surprising by now in Pereda. In fact, the personages resemble more closely actors in the *Escenas montañesas* than in any other novel, including *Don Gonzalo* where the motley would-be republicans were not as prone to rough language and violent outbursts, except upon the prodding of their leaders. These personages in *El sabor de la tierruca* demonstrate that Pereda, unwittingly, has added a naturalistic dimension to his novel, not by imitating the French models or even the few Spanish sources at this time but instead by resurrecting the original, credible types of "The Levy," "The End of a Race," and other pieces of *Escenas montañesas*. Unfortunately, Pereda has sketched horizontally instead of vertically in his characterizations, a decision necessarily affecting the plot. There are too many characters with too many subplots, and this unsatisfactory technique is compounded by the lack of any unity in the form of a main thread of action or a thesis. Pereda has omitted forceful, possibly controversial themes as a reaction to the negative reception of *The Bachelor, Don Gonzalo,* and *A Chip off the Old Block*. He has again made a complete about-face, too abruptly and too extremely, by now a recognized literary and psychological trait of the writer.

The result, apparently detected by several critics,[23] is confusion in any effort to summarize the sudden comings-and-goings of the types, who are identified briefly and without any indications of either their role or their importance in the novel. A certain dynamism, reminiscent of the *comedia* of the Golden Age, attends these scenery changes; and the complex loves of the young men and women, frustrated by circumstances or an unresponsive object of their affections, also recall the intricate stitchings of the pastoral novel. The possibility of such models is not bolstered by evidence in any letters or works of Pereda; and an alternate explanation may be one more sharp turn by the author from one procedure to another. In the three previous novels, the plot is easily followed and the characters are limited in number, sufficiently for convenient reading and better individual understanding; in fact, the story in *Don Gonzalo* is logically told and still readable today. Paradoxically, then, a superior setting, with an improved poetic style is compelled to support a mediocre plot and the mistaken inclusion of a vast supporting cast.

Nevertheless, the plot can be traced in some general outline, striving to point out main characters and principal elements — an emphasis lacking in Pereda's composition. It is not feasible to recount the plot chronologically, as Pereda narrates the happenings, chapter by chapter, for he does not call attention to the vital parts. Thus, the introduction of Baldomero and Pablo in the second chapter includes an extensive dialogue about their individual plans, all of which bears little on later episodes and leads astray the unwary or too attentive reader. Another example of the Peredian love of description is the first chapter, appropriately titled "El escenario" (The Setting), with much emphasis on the *cajiga*, "gall oak," as the epitome of the Highland spirit. Two *hidalgos*, Pedro Mortera and Juan de Prezanes, control the life of Cumbrales; but they are estranged, mainly due to the irascible behavior of the latter, exacerbated by political waves from the capital. Pedro is more open to change and to acceptance of democratic methods, such as elections; Juan is stubborn in his pessimism about any deviation from the traditional way of life, domination by his social class for the good of the people. Valentín Gutiérrez de la Pernía, a quixotic local hero of an obscure battle, is enthralled by the premonition of a renewed encounter with glory, especially on behalf of freedom against tyranny, his interpretation of the polarizing politics in the area. The children of these *hidalgos* are unconcerned; the younger generation is too involved, romantically, with each other. Pablo and María are the son and daughter of Pedro; Ana, the daughter of Juan; and Baldomero, the son of Valentín.

At the novel's conclusion, the following couples are married, living happily ever after, presumably, in Pereda's idyllic "garden" of the *Montaña:* Pablo and Ana; María and the son of Rodrigo Calderetas; Baldomero and a widow, appearing opportunely on the scene; and Nisco and Catalina, another pair frustrated at first by outside circumstances. Two contradictory problems, ultimately resolved, have caused complications and delays for the lovers. Familial quarrels and differences, principally between Pedro and Juan, together with the timidity and uncertainty of the youths, have prevented the required, traditional consents from the fathers. In some cases, the decisions of the new generation, heirs to the heritage of the *Montaña*, have curiously effected a rapprochement among some of the interested parties, parents and offspring equally; but in other instances, an unexpected tension results because of shifting political and ideological alliances. Some slight melodrama is added by the death of Valentín during an incipient imbroglio, quite ludicrous and yet artificial. At least, the mock-heroic, accidental demise of this *hidalgo* serves to cool tempers on both sides of the enveloping fray between Cumbrales and Rinconeda, traditionally antagonistic and now with a belligerency spurred by political as well as personal matters. No real villains, comparable to the rogues in other novels, Patricio Rigüelta or Sotero, hold together the nebulous plot strings; and the bullies who goad Pablo are only local types, occupied in a typical pastime.

There are some excellent local-color sketches, however, reiterating Pereda's regionalism and idealization of the Highlands. The source, as Pereda mentions on several occasions, is again *Escenas montañesas;* and he rather defensively refers more than once to the distinction between a novel and a book of *cuadros de costumbres.* This sensitivity about classification and definition surfaces often in *Redolent of the Soil,* and Pereda has no hesitation about intruding with rather firm assertions about his art.[24] The examples of *costumbrismo* are obviously grafted on the body of the plot with success in some cases and with the best being a worthy accretion to the novel. Dances, harvests, weddings, and fiestas are described in whatever detail Pereda chooses; and the impact is that of a pleasant bucolic idyll, adding to the beauty of the landscape with which the natives are in harmony.

Other contributions by Pereda recall also the less happy but realistic, naturalistic pictures of the *Escenas montañesas;* and these believable insertions provide a welcome balance to the often disastrous urge of the author to tip his book too heavily in favor of his determined ideology. Indeed, Pereda is drawing near to the rounded structure of *Sotileza;* he is accepting, not wholeheartedly but at least encouragingly, the simple explanation that there are good and bad days and that no way of life, even in his beloved *Montaña,* is perfect. This elementary compromise or rudimentary understanding of human existence does not fit into the Peredian vision in the three previous novels, which are heavily loaded with their respective theses. Here, the *brujas* ("witches") are remembered from *Escenas montañesas;* and la Rámila appears as an important character, a mixture of town gossip, local gadfly, and potential go-between, surely a type peculiar to the *Montaña.* La Rámila likewise serves as the object of the superstitions, ignorance, viciousness, and violence of lower-class types, such as Tablucas; the "witch" (a translation insufficient to convey all the nuances of the Santander *bruja*) is feared, ridiculed, and humored by turns, although at the book's end she survives a murderous attack. Pereda sharpens his psychological portrait of La Rámila by leaving the impression that he dislikes these brujas of the Highlands on a certain level and, without contradiction, finds them a rewarding type of his *patria chica.*

The life of the people of Santander, all in all, is a monotonous, dreary, and very hard existence with only scattered days for relaxation and gaiety; the future will be a continuation of the present, even for their children. The storm which signals the end of the autumn and the beginning of winter brings added hardship to the inhabitants from the cold, rain, and battering of their humble homes; and one sees, in justice and compensation, this striking vignette of the darker side of Pereda's "garden." The description of the storm shows Pereda's artistic powers, a strong point increasingly in his favor. The effective portrayal of a mountain storm foreshadows the tempest at sea in *Fine Spun,* the high mark of that novel. The picture of the Highlands, then, offers in general an idyll; but it would be unfair not to acknowledge the presence of a more balanced point of reference in this certainly realistic, and somewhat naturalistic, rendition of the *Montaña.*[25]

There are two other advances in the Peredian philosophy, woven into the tortuous plot: the role of the younger generation in effecting a reconciliation between their fathers and in determining their own futures, illustrated by their choice of mates; and the psychology of the hidalgos, studied carefully, with a moderate characterization of these types. Both changes must be appreciated in relation to the three preceding novels, although these more enlightened views of Pereda are still far from those of Galdós, and even more so from the naturalists during this decade. While the newly wedded couples will remain in the province, their lives will not be as narrow as their parents' routines; and these young people will be more receptive to the present, and less enamored of the charming but hopelessly archaic traditions of their families. This budding generation has already made a compromise with the existing order and the nineteenth century.

Another piece of evidence, and the most surprising advance in

Pereda's outlook, resides in the characterizations of the hidalgos, no longer purely the exemplary, noble guides of their countrymen, destined to govern wisely. On the contrary, Pereda has depicted these noblemen of the *Montaña* as less than brilliant in their everyday affairs, their relations with their children, and even with their fellow hidalgos. Some political interest exists in the arguments over elections and in the disparate views of traditionalists versus reformers, but this work does not belong in the line of the political novels. Similarities do exist in the problems, however, and the characters, although monolithic unity no longer guides the actions of the hidalgos, and they are significantly divided in approach and attitude toward the challenge and defense of their traditions. They are disunited because of personal antipathies and lasting feuds, and they are sometimes painted as ludicrous and ridiculous descendants of a noble heritage. Pedro is the only hidalgo who exemplifies the spirit of the aristocracy, and the sympathetic characterization inheres in his common sense, moderation, and good will, not in his traditionalist beliefs, as was the case with the noblemen of *Don Gonzalo*. Juan and Valentín are both comical and pathetic in their isolation from reality and from the changing century, and are weak, mediocre leaders of their districts.

Whatever may have been Pereda's intentions in his portrayal of the hidalgos,[26] he has undoubtedly altered his vision of the aristocratic class between *Don Gonzalo* and *Redolent of the Soil*. In the latter the nobility are more realistic and, despite the author's strictures, closer to the decadent hidalgos of Clarín and Pardo Bazán. Both the poorer classes and ruling circles by turns dominate the confusing, complex plot of this novel. They are very human individuals with foibles and faults — a different vision for Pereda — counterbalancing the romantic, youthful figures of the next generation. Within this group of Pereda's novels preceding his masterpiece, *Fine Spun*, the first three stand clearly as theses novels, with controversial publicity and without enduring aesthetic principles. *Redolent of the Soil*, while faithful in certain ways to the three previous books, takes a new direction, luckily a throwback to the positive elements in *Escenas montañesas*. This is a novel without an overt thesis, but still lacking a masterly control of the novelistic genre.[27]

V *Pedro Sánchez*

The fifth and final novel of this group, *Pedro Sánchez*, surprised the critics of Pereda without exception by the sharp turn from the thesis novel and from the idyll of the *Montaña*. Pereda's two most prestigious critics, Clarín and Pardo Bazán, startled and pleased by *Pedro Sánchez* in 1883, only a year after *Redolent of the Soil*, showed their admiration in very flattering reviews. Clarín wrote: "What is *Pedro Sánchez?* In my humble opinion, the best novel of Pereda, and one of the best that have been written in Spain in these years of the flowering of the genre. For me, *Pedro Sánchez* is to Pereda what *La desheredada* [The Disinherited Woman] is to Galdós"[28]; and Pardo Bazán, no longer critical of Pereda's "well-tended garden," thought instead that he had taken her previous advice: "The firm purpose of broadening his horizons; the wise precaution of not allowing himself to be enslaved by a thesis and secondrate morals; mild indulgence and human sympathy, muses which Pereda was unaccustomed to invoke; the especial life of the narration, which is somewhat autobiographical; and finally, the inspiration, the yeast that makes the realistic mass ferment, are united to produce in *Pedro Sánchez* one of the most beautiful novels ever written in Spanish and the pearl of Pereda's collection."[29] Menéndez Pelayo, however, while he predictably agreed with these flowery appreciations of Pereda's success in *Pedro Sánchez*, did not share their enthusiasm for all the implications of this new work: "All that is true, and nevertheless, esteeming *Pedro Sánchez* more than anyone, I do not end up convincing myself that Pereda and I are so completely mistaken; and whether it be because I am so much of the *Montaña*, or because of childhood memories, I always lovingly turn my eyes toward the poet of "La robla" and "La leva" . . . *Pedro Sánchez* seems to me a much better novel than *El buey suelto;* but I will still take *El sabor de la tierruca* and *Don Gonzalo.*"[30] *Pedro Sánchez*, the closest of these five works to a novel, does not please Menéndez Pelayo fully because the setting is not that of the *Montaña* or the idyll, a point criticized harshly by other important critics. Literary history has not followed this judgment of Menéndez Pelayo for Pereda's more durable reputation, at least about the five novels of this phase. The interesting question again arises as to the ultimate benefits of the well-intentioned influence of Pereda's compatriot. Menéndez Pelayo determined the novelist to a manner of writing that has not often survived in the jungle of criticism.

Pereda's own feelings about *Pedro Sánchez* resembled his previous complaints about the agonies of composition of all his novels, and he was apparently surprised very happily by the overwhelmingly favorable reception of this latest effort, critically most of all but also popularly.[31] Little evidence has appeared to show

why and how Pereda, changing course this time to strikingly benefi-
cent advantage, composed such a different novel. Conclusions about
the differences among the other books, as Pereda decided upon a try
at this and that, have been made at various stages of his career; but
this time the novelistic result is revolutionary. There are no sure
clues and sources for the form and content of *Pedro Sánchez* in his
work before 1883. And after that date Pereda did not further exploit
the artistry and techniques of *Pedro Sánchez*. The irony is that this
novel is still accorded high acclaim; and Cossío, for example, justifies
his selection of *Pedro Sánchez* as representative of Pereda for the
Clásicos castellanos ("Castilian classics") in this reasonable analysis:

> I could have thought of *Sotileza* or *Peñas Arriba*, without doubt his most
> perfect novels, or of some of his sketches or scenes; but in addition to being a
> question of local environments, less appropriate for foreign readers, or at
> least not from the *Montaña*, a jargon, or local dialect, so pronounced that the
> author believed himself in need of accompanying some of these works with a
> vocabulary, is used in them. *Pedro Sánchez* partakes of the virtues of the
> Peredian novels of the *Montaña*, and it continues at the same time a classical
> tradition within the manners and novelistic spirit of its time.[32]

Two differences in *Pedro Sánchez* remove this novel from the
idyll, so admired by Menéndez Pelayo. The setting in the *Montaña*
and the reproduction of not only the popular language but the
peculiar speech forms or dialectal words were beginning to be
recognized as Pereda's trademarks. One explanation of the novel's
success is the location of the action in Madrid, for the most part, and
in the provincial capital where the main character has been appointed to a government post; and the story takes place among upper social classes and in intellectual circles. Pedro Sánchez, the
protagonist, controls all the events of the plot; the novel is narrated
from his point of view without exception. He has deliberately abandoned his *patria chica* and uses a more polished Spanish, avoiding
linguistic slips into the dialect of his region, errors that would cause
him to lose prestige in his climb to the top. Everything in the novel is
learned through Pedro Sánchez, and this first-person narrative
technique gives a sound structure and artistic unity to the book, thus
eliminating a justifiable complaint about *Redolent of the Soil*, and
reducing Pereda's tendency to include too many characters with
attendant subplots.

The form of *Pedro Sánchez*, with the narrator at the center of all the action, happenings, and interpretations has led to several attempts at classification by critics, showing thereby the richness of this creation. In the absence of any indication from the author of his intentions, all the possible definitions would seem to have value in understanding Pereda's superior piece of prose fiction; and the various generic categories help to illustrate that Pereda has certainly more potential literary talent and techniques than a mere follower of the *costumbristas*, realists, and regionalists.

The first reaction to *Pedro Sánchez* is a recognition of the autobiographical features of the novel because the adventures and thoughts of Pereda's narrator reflect closely those of the author himself, probably as a youth in Santander and obviously as an adult, at least insofar as the principal facts of his residence in Madrid from 1852 to 1854 are known. This clear utilization of his own experiences to tell the story of Pedro Sánchez lasts, approximately, until the twenty-seventh chapter, when the hero, at the end of the revolution, begins to realize his ambitions. Pereda himself had fled from the capital after the fighting in 1854 and had returned home to the *Montaña*. Thus, the parallelism, while not limited exclusively to the first twenty-six chapters, nonetheless is more pronounced and recognizable in them.

Pedro Sánchez lives in a small village of the Highlands where his early existence is prosaic to the extent of restlessness. His ambitions (that fatal malady of nineteenth-century civilization for Pereda) are aroused by the reading of novels, excursions to the city of Santander, and an encounter with summer tourists, those *tipos trashumantes* whom the author ridiculed in a book of sketches. The descriptions of the province, in which Pereda employs names found in other works and thus contributes a connecting link with his growing world view of the *Montaña*, are modest in comparison with the expansive local-color additions to *Redolent of the Soil*, because Pedro Sánchez is the axis around which all other aspects of this novel revolve. In short, the description serves as a backdrop for the main character, not as an isolated, independent unit.

Some of the references bring to mind sources in Pereda's prior writings, such as the ubiquitous railroad (this time a symbol both of change and also a means to join the provincial microcosm of Santander with the macrocosm of Madrid). In fact, almost all of the elements of the first seven chapters, when Pedro Sánchez, at the age of twenty-five, leaves for the city, can be found in earlier works. Even the theme of the Highlander departing from his homeland for the lure of the big city with money, glory, and power as his aims is essentially that of *Men of Worth*. But the verisimilitude is striking, as Pedro Sánchez wavers between the love and security of family and patria chica and his great expectations in the capital, built on the promises of Augusto Valenzuela, a flamboyant politician who has spent part of the summer in the province. The farewell and departure of Pedro Sánchez are poignant and reminiscent of any young person's first ventures beyond the home, independent and alone.

This sense of loneliness afflicts Pedro Sánchez as he, traveling by coach with six types (another skillful blending of the costumbrista preference with the requirements of a unified novel), leaves the familiar geography of his native province and views the austere, arid land of the two Castiles. The place names lend authenticity to the narration, and Pereda's interpretations of the Castilian landscape offer an interesting comparison with that same preoccupation of the writers of the Generation of 1898, such as Azorín (who was impressed by Pereda's descriptive talents).[33] Description is more than a separate entity in *Pedro Sánchez:* the scenery is intimately connected not only with the mood of the hero but becomes a causal factor in his deepening melancholy.

The plot is broadened by the introduction of Serafín Balduque and his daughter, Carmen. The dialogue with Balduque, realistic, natural, and pertinent, shows Pedro the problems he will face in the capital. Balduque and Valenzuela, throughout this novel, offer an example of counterpoint: the former is a forthright, honest public servant; and the latter is an opportunistic bureaucrat. Both are victims, however, as Balduque explains to Pedro during the trip, of the lack of any civil service in Spain during this time. The two men are *cesantes,* government employes who are fired upon a change of government or ministries; and the very frequent changes of administration during the nineteenth century made the tenure of all officeholders of short duration, undoubtedly a cause for inefficiency and limited output in all branches of the central régime. This problem of the cesantes, in fact, emerges as a persistent theme in many novels of the period, including those of Galdós. Pereda has learned to describe and to criticize his own views about politics, humorously and with telling force, keeping in mind the central character and the advancing plot. There is no overt, digressive outburst on the author's part, as in other writings; and the effect augments the value of *Pedro Sánchez*.

The plot has now progressed to the added complication of two women, both attracting Pedro's attention. The coincidence is too open, as well as suspiciously reminiscent of romanticism, with the contrasts between these feminine characters too noticeable. Clara and Carmen are the daughters, respectively, of Valenzuela and Balduque so that the counterpoint in the four characters, technically a mature feature, may be weakened psychologically. A shortcoming of Pereda, observable in all the works to this date and even later, is his inability to paint compelling pictures of women. Only, in fact, in *Sotileza* does the heroine appear as a credible type with an independence and personality of her own. This artistic defect may be explained possibly by his ideological stances; he would surely draw masculine actors more forcefully than any female personages, the women being the traditional support of their men rather than persons in their own right.[34]

Indeed, one of the few defective parts of *Pedro Sánchez* is the hero's naive and unrealistic attitude toward Clara and Carmen, an attitude which is not romantic, but nonetheless difficult to accept as worthy of credibility. Pedro is overwhelmed by the physical attractiveness of Clara, although he sees her very little in Madrid, and their relationship is limited; she probably exists for him as another facet of his ambition, as a prize to be won in proof of his success in the big city. Carmen becomes a recurring image for Pedro, and he thinks repeatedly of her, first out of gratitude for her father's kindness and later out of pity for her plight. He never tries to analyze his sentiments and reactions about Clara, and he is constantly obtuse about Carmen's unexpressed but obvious love for him. The love triangle, nevertheless, is not a major idea in Pereda's novel, and only at times, almost as a relief from the other actions, does he — or Pedro — occupy himself with these amorous interests.

The scenes in Madrid, beginning in the ninth chapter, provide some of the best and most valuable commentaries by Pereda in his complete works; and the analysis of the ambiance — literary, political, and social — remains an astute, revealing, reliable guide to this decade, and not only the specific year, 1854, in Spanish history and culture.[35] Of course, Pereda is relying strongly and wisely upon his own observations, insights, and reactions about this period in a work of the creative imagination; clearly, the many references have a direct relevance to his own life and to his development as a writer. For example, he mentions the popularity of novels, especially the French books; but the only serious Spanish author whom Pereda discusses is Fernán Caballero. Although Pereda's rather unfavorable criticism has been justified by some of his successors, the points that he dislikes in Fernán Caballero's novels are ironically encountered in his own writings, for example, weak characterization, too-idyllic sketches of the countryside, and a moralizing, sermonizing content. The acknowledged influence and a debatable imitation of Fernán Caballero in Pereda's literary output are admitted by among others, Menéndez Pelayo and Montesinos in the nineteenth and twentieth centuries respectively.[36] One should bear in mind that Pereda may indeed be a defender of Fernán Caballero, and other literary figures, because Pedro Sánchez is being depicted unfavorably, as a snob and as a would-be intellectual; therefore, the reverse of his opinions may represent Pereda's real feelings and attitudes. Again, the originality and maturity of this acclaimed novel are demonstrated if one could imagine an eclectic plan on Pereda's drawing board, or speculate that he may be concocting a *puchera* ("a mountain stew"), about which he writes at times, and around which he created in 1889 his last worthwhile novel, entitled *La puchera.*

The references to the Madrid world have held up very well in literary history, and Pereda is indeed an excellent observer and critic of all the aspects of the 1850s. In these chapters, Pereda himself dominates the thinking of his main character, and so personal and penetrating are the reactions that Pedro Sánchez almost disappears from interest, not as a defect of the novel but simply because of the author's pungent opinions. Regretfully, Pereda turned his back on this stimulating, fermenting hubbub of the city; the possible loss of a broader, Galdosian realist novel is suggested by this urban apprenticeship, at least in terms of ideas. This autobiographical novel, still with Pedro as the central axis, also becomes an historical *episodio nacional*, perhaps superior to the forty-six "national episodes" of Galdós because of the technical unity of the main character's development and dominance.[37] Autobiography and history merge with another interpretation of *Pedro Sánchez* as a picaresque novel of the nineteenth century, the blending of the classical example into a modern setting, as Cossío indicated in his already-cited explanation of preference for this particular work.

The brilliance of this Peredian creation, a fusion of the very personal, and the historical with literary authenticity, and including something of the picaresque genre, is never disturbed by artistic imbalance. The three components complement each other to impressive advantage for Pereda's literary reputation in the chapters detailing Pedro's experiences before and after the Revolution of

1854. The hero's adventures are quite believable as he drifts from group to group, listening, talking, and absorbing all the details; and his pecuniary difficulties are very realistically described. Pedro's connection with Valenzuela brings him nothing because the latter ignores him; Balduque is without any influence even for himself; and the disillusioned Pedro gets a job with a newspaper, *El Clarín de la Patria* (The Clarion of the Fatherland). The grandiloquent name reflects the turgid style of this journal, typical of similar publications, according to Pereda, who then comments sardonically about journalism (his own beginning in literature in Santander) throughout these Madrid chapters.

Two loyal friends have come to Pedro's help: Matica, a student, who finds Pedro the job for *El Clarín;* and Redondo, the editor of the newspaper. More doors are opened for Pedro as he wanders around the city in connection with his duties; and he is soon involved in the growing political agitation, which now receives the attention that the literary and other cultural activities previously enjoyed. Although political complications enter into the description of historical events in Madrid during 1854, *Pedro Sánchez* does not belong to the type of political novel that Pereda developed before 1883. Once more, the balance is maintained against any ideological intrusions that could weaken the effectiveness of the autobiographical, historical, and picaresque structure. The dynamism, in terms of action to which the style, Pereda's later forte, becomes secondary, creates a physical confrontation between the mob and the army, with Pedro as a witness and a participant. The level of the vivid descriptions recalls other revolutions, such as described in *A Tale of Two Cities* and *Les Misérables*, with which the author could have been familiar. In any case, the parallelisms put Pereda in the same class with better English and French novelists.

The restoration of law and order, with the arrival of the military forces, brings Pereda to change the direction of the hero's experiences. Not unfavorably, however; the story of Pedro is more imaginative and, obviously, not based upon the author's own life. The hero's success unfolds realistically and not romantically so that Pereda stays clearly within the arena of realism; he does not retreat into romanticism for this narration, and there is even a mild dose of naturalism detectable, a conclusion never desired by this novelist and, consequently, interpretative. Balduque is killed accidentally in the street fighting, and Pedro secures a small pension for Carmen.

Valenzuela's family was saved by Pedro, even though this unreliable politician belonged to the opposing party; and Pereda's main character illustrates his honor and bravery by risking himself not only physically but also in terms of his future. Pedro is rewarded by the new authorities after he has comically and accidentally acquired a reputation in the newspapers for his defense of the government. He is appointed a provincial governor, marries Clara, bids farewell to Carmen, and naturally quits his position with the newspaper to the sorrow of his true friends. Matica and Redondo have foreseen that Pedro, by joining the government gradually, has progressed from an ally to a deputy and, finally, an administrator, shutting his eyes to the pitfalls of this alliance with power and prestige. Pedro, for them, faces a compromising and, in the end, heartbreaking future, because the political establishment is corrupt and the followers are scoundrels.

The higher Pedro climbs, the less aware he becomes of the quicksand upon which his whole existence is supported. He endeavors to be a competent governor, but Pedro is not a practical politician, trusting those who do not deserve his confidence. Barrientos, his secretary, takes bribes and becomes the lover of Clara, both deceptions completely unsuspected by Pedro. Slowly, however, Pedro's suspicions are aroused by the presence of Barrientos so often in his residence, and the extravagant expenses of his wife and mother-in-law; and finally the governor learns the truth about the source of the funds for his household, the graft extracted by the closest member of his staff. Shattered, Pedro fires Barrientos and separates from the unfaithful Clara. The confrontation between husband and wife is one of Pereda's superior scenes: the psychological motivations and conflicts of Pedro pleading for the intimate relationship with Clara and the latter's embittered, mocking comments; the dialogue, dramatic and naturalistic, with both sides presented honestly and fairly; and the resolution of the couple's problems by the only logically motivated possibility, separation. The contrast between this description and Pereda's dogmatic stances in other novels is very striking, and no prior preparation for this frank, artistic treatment of marital incompatibility appears before 1883 in the author's writings.

The rise and fall of Pedro Sánchez is complete at the collapse of his marriage in the thirty-third chapter, because the hero is now disgusted with his way of life. In the following chapter, nevertheless, he is so ashamed of his failure as a man and a son that he cannot bring himself to return home to the *Montaña* and confront the disgrace of

his patria chica and his father. Pedro leaves the governorship
without having been made a cesante by another spin of the erratic
political wheel of fortune, but he departs poor by not having
enriched himself in the customary manner of the provincial rulers.
This thirty-fourth chapter could have provided a better ending to
Pedro Sánchez, structurally and thematically; and the picaresque
tradition would have been strengthened by the hero's decision to
wander in search of legitimate happiness to replace the veneer of
success he sought foolishly. Seemingly, at the very moment of concluding this most effective novel, his best effort to this date, Pereda
was unable to resist the lure of the past, his previous theme of the
Montaña as security and an idyll. Thus, Pereda might have stopped
at this third from-the-last paragraph as the most compelling end: "I
spent the rest of the day with my friend, and on the following day,
very early, I left Madrid along the road to Andalusia, my spirit op-
pressed under the tyranny of memory, which did not tire of placing
before my eyes the most smiling illusions opposite all the errors and
disillusionments of my life" (II, 181).

The penultimate paragraph raises the level of anguish to a
somewhat melodramatic point: "And as the sole consolation in this
crude battle of opposite ideas, the mystery of my future toward
which I was going without any direction or bearings, like an inert
mass cast into space by the brutal force of my misfortune. . . . Where
would I be falling? What would become of me?" (II, 181). But if
these two paragraphs immediately before the final one in this thirty-
fourth chapter remain psychologically within the realistic and
picaresque borders, uniting a modern and a classical technique, the
last paragraph shifts, though still with effectiveness and
verisimilitude, toward the Peredian obsession with the return home.
Pedro at last comes to this attitude: "Then I turned aside from consideration of the miserable dust of the earth; and with the immortal
eyes of the soul, in the light that I always guarded with Christian
love in the sanctuary of my faith, I saw the providence of God, who
does not abandon even the birds of the air, and gave myself over,
confidently, to his designs" (II, 181). This last passage is of course an
evident paraphrase of the New Testament belief; and Pedro, keeping his religious faith, very orthodoxly (not a necessary ideal with the
pícaro), begins to turn full circle, first from the city and then to the
country.

The thirty-fifth chapter, a dubious ending for *Pedro Sánchez*, is in
accordance, nevertheless, with Pereda's ideological and personal

feelings, which are too strongly rooted for the novelist to avoid this moralizing, uplifting conclusion. In this epilogue, since no action occurs and twenty-five years have passed between chapters, Pedro explains the "second period of my adventurous life": Barrientos abandoned the Valenzuela family, Augusto died three years later, and Clara also died, impoverished, humiliated, but with no redeeming change in her negative personality. Pedro, who shows an uncharitable relief at the fates of these sinners, describes how his business ventures prospered so that he decided to marry Carmen. The marriage is very happy, but misfortune pursues Pedro because Carmen and their son, Quica, die in an epidemic.

Travel fails to assuage his grief, and, at last, Pedro goes back to the *Montaña* (even in prosperity he apparently did not feel the urge to return in triumph), where the remainder of his life is spent in the contemplation and love of the patria chica. He is rich but without heirs, and his philosophy of life is summed up in the concluding lines thus: "The wealth of human life is composed of brief pleasures and bitter, very great sorrows. . . . I shall consider as useful any such way that the example of my disillusionments may serve anyone as wisdom" (II, 185). The brevity of this thirty-fifth chapter saves Pereda from a dangerous retreat into the artistic traps of his past novels; but the psychological motivations and experiences of Pedro are contrived for an overly didactic, ideological purpose. Pereda lapses into a sentimental revolt about the changes wrought by time, especially the Revolution of 1868; and Pedro laments, upon his return to Santander, that "the customs have been radically transformed," surely the author's old, familiar refrain. There is nothing original in this crowded, needless conclusion, and none of the many explanations about almost all the characters serves any aesthetic and thematic purpose.

By the end of this novel, however, another penetrating contribution is observable, offsetting the unimpressive thirty-fifth chapter, which does nothing to enhance Pereda's mastery of the novel as of 1883. The influence of Cervantes's masterpiece enters almost immediately into consideration of the ideas and plan of *Pedro Sánchez.* Initially, the hero (who appears superior on all counts to the classical pícaro and does not deserve the unflattering classification of the antihero) reminds one of Don Quixote setting out on a sally, optimistic and idealistic, journeying through the barren plains of Castile. The experiences of the quixotic protagonist also resemble some of the bumbling adventures of the knight-errant, such as the rescue of the Valenzuela family and the involvement in the arguments of the opposing social groups. Then, as Pereda alters his plot from the autobiographical to the imaginative, Pedro's career as a politician, and most importantly, as governor, parallels the rule of Sancho Panza at Barataria. The possible Cervantine example has been shifted from master to servant, from Don Quixote to Sancho Panza, at the time when, ironically, Pedro becomes a master as a provincial administrator instead of an employe on a newspaper. Pedro's disillusionments, indicated by the above quotations from the end of the thirty-fourth chapter, can be correlated with the mood of the battered knight after Sansón Carrasco's victory. One more hypothetical clue is acceptable evidence of this Cervantine inspiration if the inversion of the names, Pedro Sánchez and Sancho Panza, is an admissible technique or perhaps a play on words. Pereda, at any rate, would have been immeasurably pleased at such an hypothesis, priding himself on the frequent comparison with Cervantes.[38]

Only the serious slip in the last chapter, together with the tepid Carmen and the too contrasting Clara in *Pedro Sánchez*, mars this first-rate novel of Pereda. The past was not only too potent, as has been suggested, but another explanation or excuse, equally valid, may be that Pereda was already so engrossed with the inspiration and slow beginning of *Sotileza* that he neglected the remaining structure of *Pedro Sánchez*. In short, Pereda was either preoccupied with his new book or he was developing the views of the *Montaña* presented in *Sotileza*, completed a year later, in 1884, and published with immediate success early in 1885.

The Seas of Santander: Sotileza

A NOTHER lacuna concerns the creation of *Sotileza* (Fine Spun), namely, the trajectory of Pereda's novel from the first inspiration to the published book. Fortunately, letters provide some material about the composition of the new work: the slow maturation during the writing of *Pedro Sánchez* of a story about the maritime life of Santander; the return to the earlier short stories, "The Levy" and "The End of a Race," as a starting point for themes, dialogue, and characters; the excited days of accumulating pages of this manuscript; the encouragement of Menéndez Pelayo, probably the major influence upon the author; the pride of the local residents upon hearing details about the chapters; and the unusual reaction by Pereda that "at least I am pleased with my work, something that has never happened to me until now. Tomorrow I will be finished . . . the job has left me dead tired."[1]

The favorable reception in Santander of Pereda's tribute to his province revived his exhausted spirits; and he exulted in the unanimous praise of the flattered readers from his patria chica. Menéndez Pelayo penned the expected laudatory review; and Clarín also praised the artistry of *Sotileza*, calling attention to Pereda's acceptance of naturalism, an awkward compliment in view of the latter's antipathy toward these doctrines.[2] Although other reviewers added to the affirmative chorus, and Pereda's name was now mentioned repeatedly for membership in the Spanish Academy, the issue of naturalism as the classification of *Sotileza* within literary history rankled and obsessed Pereda; and the issue remains as a critical question, summed up convincingly by Pattison as "Is Pereda a Naturalist in spite of himself?"[3]

I *The Defense of* Sotileza

Pereda himself prepared a defense against naturalistic categorizing of *Sotileza* in the brief dedication to "my contemporaries of Santander who may be still living"; but his rhetorical ambushes should make the cautious reader ponder the novelist's possible afterthoughts regarding similarities with naturalism. He alternates between his intentions to depict honestly "my garden" of Santander and his denial of any influence of the current naturalistic modes. The bases for the author's judgments are founded on his own observations and knowledge; and there are no antecedents in other literary models and styles, even though "from a distance they might seem displays of a determined school" — a typically oblique reference to naturalism. He is likewise veering from the realists who, like his friend Galdós, drew upon the contemporary scene: "After all, what happens in it is only a pretext to revive people, things, and places which hardly exist now and to reconstruct a town buried unexpectedly during its patriarchal repose under the great weight of other ideas and other customs carried along, up to here, by the onrush of a new and strange civilization." *Sotileza* is thus defined not as a naturalistic or even a realistic venture but as a personal "remembrance of things past." This truth is not encompassed within the confines of art but, instead, within the mind and heart of the artist, Pereda. Astutely, the local son requests his local audience (his only concern as readers, to whom he makes appeal in the first paragraph) to supply "with their faithful memory" whatever his pen may fail to represent. In short, Pereda is trying to fend off any possible thrusts from critics beyond the *Montaña;* and he also speculates that older readers will more accurately comment upon his mistakes. This literary brief is probably a mixture of flattery toward the hometown readers, a sincere admission of any erroneous reproductions of dialect in particular, and a recurring fear of adverse criticism, especially mentioning ideas repugnant to Pereda.

In addition, Pereda attacks present-day standards of art, rather strongly, but he is less effective in proposing his own theory of the novel or, more pertinently, of *Sotileza.* His aim is to avoid on the one hand the picture of "good society," a euphemism for the modern types living in the cities; and on the other hand, to omit the naturalistic characters with their attendant vices. Pereda seeks to describe the "unknown persons" who have neither the disagreeable traits of the new urban class nor the prominent vices of the proletariat; he proposes the employment of "the little people," without many material advantages but with their own normal human problems. It is doubtful if Pereda is anything but defensive when he claims that he does not aspire "to write a book to please everyone"; and on the contrary, the conclusion emerges that he "doth protest too much" in fear of the critics.[4]

II *The Tangled Nets*

The plot of *Sotileza* resembles closely the usual pattern of the nineteenth-century novel, both naturalistic and realistic, as well as the preceding romantic models, in the construction of varied subplots interconnected with many characters following their courses of action, leading to uniting and conflicting confrontations. Structurally, nevertheless, a logical division of the book can be made in two parts, chapters 1 - 11 and chapters 12 - 29, because the title of the first chapter, "Crisálidas" (Cocoons), introduces the four main characters as youngsters and the twelfth chapter's heading of "Mariposas" (Butterflies) shows them in the awkward time between adolescence and adulthood. In fact, a central aspect of the complicated plot is precisely this difficult transition, above all for Andrés, into maturity; and the high point of the action at sea in the twenty-eighth chapter concerns his decision about the future direction of his life. The many other personages who are also woven into the fabric of Pereda's novel appear initially in this first part, and no additional actors appear in the following part. Although the setting and the participants are early presented in detail, the conflicts are not developed in these eleven chapters that constitute the first part.

The only unpleasant problem of this part, indeed, has been successfully solved, or is rendered less serious, by the transfer of the orphan, Silda, from the brutal guardianship of Mocejón and his equally cruel wife, Sargüeta, and daughter, Carpia, to the childless, charitable family of Mechelín and Sidora — who unfortunately live in the same building as the previous foster parents. The enmity of the latter family continues implacably but with no outward injury to Mechelín, Sidora, and Silda at the conclusion of the eleventh chapter, when the orphaned girl is nicknamed "Sotileza" because she is a delicacy, "una pura sotileza" ("a pure subtlety") and because she is "fine spun" like the leader or transparent fiber of a fishline. All the fortunes or circumstances of the characters have improved during the first part (with the deserved exception of the Mocejón clan), and the story interest must thereby lie elsewhere.

A wry, warm humor has characterized Pereda's leisurely description of the various personages in this first part. The first chapter offers a vignette of a classroom, limited in physical assets and in the abilities of both teacher and recalcitrant pupils, that calls to mind the comical features of Mark Twain's schoolboys in *Tom Sawyer* and *Huckleberry Finn*. The hapless Padre Apolinar, the teacher, another of Pereda's exemplary priests, strives to impart his strong enthusiasm and weak knowledge to the town's hopes for the future: Andrés, whose father is the captain of the best ship in the province; Cleto, a surprisingly improved offspring of the Mocejón family; and Muergo, occupying the bottom rung of the educational ladder on all counts, with a repulsive physical appearance to complement his lack of talent. The remaining members of the class, Sula, Cole, Guarín, and Toletes, only add to the general lack of interest in studies since all these youngsters, with the supposed exception of Andrés, know they are destined to lead the dangerous, harsh, and penniless careers of Santander fishermen, the toilers of the sea. They are not unhappy about their prospective lots in life, however, because the sea is bred and instilled in them by experience with their fathers and relatives and their daily observations of the maritime comings and goings in Santander.

This warmth extends to Padre Apolinar, undoubtedly the most appealing character in *Sotileza*. This attraction is not due to any stereotyped symbol of the priesthood, a defect in the previous novels, such as *Don Gonzalo* and *A Chip off the Old Block*. In these introductory chapters, the priest emerges as the main actor because he appears so frequently and also because he solves the orphan girl's predicament after she has fled from further mistreatment at the hands of the Mocejón trio. Padre Apolinar reflects in these chapters what he represents in Santander, a magnet for all the dilemmas, problems, and troubles of the people. In this first part, and with his more subordinate role in the second part, this character is the model priest in that he practices completely what he preaches; but Padre Apolinar also reveals a very human, credible portrait of an *alter Christus* ("another Christ"). His virtues struggle winningly in all the trials of the humble labyrinth of his daily existence; and yet the psychological understanding of a priest's feelings and reactions is superbly described. For example, Padre Apolinar grumbles about the lazy, unkempt pupils he is teaching; their lack of any motivation for learning causes him to lose his temper; his language is, though never vulgar nor obscene, certainly outside the anticipated pale of priestly patience; the difficulties of dealing with unending woes from his ungrateful parishioners enervate him; the disgust at oral beratings and threats from the Mocejón tribe leads him to see no divine spark in these brutes; and the lack of enough money to eat and live not lavishly, but adequately, depresses this exemplary priest.

Pereda has unexpectedly unveiled, without prior types in other works, a living representative of the clergy who suffers and agonizes from the mounting, frustrating obligations of his vocation, baring his bruised feelings, his weaknesses, and his liabilities as a man. The fact that Padre Apolinar never surrenders, continually demonstrates by good example the Christian message that he believes un-questioningly, and, ironically, never sermonizes at length or formally (his only prepared sermon in part two is a dull exposition and dreary failure because his listeners feel that he is speaking out of character with so many erudite references and flowery lines) are the keys to his authentic Christianity.

The action, then, centers around Padre Apolinar in this first part: the introduction of the youngsters in the classroom in chapter 1; his sympathy for Sotileza, who is led to the school by Andrés; the meeting with the Mocejón guardians for redress; the decision to place the orphan with Mechelín and Sidora; his complaint to the town council about the Mocejón protectorship with the suggestion of the new foster parents; and the link that binds Muergo to a semblance of acceptability and presentability. This last relationship preserves most clearly the humanity and religious idealism of the good priest: he detests openly the language, appearance, and rudeness of Muergo; but Padre Apolinar sympathizes with the urchin because the latter, like Sotileza, is also an orphan and he endeavors to win for the youngster a welcome in the home of the boy's uncle and aunt, Mechelín and Sidora. The most touching, and rather humorous, vignette occurs when Padre Apolinar takes off his own trousers under his cassock to give to Muergo, hiding thereby the latter's nakedness — a Peredian variation on the lesson to take one's shirt from one's back to help a neighbor. At the same time, Padre Apolinar cannot deny his repulsion for the distressed creature, which adds to a brilliant sketch of sincere Christianity, rather than some angelic, saintly, unreal figure as the doer of the act of charity. Pereda's Apolinar, one of the best types in his entire writing, is closer than he probably realized to his friend Galdós, in the latter's characterization of the quixotic curate in *Nazarín* and of the lay saint in *Angel Guerra*.[5] Eoff misses the literary and ideological mastery of a type when he fails to discuss Padre Apolinar as a major element in "a fatherly world according to design" and when he dismisses this character as "a fussy, good-natured secularized priest."[6]

Other preparations for the second part are established in these eleven chapters without the appearance of Padre Apolinar, however, by extensive digressions on the histories of the Mocejón and Mechelín families in the third and fourth chapters, respectively. The contrast between the two households is very sharply drawn; they are the epitomes of good and evil, too romantically and too overtly, and the only relief from the overwhelming kindheartedness of Mechelín and Sidora is to be found in their antipathy toward Muergo. Admittedly, Muergo has no winning cards in the game of life, but he is a blood relative of this family; and they have taken joyfully into their quarters a fellow orphan, Sotileza. This irony in Mechelín's and Sidora's one failure to show love and charity brings them to a human level, making them not only symbols of goodness but real people, like Padre Apolinar, with normal weaknesses in the practice of ideals and religious teachings. Pereda sketches all these types from the lower classes of Santander with vivid realism, and a probable explanation for the evident contrasts is that he could offset any local criticism about an uncomplimentary panorama of the *Montaña* by using the two sides of the coin. His portraits are certainly successful and believable, despite the heavily intended examples of virtue and vice.

A shift to the nautical residents of Santander, the people whom Pereda sought to describe principally in this novel, first takes attention from Padre Apolinar, the schoolboys, and Sotileza, then from the Mocejón and Mechelín imbroglios, to those dependent upon the sea in the Lower Town, the better section of the city. Actually, however, the fishermen, sailors, and their families in the Upper Town (Pereda makes a very clear social distinction between these two districts throughout the book), where the less fortunate citizens of Santander reside in varying degrees of poverty, with or without respectability, have been symbolized contrastingly by Mocejón's and Mechelín's histories and households. The progeny of this depressed quarter of Santander appears as the strand uniting the old and the new, evenly, in the first chapter at the school and in the second chapter after the escape from Padre Apolinar's futile lessons.

This second chapter, again resembling the boyhood adventures of Tom Sawyer and Huck Finn, offers a charming reminiscence (Pereda's nostalgic intention at varying points in *Sotileza*) of the careless innocence of these youngsters, joined by Sotileza in roaming the docks and beaches, playfully diving for a coin and smoking surreptitiously. Andrés, the lad from the Lower Town, joins easily the group of boys from the Upper Town who snobbishly (and inaccurately) laugh at Sotileza because she is an "Uptowner" who possesses fewer advantages than they do; Andrés, with an amusing touch of social irony, welcomes and protects Sotileza as an equal, a foreshadowing of his attitude in the second part. The highlight of this same chapter for which the youngsters have hastened to the sea is the thrilling entrance of the *Montañesa* ("Highlander") into the port, the ship whose captain, Pedro Colindres (more popularly known by the surname of Bitadura), is Andrés's father.

After the usual résumé of this new character's early years, his marriage to Andrea, and his nautical career, leading to command of the *Montañesa* as the culmination of his success, Pereda interestingly connects the society of the Upper Town and the Lower Town, "the 'mariners' of that time" (as he titles the seventh chapter) in a humorous and instructive reception at Bitadura's home. The common seamen, welcomed graciously by the captain and his wife, nevertheless feel very uncomfortable in this social setting, confined by manners and customs foreign to them; their talk concerns their days on the *Montañesa* or other vessels, and their language is restricted to these experiences with the peculiar idiom of their environment. Pereda, sympathetic to honest, simple folk on land and sea in all his writings, again conveys subtly but clearly his faith in certain classes of society where members of those groups are happiest. This conservatism is rooted, according to Pereda, in an innate democratic individualism by which men treat each other as equals in their work and their talk, but by which they remain profitably and idyllically separate in their social and group patria chica.[7] Bitadura, for instance, is still uneasy in the same polished circle, and his mood, though less uncomfortable, parallels that of his comrades from the *Montañesa*, who are different in appearances but similar in their inner feelings.

This contrast between a life on land — synonymous with civilization, refinement, restrictions, and external conduct — and a career at sea — equalling untamed nature, rough ways, freedom, and individualistic behavior — is brought home more clearly for the Bitadura family when Andrés, the only child, goes against his parents' hopes by an attraction for the fishermen's and seamen's punishing existence. Captain Bitadura had prayed that his son would follow in his footsteps as a seagoing officer, especially since the parental influence, knowledge, and experience could make a maritime career less arduous and more rewarding than his own difficult years at the mast. The vagaries of their offspring's desires, the boy's wanderings with the youngsters from the Upper Town, and the general adolescent uncertainties of Andrés unite to frustrate both his father and mother. Andrea, who is totally against any maritime vocation for her son, had pleaded with her husband's employer, Venancio Liencres, to take Andrés into his firm as a clerk and to convince Bitadura that the opportunity was the merchant's idea. The two scenes are psychologically motivated, skillful and humorous, as Liencres and Bitadura spar about the merits of their respective careers until the captain slowly grasps that Don Venancio and Andrea are proposing the same future for Andrés. Along the way, Pereda indirectly attacks (via Liencres's materialistic opinions and attitudes) an old foe, the encroachment by the commercial interests of the nineteenth century on the traditions, manners, and ways of life in the *Montaña*. Pereda had learned much since excessive caricatures in earlier works, because Liencres is not an unsympathetic type, although the reader instinctively rebels against the shipowner's belief in progress, change, and business, so artful is the characterization. The subsequent interview between the supposedly irate husband and his timidly defensive wife provides a model of a happy familial confrontation — the advocacy of mutual felicity in a marriage is a pattern in the Peredian novel — as the two agree that the best solution for Andrés's future is on land, in Liencres's office, with Andrea the easy winner and Bitadura the good-natured loser.

The loser who is not overjoyed at this turn of events, still unknown to him, is the hapless Andrés, who has just finished bragging to everyone he meets, adults and fellow adolescents, in the ninth chapter, "The Enthusiasms of Andrés," that he is going to be a sailor. Andrés was innocently convinced that his father, after returning from a voyage on the *Montañesa*, would welcome his decision to follow in his father's footsteps, something Andrés believed that his father quietly wanted. Thus, the vagaries of the human condition through Pereda's compelling comprehension of the young minds in these chapters match the equally labyrinthine conditions of adult behavior, for Andrés and for his parents.

Andrés, nevertheless, adjusts quickly to the unexciting routine of a business office, where his lack of enthusiasm for daily chores is compensated by a rather agreeable new friend, Antolín, or familiarly, Tolín, the son of Liencres, and the latter's boat, a *patache*, which the two apprentice clerks use to explore around the harbor. Tolín, despite his amiability and cooperation, is a determined landlubber;

and the two boys with all their compatibility supply another example of Pereda's technique of contrasting characters. Also, Cleto is slowly and mildly opposed to Andrés; and the ubiquitous Muergo is the foil for the other boys — all of whom, however, join in the fun around the waterfront and in the boat. The drawing card for the future rivals — unaware of their nascent interests in the opposite sex because of their age and boyish pranks — is the presence of Sotileza, never prominent for long in these eleven chapters but still a stimulus. Her relationship with Andrés remains one of appreciation for his help.

Tolín has introduced Andrés to his mother and sister, Luisa, and at the same time the plans of the Bitaduras (thanks to the instigations of Andrea) have broadened to the hope for a later business partnership between the two boys. Andrés is thus torn gently between the worlds of the Upper Town and the Lower Town; his enthusiasms for the unambitious occupations of the sea and the financial possibilities of a business career on land; the sympathy of his father and the hopes of his mother; and the attractions of his playmates and the lure of more affluent society, between the games of childhood and the seriousness of adulthood. Sotileza becomes for Andrés both a link with the past and a problem for the future.

The subtleness of these tangled strands of the Peredian plot are not fully apparent as yet, and only the wary reader will grasp the possible complications of the story later in the novel. Sotileza, reflecting already her nickname, does not adhere to the favorite types used as characters in Pereda's other works and in the costumbrista literature as a whole, a major influence upon Pereda's artistry.[8]

In these eleven chapters, curiously, the adult characters are primarily types with the prominent exception of Padre Apolinar; but the young people, although they follow certain recognizable patterns of adolescent behavior, are depicted more compellingly as individuals. This individualism stands out clearly in the portrait of Sotileza, although some conclusions about her psychological reactions can be attempted. The major surprise about Sotileza — and the foreshadowing of the big net that Pereda casts in the second part — revolves around her conduct with Muergo whom, of course, the noblest and most idealistic personages, such as Padre Apolinar, Mechelín, and Sidora, cannot stand and, in fact, detest with constant, open (and very unchristian) remarks. The power of Sotileza's magnetism attracts not only the kind Andrés but also the crude Muergo — two distinct opposites — and, then, at the end of the eleventh chapter, Cleto, who first kicks her on the stairway of their building, and later returns to have her sew a button on his trousers. The three boys, companions, are being drawn apart without being aware of it by Sotileza, who is, of course, innocent of any deliberate interference (even Muergo has to be counted a friend because of his perennial presence at their activities). This variation on an eternal triangle theme with Sotileza, Andrés, and Cleto as the components should be the logical development; but again Muergo enters the arena, rationally a figure of no importance and, instead, the cause for the mysterious conduct of Sotileza.

Pereda's success in delineating the fascinating Sotileza was proudly recognized by him when, in a postscript in 1888, he referred solely to this feminine character as the explanation for the book's warm reception, "the enumeration of the honors accorded to the humble Uptowner in so many forms, from so many parts, and by so many and such different people" (II, 189). Although the cast of actors are older and changed in the second, Sotileza alone reveals most fully in the first part the complexity of her personality. Her male companions later flounder in the varying degrees of their immature, awkward emotions; Sotileza herself falls victim to the onslaught of love as a normal, human problem.

She has been analyzed in some interesting ways: Bassett relates her to the Spanish background, "This, the heroine, is the most notable of Pereda's women. With an enigmatical character both attractive and repellent, she is a lineal literary descendant of Cervantes' Esmeralda and *Ilustre Fregona* [Illustrious Kitchenmaid], a modern embodiment of the most classical Spanish traditions in the field of feminine realism"[9]; and Eoff views her as lending small weight to the story, despite admittance of the social psychology involved:

These sociopsychological aspects individualize Sotileza but they appear as the static result of environment and not as a process of growth. Nor do they give the heroine's characterization any special importance in the narrative development. The author is less interested in her as an individual personality than he is in the group activity for which she is responsible. Hence, despite the nominal position of heroine, she is scarcely more than a representative local element in a corporate body of mutually independent parts, on equal terms with all the other elements.[10]

The primary trait of Sotileza in the first part is her taciturn nature, described on different occasions as "a cold nature and keeping her own counsel" and "satisfied to be present at everything, knowing everything that the little scamps were doing, fearless and unresponsive, by nature, as was said, not because of virtue" (II, 208). In chapter 3, the tragic history of Sotileza supplies significant clues about her behavior: the loss of parents, with the semblance of a home and the bare necessities of a meager existence; the cruelties and deprivations with the guardians; and the escape to solitude and perhaps death, a fate averted by Andrés's intervention. Sotileza has several attributes of a Dickensian hero,[11] but she is a romantic offspring and not a child of the naturalistic school. Sotileza also possesses the marks of realism with this psychological depth, never probed fully because Pereda did not intend, according to the available evidence,[12] to compose either a character study of one person or a novel with psychology as the main emphasis.

The romantic similarities of Pereda's heroine with her predecessors of that earlier nineteenth-century movement are restricted to her circumstances; but a naturalistic future is thwarted by the mysterious ways for Pereda not of fate but of free will. Two things support this conclusion: the author's firmly held beliefs with no unorthodox variations, stated repeatedly in his letters; and the prior practice in other novels of this fundamental principle of his religious philosophy. For example, Sotileza surprises everyone, already in the first chapter, by her cleanliness in contrast to her companions from the same background. The Mocejón and Mechelín families, seen outwardly in the third and fourth chapters, stun the inhabitants of the Lower Town, and even some of their impoverished neighbors, by the innate evil and radiant goodness of the two households. There is no moralizing explanation for these differences in behavior, happily for Pereda's psychology, and the reader is wisely left with only implied interpretations, about the uncertainties of human personality. No individual is foredoomed to defeat by destiny; the person can rise above surrounding conditions by the exercise of virtue, both moral, as in the case of the Mechelín couple, and physical, as in Sotileza's case, with her wish to be neat and clean.

This unfathomable quality of the rise and fall of each character is translated by Pereda effectively by omission of full didactic explication and by a nebulous observation of a person's reactions, such as Sotileza's laconic dialogue at times. Thus, in the fifth chapter, Padre Apolinar, with all his helpfulness, is frustrated by his inability to understand Sotileza because she seemingly fails to show appreciation for his efforts and, more vexingly, does not want to communicate

openly with him. Sotileza suggests to Mechelín and Sidora, after
their proposal to buy her a blouse, that, instead, they purchase a shirt
for Muergo. Sotileza is unwilling, and perhaps unable, to explain her
charity toward Muergo; but her few words add an instructive depth
to her psychological characterization. Finally, this complex attitude
is analyzed tantalizingly, with significant indications for the second
part, in the third chapter:

Among so many dirty, shirtless youngsters roaming around there, she only
felt sorry for the filth and nakedness of Muergo. And Muergo reciprocated
these relative niceties of Silda by laughing at her, giving her a kick, or
pushing her as on the day at la Maruca. And the preference continued on the
part of Silda! For what reason? Maybe you can know why. Perhaps the attraction of opposites; the very monstrosity of Muergo; an unconscious
desire, the offspring of human vanity, to tame and make submissive what
seems wild and rebellious, and to make beautiful what is horrible; to make of
Muergo what some women, of the so-called elegant in the world, make of
certain woolly, very ugly dogs: to take pleasure from seeing them stretched
at their feet, growling from affection, cleaned and combed very well,
precisely because they are horrible and loathsome and should not be there.
(II, 209)

III   Storms Ashore and at Sea

By the second part, the innate predilection for cleanliness has
helped to make the heroine at the age of twenty a very beautiful girl.
Maturity has also changed the attitude of the three male friends of
Sotileza into a more serious rivalry for the girl's attention. This complicated situation provides a dynamic plot through the change of
scenes and a shifting point of narration, although Andrés remains at
the center of the action.

Necessarily, and for the interest of his audience, Pereda has constructed a complex series of scenes, retaining consistently a high
degree of human interest and credibility, motivated by psychological
realism. Three chapters, in particular, provide this rising action with
an increase of anxiety for the three male rivals, Andrés, Cleto, and
Muergo; and these three episodes take place at sea: a trip by boat for
a picnic on an island; a boat race between the Uptowners and the
Downtowners; and a storm at sea, the climax of the novel. This
twenty-eighth chapter is still considered as one of the best chapters,
in terms of style, description, and excitement, in the nineteenth-
century Spanish novel; and this same chapter is without doubt the
apex of peninsular sea fiction, ranking also with the nautical stories
of Cooper, Melville, and Conrad.[13]

It is possible, then, to reconstruct for story purposes the plot emphasizing these three decisive chapters. Cleto, living in the same building as Sotileza, has enjoyed seeing her more often than Andrés; but he never suspects the latter of any sentimental feelings toward the girl because of their social differences. Cleto, on the other hand, observes that Muergo is always the sole person who effects a noticeable change in Sotileza; she behaves toward the person who should logically repel her with the warmest solicitude. This mystery about the attraction of Sotileza for Muergo at first annoys Cleto, and later, he becomes jealous. The shy Cleto confides in Andrés, who has visited Sotileza to observe how she is progressing and likewise to show his concern for the aging Mechelín, a seagoing comrade of the young man's father. His visits, however, do not go unnoticed: Sargüeta and Carpia, embittered still and spiteful as ever, watch for an opportunity to discredit both Andrés and Sotileza through scandal. Cleto's warnings to Andrés about the former's disreputable family together with his own admission of his love for Sotileza have an ironic result — Andrés realizes that perhaps he, too, is enamored of the same girl.

Cleto is relieved after confessing to Andrés about possible gossip, his feelings about Sotileza, and Muergo's presence as an obstacle; but Andrés is left now in the conflict of emotions from which he has just rescued Cleto. Andrés is caught increasingly in this net of his emotions, while Cleto asks Padre Apolinar to intercede with Sotileza directly, and with Mechelín and Sidora indirectly, for permission to marry Sotileza, which is a shocking proposal because of his ostracized family.

During the first crisis, during the excursion to an island picnic, Andrés is angered by the glances exchanged by Sotileza and Muergo; and his ire is raised to the point of a verbal outburst when Muergo flirts with Sotileza, carrying her ashore. Later, when Andrés tries to embrace her, explaining awkwardly his feelings, Sotileza upbraids him, and the uncomprehending youth is unable to reconcile her laughing reactions to Muergo's boldness and her opposite attitude to his own flirtations. That evening, in another of Pereda's contrasts, Andrés escorts Luisa to the theater with her family; and he, failing to notice her love for him, irritates the girl by his moroseness. She, in turn, teases Andrés by referring to her view of him and Sotileza together in the boat and, finally, by alluding to the heroine as vulgar. This scene ends disastrously for Andrés with harsh words exchanged, paralleling closely the dialogue with Sotileza. Andrés, upset by his failures, goes to see Sotileza; and the latter completely overwhelms him with her arguments, centering about the question of her honor. Ominously, Andrés's visit has been noted by the Mocejón women, and they promise themselves to be doubly alert from now on for a chance to destroy the reputation of their two enemies, precisely the danger about which the young man and Sotileza were debating.

The irony, built into the situation by the triple rivalry, is accentuated by more immature fears: Andrés and Cleto vent their wrath upon Muergo as the supposed winner of Sotileza's emotions; Andrés loses sleep from worry about his defeats, alienating his own family by his moodiness and the Liencres family by his withdrawal from expected contacts; Cleto makes the same error as Andrés when, because of Padre Apolinar's lack of success in promoting his cause, he presses his own case with the girl, suffering thereby almost the identical defeat as his friend; and the youths do not repeat their previous meetings with each other.

The psychological balance and delicate humor, never carried beyond credibility, are next expanded by the second critical moment, or point of high interest, in the boat race between the Uptown and Downtown crews. This spirited but friendly contest, perhaps symbolically representing (and foreshadowing) the still nebulous rivalry between Cleto and Andrés, offers a local-color sketch, inserted pertinently within the main story, and contributing to the dynamism of the plot. Pereda also comments appreciatively and subtly about the importance of these regional entertainments for the social unity of the province, bringing together the people without regard for any latent class complaints. The outcome of the race alters considerably the direction of the action because Andrés, upon seeing how Cleto has presented the victory flag to the girl before a large audience, grasps the fact that his friend is a serious opponent for Sotileza's hand. Muergo, groomed by Sotileza for an acceptable appearance in his version of Sunday-best clothes, has been thrashed by the girl for flirting boldly and crudely. Later Muergo performed laughably, falling into the water, in an effort to win a prize for Sotileza in a competition that was far above his capabilities.

Andrés, frustrated beyond reason, again determines to talk with Sotileza alone at the Mechelín home; and the consequences (Pereda's word used in four consecutive chapter headings to emphasize the gravity of this decision) come to a head when, with the two young people in a compromising situation, Carpia seizes upon the chance for the Mocejón vengeance. The appearance of scandal is caused by Carpia's locking of the door to the rear of the Mechelín apartment, where Andrés and Sotileza are conversing innocently. Then, "the two furies," as the author disdainfully calls the Mocejón women, shout in the street about the dishonorable conduct of Andrés and Sotileza. Although their neighbors realize the hypocrisy, the mother and daughter succeed in embarrassing the couple, who, released from their prison by Carpia's pushing of the key under the locked door, cannot face the crowd without evident shame. Sotileza with unanticipated anger attacks Carpia and turns the onlookers' sympathies against the villainous pair. However, the damage is done, and the scandal spreads quickly.

Sotileza is crushed by this evil blow to her many efforts to maintain her honor, with Andrés, Cleto, and Muergo. All her painstaking cares to present a neat, respectable personal figure, in conjunction with her moral virtues, now seem doomed because of this scene. Andrés is blamed by Sotileza, and he readily accepts responsibility for his improper visit, having waited for Mechelín and Sidora to be absent from the house. His depression is deepened when Captain Bitadura confronts Andrés with a demand for the truth. The interview between father and son, with the agonizing Andrea on the sidelines, offers a model of realistic dialogue.

Pereda has not tilted his arguments for or against either of the contestants, and this artistic impartiality also extends to the mother's role. Andrés cannot be entirely frank with his father about his purpose in visiting Sotileza, because the son would thereby lose honor — the increasingly major issue for all the characters after the twenty-third chapter — since he was irrationally enmeshed in the net of his adolescent feelings about the girl. Bitadura shrewdly comprehends that his son is lying, and the father's suspicions are consequently aroused about the accuracy of the gossipy stories.

Bitadura now makes a visit to Mechelín, a seagoing companion whom the captain has helped previously, and the two sailors discuss the redress for the scandal. If necessary, Andrés would marry Sotileza for the redemption of her honor as well as the reputation of the families. Sotileza, quiet as usual, comes to life in one of her best scenes in the novel when she defends herself against any imputations of misbehavior with Andrés (and thereby supports the son's defense against Bitadura's accusations and fears) by challenging the facile solution of marriage. What about her opinion in this matter? The bubbling wrath of Sotileza, always present, though dormant, as a key to her personality throughout this second part, erupts like a volcano when she demands that everyone state openly and fully future plans for her. Then, Sotileza argues her own case:

> I want you to know, hearing it from my own mouth, that I have never let myself be tempted by covetousness nor did the airs of gentry ever turn my head; that I esteem Andrés for what he is worth, not for what he can be worth to me; and that if there were no other way to save my good reputation than the one he could give me by taking me along to be the wife at his side, I would rather remain with my honor in doubt than to burden myself with such a heavy cross. (II, 346 - 47)

The shocked reaction from Bitadura, Mechelín, and Sidora is due to Sotileza's outspoken manner and views, a rejection of the established pattern in this conservative society and a refusal to follow docilely the judgments of the hierarchical chain of elders and superiors. Pereda has created a dynamic personality in his heroine, but the premises of Sotileza's argument go against the grain of his ideological beliefs. There is no precedent in his novels for such a winning portrait as that of Sotileza (Pereda's recognition of this surprising achievement can be once more confirmed by the 1888 postscript). Bitadura is very favorably impressed by Sotileza's honesty and forthrightness and grants the falseness of the town gossip.

Andrés, meanwhile, is in the depths of youthful despair: his reactions are juvenile, contrasting sharply with the mature comments of Sotileza. For example, Andrés decides not to go back home, concluding that his parents will worry, search for him, and appreciate him better; then, he determines to join the seagoing crew of Reñales on the next day for some practical experience as a sailor. Andrés spends the night before joining the fishermen on a hard bench at the Zanguina Bar, although he had promised his father not to frequent this Uptowner local tavern in exchange for Bitadura's offer of a boat. Ironically, his comrade during these uncomfortable hours is Muergo, also a member of the next day's fishing trip. In the following twenty-eighth chapter, Andrés is totally enamored of the freedom, beauty, and excitement of the sea until a sudden storm traps the boat far from shore. The description, a dynamic example of the Peredian mastery of language, provides one of the best pages in his literature:

> His ears suddenly perceived a distant, frightful noise as if gigantic artillery batteries were rolling along hollow ground. He felt upon his face the impression of a cold, wet gust of wind; and he observed that the sun was growing

dark and that big, wavy spots, almost blackish green, were advancing over the sea along the northwest. At the same time Reñales was shouting: "Lower those bigger sails! Keep only the one for the wind!"

Andrés, frozen from fright, saw those very valiant men drop the oars and scurry, pale and quickly, to carry out the skipper's orders. One single instant of delay in the maneuver would have resulted in the feared disaster because the mainsail for the wind hardly had been raised when a strong burst of wind with pouring rain struck the sail, enveloping with its force the boat in roaring whirlwinds. A very thick mist covered the horizon, and they could guess at rather than see the coastline because of the crashing of the water beating against it and the boiling of the foam assaulting it with all its fury.

All that his sight could then take in around him was a terrifying stretch of waves pursuing each other in a confusing race, and they lashed each other with their white crests shaken by the wind. To run ahead of that unbridled fury without allowing oneself to be assaulted by it was the only means if not to save oneself at least to try to do so. But the attempt was not easy because only the sail could give the necessary thrust, and the boat would not withstand the impulse from the small sail in the center without capsizing.

Andrés knew it very well, and upon observing how the mast creaked in its base, swaying like a willow rod, how the sail was crackling, how the boat was plunging with its bow, then leaning way over to one side, and how the sea was battering it on all sides, he didn't wonder why the skipper had ordered the sail for the wind to be raised and why the canvas called "extreme unction" was being prepared in the small cabin at the bow. More than what the operation signified at that agonizing moment, the terrible name of that narrow piece of cloth unfurled at half-mast on a very short pole froze the blood in Andrés' heart. Extreme unction!

That is to say, between life and death. (II, 362 - 63)

Pereda has achieved in this passage what he had failed to do in other novels, namely, the reconciliation of art and ideology, or, in this particular instance, theology. Extreme unction in Roman Catholic teaching is the last of the seven sacraments, last because the rites are normally given to a dying or seriously ill person; and the call for this sacrament indicates to all concerned that death is near or is an evident danger. The name of the sail symbolizes the final help for a ship in distress, bringing either salvation through the power of the wind or becoming the fruitless measure in the battle against the onrushing storm.

The vocabulary of this descriptive excerpt stresses the almost Gothic terror of the potent, senseless monster of nature; and the vivid words bring close to hand the image of the small craft struggling to remain aright with the many technical terms providing authenticity to the narration. At the most critical moment, in which the thrust from the wind can either impel the boat toward land or shift the balance disastrously, Reñales is knocked unconscious as he tries to grasp the body of Muergo, adrift in the waves after the capsizing of the other boat he had joined in the fishing fleet. Andrés takes command of the vessel and courageously manages to give the correct orders in time to prevent destruction from the waves. Entering the harbor, Andrés is greeted joyfully and proudly by his father; and the town, despite sorrow about the human losses from the other vessel to the inscrutable sea, exults in the safe return of this part of the flotilla.

In the last chapter, as in the last scene of the *comedia*, all the strands of the tangled nets come unwound after a mounting series of complications and centrifugal events; and these resolutions are felicitous or satisfactory for the characters, maintaining at least the fabric of society for the present but, sadly for Pereda, not for the future. The only weed in the Peredian garden (that metaphor he had at first resented from Pardo Bazán) has been conveniently eliminated by Muergo's death, because, psychologically, he could have offered a problem for Sotileza throughout her life, although no amorous relationship is implied in light of the girl's code and the author's philosophy. Nevertheless, Muergo is (perhaps cruelly) the ugly duckling in this idyllic world, owing much probably to Victor Hugo's Quasimodo, with whom Pereda compares his Spanish creation in the sixteenth chapter; and this unfortunate outcast in Santander is indeed mourned little and forgotten quickly. There is, however, no lack of verisimilitude in this solution; and casualties from the violent storm were certainly expected as the normal consequence.

Andrés, through Tolín's intervention for his sister and the wishes of the two families, settles down in the city and plans to marry Luisa. Andrés attained maturity during the storm when he seized control after Reñales was knocked unconscious; but again, this disentanglement of Andrés's troubles can be logically justified: the son has come of age in a flash because of an exceptional crisis, and the boy has imitated the man, his father, who would have behaved thus in a storm. Pereda has cleverly worked one of his favorite proverbs (used in his controversial novel of the same title) — into a psychological proof that Andrés is "a chip off the old block." Ideologically, Andrés's trial under stress also illustrates that blood will tell, that honor, courage, and virtue are not transmitted by the methodology of the nineteenth-century social and political theories but by heritage, tradition, good breeding — another basically conservative tenet of his world illustrated in *Don Gonzalo*.

Andrés, nevertheless, does not emerge as the hero of this novel; and the shift has been slow and subtle because, initially, he appeared to be not only the principal character but the one destined to win Sotileza. The story is narrated principally from the point of view of Andrés, and he is certainly in the center of action. But Andrés has veered fatally from the path of a gentleman, violating the social code in several instances: his dishonest absences from the office to visit Sotileza; the surreptitious interviews with the girl; the emotional intentions to court her for his own satisfaction; the selfish disregard for her feelings about their families and status; and the humiliations caused to his parents and the guardians of Sotileza. Thus, at the end, Andrés is no longer permitted to pay a visit to the Mechelín household, a decision painful to the latter couple and to himself. Cleto, never prominent despite his serious rivalry for Sotileza, asks her to marry him; and Sotileza accepts rationally but not emotionally, knowing that he will be a good husband but that she is not overwhelmingly anxious to wed anyone at this particular time.

This potential "happy ending" is marred, however, by an outside force; Pereda avoids a sentimental, syrupy final curtain with the insertion of an old foe of the simple people in his patria chica — the draft or military service. Once more, Pereda has mined the earlier two short stories for his conclusion to *Sotileza;* and the result is a novel clearly within the vein of realism, skirting around naturalism and eliminating romanticism. Cleto, together with a large group of conscripts from the area, one of the largest draft calls in years, will leave for three years in the navy. Mention was made in other chapters about the coming lottery to select the unlucky numbers (none of the recruits expresses any enthusiasm and any patriotic outbursts for this onerous duty), and this cloud hangs over the young men of Santander as a matter of perennial worry, so that Pereda's utilization of the draft is solidly founded within the framework of the novel. Sotileza will loyally wait for Cleto, and her betrothed will be just as faithful to her during these three long years. But who knows? Pereda indicates that these optimistic plans may be altered by time and circumstances — as in the changes between "The Levy" and "The End of a Race" caused by the military conscription — with, sadly, the worse fate being the death of some of the recruits.

Changes may also come with injury, moral degradation, or a second look at the previous promises.

The farewell to the departing conscripts (Pereda's antipathy to this disruption in the lives of his simple, poor fishing folk and in the continuity of tradition in Santander pervades artistically this last chapter) presents a colorful ceremony with those at home endeavoring to build up the morale of the young men. Padre Apolinar lends his personal wishes and the blessings of the church to the men he knew as boys, and a melancholy *déjà vu* permeates this scene at the wharf. Even this symbolic disruption of the old life is only the dimly understood end of it all, unrecognized by the characters but grasped repeatedly by their creator.

IV *"My Garden"*

This acceptance by Pereda of a critical metaphor was converted by him into an expression for the regional novel, generally, and for his particular interpretation of the *Montaña* as well as his art in molding this edifice of the past.[14] Thus, the consummate irony (among so many uses of this technique in the novel) is that all this civilization, so fragilely maintained at the end and facing the outside storms of change, so much more dangerous than the physical tempests at sea, will vanish by the time the author is actually composing, using the materials of observation, imagination, and nostalgia. There are many examples of this philosophy, wedded with aesthetic success to the plot throughout *Sotileza;* and Pereda convincingly links his ideas in the first and last chapters, initiating and reinforcing for his audience some of his purposes. Concluding the first chapter, Pereda stresses his love for "the Santander that I have here inside me, very deep, in the deepest part of my heart, and engraved in my memory in such a way that I would dare to trace it all with my eyes shut" and laments that "it is the only refuge remaining to art when, with its resources, it tries to offer to the consideration of other generations something picturesque, without ceasing to be correct, in this race, a fishing folk, disappearing among the motley and tasteless confusion of modern customs" (II, 196). Here, within a single long paragraph, is the synthesis of Pereda's realistic but nostalgic proposal in *Sotileza:* to recall the past, vanishing without trace, in the shabby present, while offering a pessimistic survey of the nineteenth century. Still, this evocation of another Santander is elevated beyond the prosaic narration of a story to the heights of the epic, for Pereda's higher purpose is, as he ends his novel on this theme, a modern epic in prose:

And as there are no other matters to air concerning this book, let us leave it here, compassionate and complacent reader, for it is certainly time for us to leave it; but not without declaring to you that, on giving a rest to my tired hand, I feel in my heart the heaviness engendered by a very deep misgiving that I have not maintained in myself the enormous enterprise of singing, in the midst of these unbelieving and colorless generations, the noble virtues, the miserable lives, the great weaknesses, the incorruptible faith, and the epic labors of the valiant and picturesque seaman of Santander. (II, 373)

This thematic ambition is found earlier in the novel, and the references, scattered throughout the chapters, are very tellingly summarized in this conclusion of the seventh chapter:

And those big lads were the men who knew how to take a ship to all the ports of the world and, with a fervent prayer and a promise to the Virgin, face death a hundred times, with a serene face and an intrepid heart, in the midst of the fury of storms!
Has poetry ever considered anything greater and more epic than those trifles? (II, 235)

So Pereda, then, is very cognizant of the potentialities of the modern novel; and this appreciation of the open doorway now made available to the nineteenth-century writer should rank him with his Spanish contemporaries, like Galdós and Valera who also grasped this fact about the age of the novel, and with European novelists who took this genre as the path to greatness. It is true that Pereda's romanticized concept of the possible superiority of a prose epic dedicated to the humble, forgotten, fishing folk of an inconspicuous region of Spain, unexploited up to this time by authors, creaks occasionally under the weight of a yearning for the past; but *Sotileza* retains so many valid traits of the realistic novel, while never abandoning the regionalism so familiar and preferred by the novelist, that his effort has successfully survived the criticism of almost a century. Menéndez Pelayo stressed this Peredian success and, prophetically, recognized the ability of this single novel to raise the author to a major role in the nineteenth-century novelistic field, with the book itself, standing alone, one of the permanent novels of the modern period.[15] Montesinos, on the other hand, while his critique of *Sotileza* reflects acumen, does not see, even in this novel, any originality or durability.[16]

Although Pereda later accepted and exploited the originally adverse critical metaphor of "my garden," within the novel itself, the metaphorical mode is concisely defined as nautical. If most of the action occurs on land, the three crises, turning points, or sensitive chapters for plot development, take place at sea; and these episodes are among the best descriptive pages in *Sotileza*, providing thrilling moments, laughter, revealing traits of the characters, and providing sustained reader interest. These three chapters, as indicated earlier in this discussion, are central to the whole novelistic structure; and they are masterly, as individual units in an anthology without the whole frame of reference. The nautical metaphor also pervades all the activities ashore for various reasons: the life in Santander is joined economically to the fortunes of those who go to sea, both in long voyages such as those made by Captain Bitadura and in shorter trips made by Mechelín, Mocejón, and others, as well as in the commercial ventures of Liencres; the families and relatives of the above-mentioned characters depend for their livelihoods and futures on the maritime enterprises of these men; the thoughts, plans, and prospects of all the residents in the city reflect the successful or unsuccessful catches of fish and the losses of vessels and men from storms, cold, and winds; and the people live close to the physical world of water, always noting the cloud formations, sunny, windy weather, and the attendant change of seasons.

Nature is essentially a stable, unchanging phenomenon, although there will always be the anticipated alterations of the time of year, particular conditions on a given day, or the variable measure of sunshine, among the myriad possibilities within the range of this permanency. Yet everyone in Santander loves the challenge and response to nature, and the life at sea attracts, most importantly for the Peredian hope of continuation, the youth, both the bright and less gifted. There is a very minor (but surprising for Pereda) vignette about Colo, a chum of Andrés and the other youngsters, who hates his uncle, Don Lorenzo, for the latter's insistence that the boy study Latin in order to follow in his footsteps as a priest; and after many beatings, Colo rejects the unexciting clerical studies for the lure of the sea, leaving his crazy uncle to be removed from his parish — exceptional evidence of the contrast in characters between Padre Apolinar and Don Lorenzo.

The acknowledged contribution of Pereda (long advocated by Menéndez Pelayo) to the enrichment of the Spanish novel is the employment of language to cement the structure of the regional background. The first principle of an authentic rendition of the speech of the characters is realism, and thereby, the transcription of the dialect peculiar to the *Montaña*, in this instance, the immediate area of Santander, near the sea. Pereda has gone beyond this accepted trait of the realists by converting the entire process of language into his pattern of nautical metaphor. The characters follow provincial ways by using nicknames instead of their proper names; and these nicknames are not simply offshoots of the baptismal designations but, characteristically, designate the type (that costumbrista influence so noticeable before in Pereda) called into play at this moment in the plot. Avoiding consequently the trap of a lengthy, digressive insertion (although Pereda has followed this nineteenth-century mannerism in the novel), the author can thus indicate the minor personages by a word or a nautical nickname, for humorous, appealing, satirical effect, at his will. Characterization, ambiance, and the epic novel of the sea are fused by the language into the interpretation of Santander at that point in time. Pereda has consistently and single-mindedly developed from not only the examples of dialect in the dialogues but in the seagoing slang, references, and similes a feeling and reaction about the nautical surroundings. Nautical matters penetrate every facet of the lives and histories of these people; indeed, they control the plot.

Certain linguistic patterns in *Sotileza* relate to the common language in the mountains (as later in *Peñas arriba*), the towns (as previously in *Don Gonzalo* and other stories), and even among the various classes of the city of Santander; and these similar dialectal divergences exist in other provinces of Spain as well as in Spanish-speaking areas of the New World. However, the principal dialect, with this pervasive association of the sea, is that of the fishing folk, Pereda's heroes in this novel. Pereda contributes moreover a very technical knowledge of maritime terms, some of which are peculiarly Spanish and others peculiar to the vicinity of Santander (the examples of *patache* and *unción* mentioned earlier serve as typical but not uncommon usages by the author), with the resultant strength of realism, local color, and authenticity as the virtues of this procedure.

A negative side to this detailed and complicated explanation of the seagoing terminology and metaphor arises however, in the difficulty for present-day readers, even in the Spanish world, to understand these expressions. The further limitations to Pereda's achievement are noted in the paucity of translations for English and American audiences, because, quite simply, the brilliant Peredian language lacks at times accurate equivalents in English.[17] Nevertheless, this agonizing task for translators must be equated with the problems for

Spanish interpreters of the great English-speaking writers about the sea, who, with the exception of Cooper's early nineteenth-century popularity in Spain (and throughout much of Europe), seem to have fared poorly among Spanish speakers. The old law of balances and the familiar complaint regarding the insularity of peninsular literature serve as unfortunate evidence for the lack of acceptance of *Sotileza* beyond Spanish-speaking borders.

Another facet of the Peredian world, perhaps more in accord with Eoff's approach, lies in the benevolent influence of the nautical experience. Santander is only a microcosm of the outside world, with the creeping changes of the modern age, but with the permanency of values conveyed by language, by the seagoing language. In that area, time has little impact, despite the regretful embitterment of Pereda; and one receives the distinct impression that all these characters, at heart no different from those of other centuries, are speaking the same language as their forefathers. The seagoing types and the seagoing metaphor embody the *intrahistoria* of which Unamuno writes, the *abulia*, or passivity, that Azorín describes so sympathetically; the whole atmosphere, or the metaphorical mood, symbolizes what, for Pereda, should be eternal, because the qualities of these people need preservation.

The narration, like the waves of these seas of Santander, is not only linear, that is, chronological; the story seems to go back and forth, like the waves crashing against the docks and shore that the youngsters in the first part enjoyed, and also like the crests of the storm in the twenty-eighth chapter. If not everything in *Sotileza*, at least a great deal can be explicated in the unifying measure of the sea and the nautical. This vast frame of reference is supported, primarily, by the richness, the refined and the vulgar aspects, of the language — "the infinite resources of the vocabulary . . . crude, picturesque, barefaced, smelling of small sardines and rotten fish," as it was described by Menéndez Pelayo.[18] Likewise, Don Marcelino calls attention to the explanation that Pereda acquired this language of Santander by observation during his boyhood and youth; and the true reproduction of regional, local-color characteristics must be attempted not only realistically (and certainly never by learned acquisitions) but also by actual immersion in the environment with an attendant love for the surroundings. Menéndez Pelayo labored long in behalf of this thesis for Pereda; and Pereda both followed and strayed from his advice before and after *Sotileza*.

One more notable, impressive feature of Pereda's language in his masterpiece resides in the balance of dialogue, description, and narration, all in the same popular vein, with no lack of ease of transition among these three techniques. *Sotileza,* stylistically, resembles the Galdosian novels of the Madrid settings, such as *Misericordia* (Compassion), in the use of popular language; it does not illustrate the *castizo* ("polished language") of the next great book of Pereda, *Peñas arriba,* with the interval of a decade.

CHAPTER 5

The Mountains of Santander: Peñas arriba

ESTHETICS and not chronology link *Sotileza* and *Peñas arriba*, and again, the spinning fates of criticism place these two books, in that order, as the important Peredian contribution (whether historically, intrinsically, or through a combination of factors) to the nineteenth-century novel. Pereda had by now passed beyond the stage of short stories and recognizable cuadros de costumbres, but he had also stumbled badly between *Sotileza* and *Peñas arriba* with four disappointing works. Cossío has been able to trace with remarkable thoroughness the progress of *Peñas arriba*, and he has likewise identified a great deal of the "historicity," or historical genuineness, the actual background and characters utilized by the author.[1] *Peñas arriba* was immediately apotheosized, as Montesinos wryly defines the reception of Pereda's new novel; and the same critic seems puzzled by this exceptional warmth of the Spanish press toward an important work of the nineteenth century.[2] Even Menéndez Pelayo climbs to these "upper peaks," as if to emulate the mountain views of his compatriot, in the routinely expected positive review of *Peñas arriba*, although there are in Don Marcelino's comments the designation of weaknesses in the novel. Both the critic of the time and the present commentator, Menéndez Pelayo and Montesinos, grant that Pereda has inserted something not only different but more profoundly philosophic about the *Montaña*.

One factor explaining the laudatory welcome of *Peñas arriba* (Pereda's best seller among all the many novels) would appear to be a common literary occurrence, not limited to Spain and unrestricted also in time, namely, the return to greatness of an author who has failed to maintain a previous solid achievement. There are, within this decade of ten years, several explanations for Pereda's inability to have kept up the first-rate quality of *Sotileza*, a summary of which was mentioned in the first chapter. The germ of *Peñas arriba* was in his mind by 1891 but grew very agonizingly and, as usual, dilatorily, so that in late 1892 and even into the spring of 1893, Pereda complained to Menéndez Pelayo about the mental block regarding the novel.[3] But in the summer of 1893 in Polanco, away from the city and, perhaps symbolically, closer to the mountains, Pereda enjoyed the stimulus of renewed interest in *Peñas arriba* until his son's suicide at the beginning of September. No critic has failed to praise Pereda for the extraordinary force of will he demonstrated in completing *Peñas arriba*, and the question of the influence of a terrible personal tragedy must be critically raised as to the impact of Juan Manuel's death on his father's work.

I   *Excelsior!*

Despite the depressing event of the son's suicide, with the resultant "dark night of the soul" for Pereda, the mood of *Peñas arriba* remains one of striving upward, a winning of the struggle for Marcelo's spirit, and the hero's enthusiasm for a future in the *Montaña*. This pattern, not only of the plot and of the characters but more importantly of the philosophy and ideology, has prompted Montesinos (following the lead of more favorably inclined friends and critics of Pereda) to declare that *Peñas arriba* is "a very considerable work, if not the best of its author, certainly the most serious, the most mature as to thought, the most planned, for these very reasons, the most magnanimous."[4] There is no doubt that *Peñas arriba*, unlike *Sotileza* despite all that novel's assets, demonstrates a superiority of the technical craft; and from that point of view, that of structure and style, *Peñas arriba* is indeed an "ascent to the heights," as the title could signify. This richness of the Peredian style is initially revealed by the book's title, a symbolic clue to the author's intentions, with the beauty of the expression also offering a problem to the translator. The present solution for an interpretation (rather than a translation perhaps) has been "the upper peaks" for *Peñas arriba*, although two other possibilities have been already mentioned in this chapter, "ascent to the heights" and "excelsior." Again, as in *Sotileza*, the language of *Peñas arriba* becomes a barrier to the diffusion and popularity of a Peredian work beyond the Spanish-speaking areas.

Stylistically, therefore, *Peñas arriba* is certainly the height of not only the purest usage by Pereda of the Spanish language but a triumph of the use of *castizo* (the classical, correct, and idiomatic

language) in dialogue, description, and analysis in the nineteenth-
century novel. Although the employment of regionalisms and popular speech is scattered throughout the book, dialect has been suppressed, in general, in favor of a more standard transcription by one
of the characters. Some language, then, is regional, but without the
difficulties of *Sotileza*, coming, in this instance, from the Highlands
of the province. Two other changes augment the solidity of the
novel's framework, again technically. The plot is linear, a direct
chronological narration, taking place within the cycle of one year,
starting with Marcelo's arrival at his uncle's mountain home, close to
the beginning of winter (and the beginning of a new life for the
hero), and lasting through the many events of the next twelve
months until the end of autumn and the quickly approaching harsh
weather. The entire novel is reported from the first-person point of
view, from the vantage point of Marcelo, the main actor and the
hero, without any doubt or any turns of fortune, as with Andrés.
Everything proceeds along this straight line without any surprising
turns in the story, though with certain exciting and dramatic
episodes.

   Peñas arriba is the history of Marcelo during the most critical year
of his life; but the hero is no youth, like Andrés, who comes of age in
the grip of an overwhelming moment, because Marcelo is thirty-two
at the time of the first chapter. His age helps to explain why he was
reluctant to answer his uncle's appeal to come to the *Montaña*.
Marcelo, settled comfortably in the capital and enjoying his established status, has no inner reasons to disturb his way of life, except for the constant need of more funds, one of the Peredian evils of
big-city civilization. Nevertheless, Marcelo is somewhat restless in
Madrid, and he rationalizes that a small dose of nature (which he
basically abhors) will cure his annoyance with any aspects of his
present life and, indeed, will make him appreciate the comforts of
his urban home. Marcelo's arrival at the last semblance of a
progressive town in the lowlands of the *Montaña* where he is met by
the faithful servant of his uncle, Chisco, is not unlike Pepe Rey's
reception in Orbajosa by his aunt's loyal neighbor, Licurgo, in
Galdós's *Doña Perfecta*. Then, Pereda presents a complete reversal
of the severe Galdosian portrait of a small town, because Marcelo is
greeted sincerely and helpfully by all the acquaintances and
followers of Celso, obviously the acknowledged master and guide of
the community; and this introduction softens Marcelo's antipathy.
Galdós deepened the conspiracy of Doña Perfecta against her

nephew each time the latter was introduced to a local inhabitant; and Pepe Rey felt and expressed his repugnance about Orbajosa more overtly with these unpleasant experiences. Once more, perhaps, Pereda is answering his friend's views by means of a novel, positively and delicately (unlike the brusqueness of *De tal palo*), without alienating Don Benito; and these reverses parallel developments of plot, characterization, and themes.[5]

Three dramatic actions, somewhat like the triple use of the sea in *Sotileza,* occur in *Peñas arriba:* the trapping of the bears with the necessary killing of these animals, a menace to the whole area, providing a close call with disaster as Marcelo proves his worth during the attack (and showing his mettle as the successor to Celso); the rescue of Pepazos (one of the familiar servants and peasants so regularly sketched in the novel) during a terrible snowstorm followed by the rescuers' entrapment in an avalanche with Chisco, Celso's most intimate retainer, narrowly saved from the edge of a precipice; and the attempted robbery of Celso's home by the blackmailing spouse of the unfortunate Facia, the housekeeper, with her mysterious past serving as a running story interest until late in the novel. In these three vividly narrated events, Marcelo's role increases in significance from the first crucial intervention during the bear hunt to his later exclusion from the rescue party, principally to alleviate any worry on the part of his uncle, now rapidly approaching the final decline of his health. Marcelo has thus in the second thrilling vignette a more important part, ultimately preserving his personal safety for a higher purpose. At the third, clearly Gothic encounter (the three confrontations resemble Gothic thrillers in the Peredian choice of language and in the menacing, narrow escapes from tragedy and destruction), Marcelo demonstrates his ability to command physically, hinted at during the search for the bears, and psychologically, illustrated by his relation with his uncle. After Facia has at last revealed her secret to Marcelo, the latter prepares against a possible burglary without disturbing Celso; and the nephew's control of the threatening situation is a masterly example of his ability to be a worthy follower of his uncle and a leader for the neighborhood. No clash takes place between the hopeful thieves, led by Facia's renegade husband, and the watchful Marcelo, because the rogues are trapped by the same storm, which so recently menaced Pepazos, Chisco, and the others; and later, the frozen bodies of the criminals are discovered, showing also the two sides of the coin of nature or the Emersonian law of compensations at work. Probably for Pereda,

from past illustrations in several works, the solution brought forth a
literary usage of irony and a moralizing proof about the labyrinthine
interventions of the God of his forefathers where a firm faith in tradition and nature will set all aright.

The unhurried pace of these three actions is normal in the
leisurely nineteenth-century development of the novel, of course;
but also, Pereda, more than in any other novel (before and after
Peñas arriba) has inserted long, detailed descriptions of the scenery.
Structurally and thematically, the geographical settings play a central part in this conflict: Will Marcelo yield to the ambiance of
nature, renouncing the city and the false gods of contemporary
civilization for a return to the past, to the true values of tradition and
a measured, sure way of life? Will Celso live long enough, first to
persuade and demonstrate to his dubious and then wavering nephew
the glories of the *Montaña*, and secondly, to see Marcelo put on the
mantle of leadership as heir to the uncle's responsibilities? Description and discussions are the bricks and mortar, respectively for this
novelistic edifice; dialogue is never a major device in *Peñas arriba*,
and the three climactic actions are only peripheral to the author's intentions. Plot, in short, is not the purpose and appeal of this
novelistic venture; and Pereda has really looked backward but in a
very modified and artistic fashion to his initial undertakings in the
thesis novels. Certainly by now, this novelist's constant, consistent
pattern of adhering neither to a successful (nor an unfortunate)
methodology is not unexpected.

II   *The Weight of Description*

These many descriptions, realistically and minutely added to the
lengthy novel, would lessen the Peredian thesis if they were excised
or abbreviated; but these extensive passages do not contribute
basically to the story, and, indeed, they slow down noticeably the
progress of the action.[6] Even the ideological significance of this
descriptive background would not have redeemed the novel from
failure without the quality of form, the poetic, chiseled language of
the artist. The stylistic greatness of Pereda has reached a culmination, "the upper peak," principally in the rendition of the mountain
settings. In the perennial question of form versus content as the
primary criterion of an outstanding novel, Pereda has here placed
himself on the side of form overwhelmingly to the detriment of content (mistakenly, in the aftermath of the rejection of nineteenth-
century formulas, a criticism that must be considered later in this

analysis). From the viewpoint of vocabulary, syntax, and general expression the descriptions comprise a lyric poem; and excerpts are usually a favorite choice for anthologies and stylistic analysis if, again, the editor can bring himself to the justification of leaving aside current, contemporary interests as a factor in the always vexing dilemma of what to include as representative selections of the times.

There are an abundance of possibilities to illustrate the above conclusions; but the most popular as well as the most revealing example of Peredian technique in this novel is the eleventh chapter. In terms of plot, Marcelo and Don Sabas, the priest, take a trip (at the suggestion of the latter) to a more desolate but more beautiful place up in the mountains; and these few words summarize the story development of this chapter, surely an episode that could be excised without harm to the narration. But the chapter is essential to Pereda's themes and his superb demonstration of style. Marcelo, despite the physical exertions and some first impressions of the priest as a rather dull companion, undergoes a near-mystical, clearly romantic, rapture upon viewing the sky, sea, and vast extension of land above, around, and below him. The grandeur of nature and the smallness of man, that dream of pure romanticism in painting and literature, are accentuated with each moment for Marcelo after his "ascent to the peaks" or to "the upper peaks," for whichever interpretation of *Peñas arriba* is preferred, the novel's title is most strikingly illuminated in this chapter.

A religious glow permeates and increasingly dominates the view and the vision, the former the more overt aims of Celso and the priest (the reader clearly perceives that this expedition is part of the bait to lure Marcelo to the *Montaña)*, and the latter being conveyed by the exaltation of Don Sabas with the desired effect on Marcelo. Indeed, this chapter is a turning point in the trajectory of Marcelo's attitude toward nature and, more vitally, toward the question of a future in the *Montaña*. It is, of course, no accident that Pereda has selected the priest as the guide for Marcelo during this journey, because, in this contrast and yet harmony between nature and man, the church, not undefined religion and certainly not any pantheistic associations of the romantics, enjoys the role of *mater et magistra* ("mother and teacher"), evident in the directional and didactic performance of Don Sabas in these pages.

The Peredian ideology is credible because the episode possesses verisimilitude in the strong impressions made on any usual visitor or tourist by an awesome view of nature, such as the Grand Canyon;

and Marcelo's depiction as a sensitive, open-minded person, ready at this particular time for conversion to residency in the *Montaña*, makes very acceptable his emotions and reactions, almost like a Joycean epiphany. But again, all these facets would be ineffective or seriously weakened without the poetic prose, almost a necessity to sustain the mounting level of rapturous contemplation; and by keeping in mind the whole of chapter 9 as loyal to this stylistic triumph, the following excerpts provide a support for the above arguments:

> Going on and on, slipping here and faltering there, and my horse sighing; at the end of an hour the profiles of the mountains began to be outlined upon the sky confusedly illuminated by the tenuous clarity of the dawn. . . . The priest, who seemed to have that quality of the mountain birds, became more loquacious and little by little began to come out with the mysterious harmonies of their songs. . . . At the first glow of dawn, he praised God with a fervent salutation and, though not at his level, deeply felt in his heart . . . and holding back the reins which he almost pulled from my hands, he said to me, pointing with his idle right hand to a very tall and distant important peak on whose tip was sparkling the first ray of sunshine penetrating those mountainous regions:
> "Look, look! . . . Look, Marcelo! Wouldn't you swear that that thing shining and blazing way, way up there, on that peak, is the last of the altar lights with which the world pays homage to its Creator while the sun is fading into the abysses of the night? A good thing! A great thing! *Laudate Dominum omnes gentes. . . . Magnificentia opus, ejus, manet in aeternum* ["Praise the Lord, all peoples . . . Magnificent is His work, lasting for eternity"]." (II, 1165)

Don Sabas and Marcelo continue to go up and up and up, to the increasing fatigue of the latter and the growing enthusiasm of the former (with a good contrast thereby between the humorous, human aspect and the serious, exalted side) until, proceeding on foot to attain the uppermost pinnacle, they are exposed to the breathtaking panorama of the sea and land, from west to east, north to south, of the entire province, seemingly. Marcelo, after contemplating the majestic picture, begins to study the details in all directions:

> All these details, and a thousand others and more, ordered and arranged with superhuman art in the midst of a flood of light, had as a complement of their grandiosity and beauty the imposing silence and the august solitude of the wild heights of my observatory.
> Never had I seen so great a portion of the world at my feet, nor had I found myself so near its Creator, nor had the contemplation of His work

caused me such deep and pleasant impressions. I attributed them to the new point of view, and not without rational and judicious foundation. Until then I had only observed Nature in the shade of its masses, in the narrownesses of its mountain passes, in the mistiness of its ravines and in the shadow of its woods; all of which weighed upon my spirit, to the point of overwhelming it, formed in the refined softness of the big cities, in whose wonders one sees the cleverness and the hand of men more than the omnipotence of God; but in that case I could savor the spectacle in vaster proportions, in full light and without hindrances; and without failing therefore to deem myself a worm by the power of the contrast of my smallness with those immensities, I was a worm, finally, from the heights of space and not from the muddy grounds of the earth. Until then I had needed the contagion of Don Sabas' fervors to read something into the great book of Nature, and on that occasion I read into it alone, unashamedly, and with great pleasure.

And reading into it, fascinatedly, I came to immerse myself in a mass of reflections that, branching off at one end in the monotonous dullness of my whole worldly life and becoming enraptured immediately with the spectacle that delighted my eyes, soared afterward above the very highest summits limiting the horizon at my back; and they even continued rising through the outright ether in which the prayers of the unfortunate and the sighs of yearning souls of the Supreme Good ascend.

At last, turning my eyes toward Don Sabas, whom I had forgotten for a good while, because he had not been thinking about me during the same time, I found him, to all appearances, reading the great book on the same page as I. He was in the whole fullness of Nature, as his resplendent eyes declared, his mouth half-open as if eager for mountain air, and that special restlessness of his muscles and even of his clothing.

"Has it all been seen well?" he asked me, coming to his senses suddenly.

"To all my pleasure," I answered him.

"Then add to the reckoning that something of the great works of God which we have around here has been seen now."

"This spectacle is indeed great and beautiful and admirable!" I replied.

"Great?" Repeated the priest; and he again contemplated [the view] with his arms outstretched to all directions, as if he should like to give in that manner the measure of its magnitude.

After he uncovered his head, whose gray hairs waved in the air, he lifted his glance to the sky, his hand with hat and all; and he exclaimed in a solemn and virile voice that vibrated with a strange sound in the imposing silence of those majestic heights: "*Excelsus super omnes gentes, Dominus, et super coelos . . . gloria ejus* [Exalted above all peoples, Lord, and above all heavens, is His glory]."

It was possibly because of the exceptional state of my spirit or whatever work of an external agent, but the certain thing is that it seemed to me that final note stamped on the picture by the priest of Tablanca bordered on the sublime. (II, 1168 - 69)

III *A Spanish Lost Horizon*

It is clear from examples such as the above that Pereda had the intention to compose a novel of idealism, in addition to a regional work exalting the *Montaña*. For instance, the local-color sketches, characteristic of regionalism and a favorite with Pereda before *Peñas arriba* have little or no place here, making the novel almost a rarity, therefore, in the author's whole canon. A common accusation is that Pereda has written an escapist novel, a retreat from the dissatisfactions of urban life and nineteenth-century civilization, so persistently abhorred from the beginnings of his literary output; and no one can deny absolutely that the almost obsessional reaction and prejudice surface as a familiar pattern in *Peñas arriba*.[7] Aside from the admitted presence of a strong regionalism, a nostalgic escapism, and an uncompromising rejection of the age, the entrance of a more mature approach to the times appears as a prominent contribution on Pereda's part toward his novelistic art and this novel, in particular. Description, of course, overshadows discussion; and this weight of description, as illustrated by the previous citation with the lengthy, beautiful, and moving pages, typical and yet a peak of the author's stylistic brilliance, intervenes too often, preventing the development of Pereda's thought about the future of the *Montaña* and of Spain.[8]

References are made to the characters in *Don Gonzalo* in the eighteenth chapter, where the previous novel's actors are described as neighbors of Celso. The turbulent events of the Revolution of 1868 with Don Gonzalo González de la Gonzalera's pompous and ambitious schemes are still the scandal of the region. Later, in the thirtieth chapter (both chapters summarize action from *Don Gonzalo* and offer Pereda's afterthoughts on this particular novel), more characters from the earlier work are mentioned with the predicted news that the results for the ruling class and the way of life have been disastrous. It is true that the upstarts have been frustrated, but "the example of the fall of Coteruco," as those happenings are analyzed by some of the personages from *Don Gonzalo* who now appear for Marcelo's further enlightenment, serves sadly as a lesson within the story of *Peñas arriba*. The revelations about Coteruco have been planned by Celso and his friends as additional pressure upon Marcelo to remain, as his uncle's heir (and more importantly to become the successor of all this heritage). The decline and fall of a neighboring, similar enclave of the *Montaña* acts as a confirmation of the previous discussions and as a warning of a possibly dismal future. Pereda has changed greatly between the publication of *Don Gonzalo* and *Peñas arriba:* the former novel portrays fearfully and nostalgically the chaos and never-to-be-restored existence of the rural, traditional areas, so that the mood is very pessimistic and negative; but the latter novel, while adhering to the concluding tones of the other work, now attacks, in a positive fashion, with the question posed as to what are the opponents of the new and the defenders of the old to do about other Coterucos. And more revolutionary upheavals are in store for the nation, as Pereda astutely and prophetically grasps in the two novels. At this late date in the nineteenth century, and close to the protests of the Generation of 1898 and the new century, Pereda has sketched briefly but tantalizingly his vision of the Spanish polarization and projects the apocalyptic outline of the civil war.

Still, the author is not completely hopeless; and this hope stands out as the intrinsic argument for Marcelo's acceptance of command and leadership after Celso's death. Command will come easily and as a matter of the traditional acceptance of loyalty to the new *mayorazgo* ("primogeniture"); but leadership requires a great deal more than the steady continuation of the past, and this is Pereda's profound and promising change between *Don Gonzalo* and this novel. The discussions up to Celso's death, and even beyond, concern an idealistic society in the *Montaña.*

Although this idealism must await the death of Celso (who recognizes that he is physically and philosophically unable to project higher goals for his sphere of influence), the invaluable aides for the improvement of these lands already live here. In fact, the various conversations oscillate between a possibly ideal (but no longer idyllic) state and a more enthusiastic crusade for a utopian patria chica. These Peredian thoughts must be collated, however, because the strands of the idealistic, utopian pattern are not developed at full length but are interrupted either by one of the three central actions or by the comings-and-goings of the minor characters. The Peredian solution has been often omitted in studies on this turning point of Spanish history; or the views expressed in this last major novel have been dismissed as anachronistic, unfeasible, a sop from the past to the growing demands of the emerging twentieth century.[9]

Clearly, the social, political philosophy is traditionalist, conservative, and medieval; but the spirit of the Middle Ages is modernized and meaningfully applied to the future, on the local and national levels. The first source for Marcelo's initiation is obviously

Celso, who, in the fifth chapter, explains his love for this Shangri-La, preserved in the mountains. Celso confides in, and then bequeaths the enclave to, his nephew. Marcelo's own explorations in the seventh chapter, especially, lead to appreciation of the retreat's traditions and history, with emphasis on the *romances* ("ballads") and the strength of the race, followed by continued observations, analyses, and conclusions.

Marcelo broadens his range of acquaintances and friends with the two representative types, the priest, Don Sabas (one of the twin pillars for the young man's leadership, a symbol of church allegiance), and Neluco, the doctor (the other buttress of the social order with his unwavering support). There is no conflict here between religion and science, that classic nineteenth-century struggle stimulated by Darwin's influence, which erupts in the Spanish novel after 1870; on the contrary the dual forces are in agreement and work harmoniously, further exemplifying the Peredian idealism or utopian quality in this novel. The ninth chapter, a long talk between Marcelo and Neluco, offers the most striking outline of the author's ideas because the doctor, not completely pessimistic about the present century and declaring that this age is better in some respects than past times (an unusual, progressive stance for Pereda), states that the real aim of Celso for Marcelo, with the loyal strength of the two members of the Tablanca establishment, is to exemplify the regeneration of the whole nation. The isolated edges of Spain remain healthy in spirit, at heart, "some of them, at least, and only with the rich blood of these members could be purified and reconstructed with much time and great patience the corrupted part of the centers" (II, 1157).

Neluco later expands this plan to the intellectuals' role in a new *reconquista* ("reconquest"), converting the small, dedicated band of individuals to a knighthood of the modern age. These updated knights-errant will be quixotic like the Cervantine hero; but they also will be practical and realistic in their undertakings because Celso, Neluco, and Don Sabas admit the defects of the humble residents of their district. No idealization about the solid peasantry exists in their reports, and the reforms must start at home, in the *Montaña*, before expansion to the cities — surely the targets of Pereda's thrust about "the corrupted part" of the Spanish homeland. Still, the peasants with their rude faults are likewise the innocent victims of neglect and exploitation, another warm, humanitarian regard on Pereda's side for his humbler compatriots, as in the attack on the oppressive naval conscription in *Sotileza*.

The commentaries expounding a visionary system are found, besides in the fifth and ninth chapters, within more general, limited episodes, such as those of the eleventh and fourteenth chapters. The importance of these guidelines for the restoration of the *Montaña*, for the brotherhood of devoted *caballeros* ("knights"), and for the rebirth of Spain inspires Marcelo to take Celso's place. First, the people "considered me no longer as the continuer but as the reformer" (II, 1305), as Marcelo realizes close to the novel's end; and then on the final pages, he eagerly seizes upon the chance to *obrar bien* ("to work well"), according to Calderón de la Barca's expression in *La vida es sueño* (Life Is a Dream), with this rationalization for exemplary future conduct:

And finally, I succeeded in telling myself, if the theories of that little doctor are well founded, if the reconstruction of the degenerated and rotting body is to come through the pure blood of the extremities, someone has to begin that eminently humanitarian and patriotic work. And why am I not to be the one? . . . And although, as the days go by, all this turns out to be nonsense, what more can I aspire to, worldly, insipid, and disenchanted, than to live in the warmth of this divine fire sparkling in my heart and mind, and which has transformed me from a soft, insensitive, and careless courtier into an active, diligent, and useful man? (II, 1315)

Following this coolly logical approach, Marcelo knows that he will be surrounded not only by a loving wife and the faithful companions of his lands but also by the beauties of nature and a strong faith in God. And after a certain number of years, in a few lines comprising the thirty-fourth chapter or an epilogue, Marcelo is still overjoyed about his fortune in making the right decision to stay in the mountains. But there is no mention of the reforming changes at home and, consequently, no outward drive of the modern Reconquest to rescue Spain. The analogy has been dropped: historical parallels have been abandoned by Pereda in a way that is perhaps explicable by the crushing personal blow at the moment of the twenty-first chapter. Whatever the explanation may be, the novel is still weakened acutely from then on, with the artistic problems prior to chapter 21 brought into more prominent relief.[10]

IV   *The Grain of a Novel*

Not only Menéndez Pelayo,[11] although his is the first and still impressive voice, but also successive critics in all hues have come to grips with the usual question about any novel: Is this an exceptional novel? Generally, the style, the description, the discussions, and the entire range of the Peredian approach, while winning praise, do not merit affirmative reply to this standard query. Today, the contemporary reader quite frankly finds that *Peñas arriba* does not possess the dynamism that Outzen claims to be the trait of Pereda's writings.[12] The story and the plot, while centering on the spiritual journey and development of the hero, do not offer the conflict and interest required to sustain Pereda's longest novel nor does the work deal with the sometimes difficult and confusing complications of the many characters. The problem, it seems clear, is that one can readily anticipate what is going to happen; and one is not too far into the novel before the surety is established that Marcelo will follow in Celso's footsteps. The rather timid love of Marcelo for Lita encounters no barriers except for the mistaken notion on the young man's part that the girl prefers Neluco. Again, the whole outline of this puzzlement is never opaque; and the other sentimental aspirations of the couples resemble more appropriately the amusing, charming loves of the less important characters in the Golden Age *comedias de capa y espada* ("cape and sword plays"). Except for the heightening thrills of the three climactic actions, noted earlier, there are no confrontations and dramatic qualities in this linear, clearly focused plot.

The most noticeable influence of the Peredian domestic tragedy, that brooding memory of his son's suicide, would seem to be in the overly extensive scenes of Celso's death — after the twenty-first chapter. It is true that Pereda, in accord with his modernized chivalric ideal, probably saw in these minutely detailed, slow-paced scenes another transfer of the medieval ambiance to the current stage. Continuity rather than change is symbolically conveyed by Celso's death within the novel; and the entire atmosphere is redolent of a medieval mood where time and space occupy no prominence. Although *Peñas arriba* obviously belongs in the nineteenth century with reference to the temporal and spatial backgrounds, no significance is attached to the century, specifically, or to an action's occurring in a certain year, for instance. Marcelo's dilemma about life in the city or in the country could have been faced in other times, and the example of Fray Luis de León in the sixteenth century is fundamentally that of Marcelo, choosing the rural over the urban.

This medieval analogy, referring to Celso's demise, can be immediately associated with the great fifteenth-century elegy of Jorge Manrique on the death of his father, so interestingly rendered into

English by Longfellow. Pereda has described in prose, in the genre of the nineteenth century, what Jorge Manrique interpreted in verse. Celso, like Rodrigo Manrique, approaches death calmly and stoically, confident of the redeeming virtues of his good works and stalwart faith; and the culminating moment, the deathbed scene, reproduces the feeling of the fifteenth-century agony for the dying nobleman, "surrounded by his family," as Celso is enclosed in the sad consolations of Marcelo and all the others. But once more, the brilliance in style of the two reproductions of a nobleman's death cannot answer affirmatively the recurring question about the novelistic art. There is perhaps, in the whole of Spanish literature, no more ineffectively prolonged depiction of the last days, hours, and minutes of a character. The effect of this account of Celso's death is a return to the romantic predilection for these pictures of a person approaching the end of existence; and too, the continued emphasis on the uncle's death draws too near the morbid and effusive.

Even the interesting similarities and attempted parallels with Tolstoy's *Anna Karenina,* as well as with novels of Dickens, Hardy, and Turgenev,[13] fail to raise Pereda's novel to the standards of the other recognizably first-class European productions. *Peñas arriba* is a contender in any race for beauty of style and setting but without achieving acclaim as an exemplary illustration of the modern novel. Form won the not necessarily inevitable conflict with content, and this work has been relegated to a more provincial level as twentieth-century interest has narrowed to a compelling attraction for psychological characterization and more associative themes, ideas, and topics.

CHAPTER 6

A Continuing Search for Stability

THIS decade between the twin peaks of *Sotileza* and *Peñas arriba* brought Pereda financial success through sales of his books, never unwelcome despite his affluence, and sustained attention from the critics, generally unfavorable as to the works of these ten years. The prevailing literary and intellectual mood now reflected the interest in naturalism, and the country was also on the threshold of the reaction against the nineteenth-century realistic styles, with the initial probings of Costa, Ganivet, and Unamuno. The diminution of Pereda's talent was matched by his anachronistic place in the national literature at the period of his acceptance into the fold of major writers of the century. The Peredian contributions between his two masterpieces provide no significant mastery and originality over his previous works, and one cannot help but conclude that these books merit attention only because of biographical considerations and as a footnote to literary history.

I   La Montálvez

Pereda was at first pleased by the popularity of *La Montálvez* (The Lady Montálvez) in 1888 and also by the recognition that he had published another *succès de scandale*.[1] However, a familiar problem disturbed him by the end of this same year, 1888, when Menéndez Pelayo expressed disappointment in Pereda's seemingly ardent embrace of naturalism; and the similar reaction of conservative critics and Santander readers convinced the novelist that he had not proved his thesis. Protest from the urban, liberal critics and audiences had been anticipated; and Pereda was attacked for his depiction of the decadent aristocracy in Madrid and the low moral tone of the capital, obsessed by social climbing, financially advantageous marriages, and amorous liaisons as the expected way of life. This noisy reception of *La Montálvez* brought a weak defense and evident retreat from Pereda as he endeavored to justify the novel as "una novela de análisis" or "una novela moral," (an analytic or moral novel), resurrecting these previously employed euphemisms for his blunt purposes. The question of his interpretation of naturalism, which many still see in this novel, added further controversial material to the debate about *La Montálvez*.[2]

The irritating feature of this novel, apparent at the time of publication and more noticeable at the present, resides in Pereda's inability to analyze impartially, or to judge charitably, his opponents in terms of the characters, themes, or settings of *La Montálvez*. This work is not even a thesis novel, because the stridency of his arguments (so repeatedly condemned by Montesinos) is unrelieved by any humanitarian, religious qualities. With cruel insistence upon the avenging hand of divine justice, the Peredian rigidity of thought turns away, instead of converting, readers to his stern orthodoxy, a repeated point in the Montesinos study.[3] There is basically nothing new here, inasmuch as internal comparisons of books of the decade before *Sotileza* with *La Montálvez* reveal resemblances in the harsh, unbending punishments assigned to sinners and wrongdoers, especially in *De tal palo*. This novel, in fact, seems a real source for *La Montálvez;* and once more Pereda appears to have reverted to a past formula. The fire-and-brimstone message is that the sins of the fathers — as in *De tal palo* — are passed to the sons, remorselessly and as a matter of unalterable belief. Resemblances with naturalistic determinism are coincidental. In *La Montálvez*, the moral vices of Verónica, the mother, are punished by the parent's sufferings at the anguish done to the innocent, pure daughter but more directly by the child, Luz, who sees all hope of a happy marriage destroyed by the family's reputation and who also dies melodramatically (in the romantic manner) in a long, unconvincing conclusion to the novel.

The story is without surprises in the development of the action, which follows the fortunes of three generations. Verónica's parents are the cause of her perdition by their ambitious and misguided social striving; the training, education, and corrupt companions of Verónica provide the background for her fall into sin. Pereda traces the liaison of Verónica with Guzmán, her lover and the father of Luz; the hasty marriage of Verónica with a dull husband; and the attempts to raise Luz in a better environment and to hide the past from the child. Some of the motives are clearly within the naturalistic mold, such as the role of familial, particularly maternal, love as a major factor in the psychological growth of offspring and the struggle of the characters to avoid their determined fates; but the resemblances are fundamentally coincidental (and Pereda's ideas at this date and prior to *La Montálvez* as well as his abhorrence of naturalism should be accepted at their face value) with this obvious referral to the author's first novelistic period. The jaundiced interpretation of the city, specifically Madrid, is reminiscent of *Men of Worth* and *Pedro Sánchez*, in particular; and the characters are only repetitions of those detested urban dwellers. Pereda's few literary excursions into the city as a story background are failures (with that surprising and successful exception of *Pedro Sánchez*); here again, he strays beyond the regional ken to his own artistic peril.

One suggestive but abortive insertion in *La Montálvez* is the ambition of Angel Núñez, the would-be fiancé of Luz, to be a novelist; and this character's description of his novel, reflecting precisely the developing complications of the story of *La Montálvez*, starts to present the dilemma between life and literature. Can the literary creation reflect accurately and instructively the problems of a real crisis? What is the balance between the writer and the man facing a similar situation on paper and in his daily existence? This tantalizingly innovative and constructive problem for Pereda is solved unsympathetically by leaving the rather pitiful Angel Núñez to be swept into the sordid history of Luz's family to abandonment of the issue without resolution. Pereda's venture into a foreshadowing of the autonomous character in the novel, a novel-within-a-novel, is brushed aside with sardonic humor, another basis for the criticism of Montesinos as Pereda's lack of fantasy.[4] The failure of *La Montálvez*, excluding the profitable sales of the novel, predictably turned Pereda back to the region of Santander.

II   La puchera

In the following year, 1889, Pereda published *La puchera* (The Stew) which pleased local audiences and the majority of critics on all sides, such as Menéndez Pelayo and Clarín; recently, Montesinos has subscribed to the opinion that *The Stew* is one of Pereda's masterpieces while commenting acidly on the defects of the work.[5]

There is again no distinct change or development in Pereda's outlook in *The Stew*, but an intensification of the regional and realistic backgrounds leads to the reaction that this novel is a culmination — so late in the century — of costumbrismo. The entire book offers an attempt to chisel the cuadros de costumbres into a semblance of a novel; but the diverse subplots (no single plot stands out clearly to attract the principal interest) never come together with unifying power, especially with the acute division, structurally, of the book into two parts. It is true that the stories of the various persons, their characterizations, and the psychological drives are constructed around the novel's title; the idea of *asegurar la puchera* refers to the regional dish of *el puchero* ("local stew"), the common, everyday fare without which an individual or family would be literally impoverished, almost hopelessly crushed by life. The regionalism of "asegurar la puchera" means to assure one's livelihood now — and for the future — by climbing the social ladder (the persistent issue in many Peredian books) through marrying well, the most convenient way in this society, through close ties with relatives to preserve estates and assets, or in one case in this novel by entering the priesthood as a rather comfortable career. All the honorable and mostly dishonorable ambitions and schemes, particularly after the first half of *The Stew*, build up to a romantic climax and a Gothic ending. The first half proceeds at a slow pace because of the extensive description of settings and characters, conveying the effect of a hard, honest life of Pereda's countrymen, in particular the peasants (another idyllic repetition from novels such as *Don Gonzalo*); and the plot complications are likewise narrated without any immediate attention to the compelling problem of achieving social and financial success but instead delineate the past and present lives of the involved participants.

The descriptions of these simple fisherfolk and tillers of the soil are no more than local-color sketches, interestingly described and sympathetically explicated, but the novelistic heart is lacking to hold readers. Later, in the second part (although no formal division of the novel is made by Pereda), the aspirations of these humble workers and servants are linked to the drives of their superiors and masters; and, in fact, the concerns of these former characters nearly vanish from view — a damaging evidence against the lengthy chapters in the first half of *The Stew*. Pereda also departs from the stress on costumbrista and realistic traits to a portrayal of types and an ugly, criminally motivated plot. Don Baltasar, or "el Berrugo," is the usurer who, like his possible predecessors in Fernán Caballero's *Lágrimas (Tears)* and the Galdosian series of *Torquemada* as well as similar characters in Molière and Balzac, dominates everything through his evil intentions, being almost diabolical and certainly pathologically motivated, with obsessions regarding "asegurar la puchera." This epitome of wickedness brings to mind the earlier

novel, *A Chip off the Old Block,* and the progression of the now
swiftly moving story confirms resemblances between the two Peredian books. Don Baltasar has caused the death of his wife, allying
himself with his equally depraved housekeeper, to maintain control
of his possessions, dominating his daughter completely; and la
Galusa, hoping to have her worthless nephew (a disreputable
seminary student eager to escape ordination) marry Don Baltasar's
child, has joined very willingly her master's conspiracy. There are no
innocent *intereses creados* ("vested interests") involved in these
schemes, and there is no humorous element, as in the first part, to
counterbalance these wicked maneuvers of the sharply drawn
villains. Pereda employs his romantic devices in the escape of Don
Baltasar's daughter, the union with an exemplary aspirant for her
hand, and the success of other story interests. La Galusa and her
nephew are thwarted by their fears and terror at Don Baltasar's insane rages about his frustrated cabals; the cowardly nephew flees
from the housekeeper's reactions; and Don Baltasar, in the last
chapter, falls to his death from a precipice while trying to search for
a supposedly hidden treasure. This last chapter provides excitement
and suspense as the priest spurs the neighbors (and victims) of Don
Baltasar in boats to row toward a rescue. The final effect of horror,
achieved through the concluding paragraph describing the usurer's
mutilated body, is justified by Pereda's use of Don Alejo throughout
the scene giving consolation to the sinner before the latter's death
and final absolution to the corpse.

All the characters are basically familiar from a reading of Pereda's
other novels: the good and the bad characters have no shades of psychological realism; and the personages are contrasted for didactic
purposes in many scenes. Of course, Don Alejo as the symbol of the
Church is another of the sterling priests observed previously; but
Marcones, serving obviously as a contrasting figure, does point out
the existence of ignoble candidates for the clergy, an occasional
balancing feature in Pereda's general defense of Catholicism. Don
Elias, the doctor, is perhaps the only complex figure, the single actor
with some tints of personality rather than a straightforward presentation; but his role is still too minor to postulate any significant influence of Galdós with the latter's interest in these apparently mad
but often perceptive individuals.[6]

Such positive traits as to types and characterizations, especially in
the second half of *The Stew,* and the more dynamic action, though
weighted so noticeably toward the creation of an effect, do not fun-

damentally compensate for the sudden alteration in structural tone between the two halves of this novel. The lack of balance, or the transition between the author's techniques, eliminates an artistic unity to the whole work, although the first part constitutes a height of the costumbrista influence, interstitched with some naturalistic texture to form the culmination, or certainly a high point, of the regional novel. This provincial ambiance, in terms of life and characters, is fortified by a realistic language peculiar to Santander; and this mingling of the two linguistic aspects, the down-to-earth, natural speech of simple folk and the moderate usage of the regional, limited patterns, has won high praise for *La puchera*. The novelistic art, however, has suffered in this Peredian contribution; and from this angle of structure, the book is very weak because of the undue length, slow pace, and unclear motives about Pereda's aims until late in the text.[7]

III   Nubes de estío and Al primer vuelo

These last two novels, though long, were written quickly and were published in the same year, 1891. There is no controversy as to the low quality of the books, similar in plot and obviously produced to satisfy the demands of publishers for more stories from an author at the height of his popularity and close to membership in the Royal Spanish Academy. A harsh conclusion would be that Pereda might have salvaged some literary immortality by not having published the pair of novels, representing the nadir of his artistry. In short, *Nubes de estío* (Summer Clouds) and *Al primer vuelo* (On the First Flight) destroyed Pereda's declining reputation in the long run; and more closely at hand, helped to mount reservations about his merits as a candidate to the Real Academia, especially among antagonistic critics. Pardo Bazán, for example, launched a bitter attack against Pereda with her previous arguments about his intrinsic lack of novelistic talent, his provincialism limited to a warped view of his "garden," and his incomprehension of naturalism with the consequent lack of inclusion in the circle of these naturalist writers. Pereda, foolishly, engaged in a polemic about these evidently indefensible two novels. He lost the fight on all aspects, artistically, and his prestige suffered because of his embittered, ineffective replies.[8]

The two novels might have been saved as short stories if Pereda had reverted again to a past manner, in this case, the short story or sketch, or a novelette. The two plots are so much alike that the ultimate judgment that the novels are mere potboilers cannot be avoided, since there are likewise no redeeming traits of originality in characterization, setting, and ideas. The prolix tediousness involved in the reading of the books is unmatched elsewhere in the extensive production of this author. *Summer Clouds* establishes a conflict between the prosperous, ambitious, and provincial family from the *Montaña,* overwhelmed by the pretentious, impoverished aristocratic summer tourists from Madrid. The family's daughter is to be sacrificed on the altar of marriage to the boring and mediocre scion of the noble household; but all ends happily as the girl's mother and the daughter herself outmaneuver the master of the home, a thoughtless husband and father on all grounds. The satire is ponderous because the opposing families are too clearly objects of the Peredian scorn and hatred for the city as well as rejection of the social-climbing citizens of his native region.

Character development is totally lacking, and the actors in this summer drama never appeal to the reader as believable persons. Of course, these problems of the polarization between urban and rural values, the representatives of upper-class circles with their moral corruption and arrogance, and their equally ridiculous country cousins, and the outcry about the waning of the strong traditionalism facing the waves of materialism have been observed often in other books by Pereda, for example, in *Men of Worth* and *Nomadic Types.*

On the First Flight is no improvement, all in all, although there is relative avoidance of the overly sketched caricatures of *Summer Clouds* in favor of the inclusion of local types, easily acceptable in their common speech and realistic manners. But the plot is immediately evident, and the felicitous outcome, while adhering to versimilitude and the reader's hopes, is also too clear early in the text. A daughter is brought by her father from the city to the country — again the polarized situation between the two environments — where she is intended as the bride for an indiano coming back to Spain. However, she falls in love with a poor young man from the town; and again, a father's pretensions are vanquished by the good sense of other members of the family in addition to good friends among the townspeople. As a short story, *On the First Flight* would have been possibly the more successful of these two dismal ventures, although the plot is unabashedly sentimental with lingering romantic strains in the scaffolding. No dynamic qualities and no rising interest detract from the few qualifying features of this novel, and the costumbrista accretions recall earlier usages by Pereda. More than a retreat, therefore, *Summer Clouds* and *On the First Flight* offer a sad regression and decline after *Sotileza*, and even more immediate predecessors such as *La Montálvez* and *The Stew*, defective as these works are. *Peñas arriba*, however, still lies ahead, following the artistically dark night of 1891, the worst time of the Peredian production. No critic, seemingly, has defended *Summer Clouds* or *On The First Flight*, either then or later.[9]

IV   Pachín González

Pachín González has been regrettably neglected as the last serious writing of Pereda for several reasons: the book was published in 1896 and was thus overshadowed by the brilliant sunset of *Peñas arriba*, which appeared in the previous year; this final book is difficult to classify as a short novel, a long short story, or an exercise in reporting due to the historical basis of the incident; and the most interesting fact that this contribution is so different, positively, from any other effort of the author.

The basis for *Pachín González* was the explosion in the harbor of Santander on November 3, 1893, of a ship loaded with dynamite and the resultant destruction in the city, resulting in the deaths of 600 people. Pereda's interest in this material can be explained most immediately, of course, by the love for his native area and the sympathy for those neighbors, known and unknown, who died or lost possessions in the catastrophe; but the attempt to relate this accidental disaster with the divine will, a tenet of Pereda's Catholic beliefs and a motive for his conservative acceptance of destiny in other stories, is also due to the brooding preoccupation about his son's suicide during the writing of *Peñas arriba*. The plot in *Pachín González* concerns a son's search for his mother in Santander following the naval misfortune; and the solution, whether the boy's parent is alive, dead, or mutilated by a cruel fate, is held in credible abeyance until the novelette's end. Any of the three possible decisions would have been logically acceptable, and the reader is led subtly to prefer death rather than mutilation for the mother because of the photographic descriptions of Pereda of scenes on the streets and in the temporary hospitals or shelters. Consequently, Pachín's discovery of his mother, safe and without injuries from the destruction, comes as a pleasant surprise after the overwhelming mood and details of the terrifying situation.

The Gothic and naturalistic devices to mount an effect convey all the feelings and reactions connected with the tragic events of this marine disaster; and the past realism and costumbrismo appear in the Peredian formula, or common lesson, to mother and child to remain in the *Montaña,* rejoicing in the providence of God and with a steadfast religious devotion. Pachín's purpose in coming to Santander was to embark for the New World to make his fortune, returning in the indefinite future as an indiano (one final use of the repeated character and problem in the author's writings). This didactic element is never so heavy-handed as to detract from the literary advantages of *Pachín González* so that the conservative, traditionalist viewpoint can be justified and accepted as a natural consequence of the traumatic reaction to the terrible destruction. Although no new qualities mark this final book, unless one insists on the brilliant evocation in stunning, minute details of the setting and the bleak atmosphere logically associated with this tragedy, the fusion of these traits and the compelling story result in a first-rate similarity with some of the permanently valuable sketches and stories of Pereda's first book, *Escenas montañesas.*[10]

CHAPTER 7

Pereda's Place in the Twentieth Century

PEREDA'S chronological development as a writer is marked by an erratic forward and backward movement, with no predictable and consistent pattern emerging as a guide from letters, prologues, or the works themselves. His two masterpieces arrived late in life, with almost a decade intervening between the very different novels, *Sotileza* and *Peñas arriba*. Debate exists, limited as is all the criticism about Pereda because of his declining reputation after his death, as to the superiority of *Sotileza* against *Peñas arriba* or the advantages of the latter novel over the former book; but the mild arguments are no more than academic exercises, often revolving around the questions of form and style. As a novel, *Sotileza* emerges as a better choice for the Peredian peak because of the compelling, dynamic plot and subplots, the variety of characterizations, the panoramic view of a passing society, and the vivid, sympathetic understanding of the sea as the center of the existences and livelihoods of all these Santander people. Pereda has successfully and artistically fused realism, costumbrismo, and regionalism, very late in the nineteenth century, and with the moot basis for some naturalism as a trait (despite his announced antipathy toward naturalistic ideas); and the axis in *Sotileza* for these several movements or tendencies is language or, more broadly, style. The stylistic or linguistic features that are difficult to grasp and to translate are primarily nautical expressions and manners, and secondarily the regional variations of speech with the precise reproduction of the dialect of the *Montaña*, maintaining the logical distinctions among the social classes and individuals throughout the novel.

This theoretical quarrel or discussion about the exact Peredian peak can be more readily and properly extended into that nebulous and perilous dimension of the "relevant" or simply contemporary applications with *Peñas arriba* because Pereda most effectively clarifies and summarizes his philosophy, ideology, hopes, and fears in this work. Although Pereda can stake no claim to being a complex, evolving, or very profound thinker (a statement he would have welcomed as a surety of his successful communication of his fearless, unyielding, and sound beliefs), an outlook and attitude appear in *Peñas arriba* that, for the first time, proceed beyond a negative glance at the past and an unhappy reaction to the present. *Sotileza* is a prose epic of the sea and of a vanishing Santander with no betterment, only decline, to replace the noble traditions and stalwart race; *Peñas arriba* is an idyll of the mountains, of a province where the old is yielding to the new with an uncertain direction yet with the hope, possibility, and plan not only to maintain good ways from the past but to improve life for the challenges of the twentieth century, civilization, industrialization, and political outcries. The latter work becomes an idyllic vision of human existence with spiritual revelations and lyrical paeans of nature. *Peñas arriba* offers a more poetical style with a richer, more cultured language and vocabulary, less employment of regional expressions and speech patterns, and many very long passages of geographical description, especially. Again, this later novel shows taut construction and rigid outlines; but the dynamic component, reader interest, and a paced plot (as a minimum requirement for such a lengthy, descriptive novel) fail to win today, as earlier in the twentieth century, audiences ready to devote themselves to an appreciation of Pereda's artistry. *Sotileza*, for present readers, retains a more convenient attraction and ease of endeavor; *Peñas arriba* can be a surprisingly rewarding venture in ideas popular at this moment, but the interest in this novel has demonstrated no increase in recent times. Both novels win first-rate attention on aesthetic bases, as works of notable merit by themselves and within the framework of the European novelistic productions of this century; and the two books gained for Pereda his lasting place in literary history.

Pereda's novels before *Sotileza,* in addition to some of the stories and sketches of *Escenas montañesas*, require extensive consideration as the key to the writer's thought and techniques in his masterpieces. For better or for worse, the prejudices, religious and social, dogmatism, and the political mythology emerge forcefully and repeatedly in novels, such as *Don Gonzalo, A Chip off the Old Block*, and *Redolent of the Soil. A Chip off the Old Block,* perhaps the Peredian novel of most unbending and, essentially, most unchristian orientation and conclusion, provides an important source for many of Pereda's other, often admittedly weak, writings. *Don Gonzalo* is a seminal novel for the Peredian political credo, found in more successful books such as *Redolent of the Soil* and *Pedro Sánchez;* and the literary characteristics of the mature Pereda are perceptible in his initial novels.

Of course, the imitative romantic procedures and creaky structures of the plots and characters cannot be ignored in the first publications by Pereda as a novelist. *Pedro Sánchez,* a unique enterprise by Pereda, has been recognized consistently as a fortunate contribution to the rich picaresque inheritance from Spain, one of the author's most significant, revealing stories. These first novels, the initial phase of Pereda's devotion to this genre, are nonetheless limited in importance, historically rather than aesthetically, within the trajectory of nineteenth-century Spanish literature and their creator's own development.

Too much emphasis has been dedicated at times to Pereda's contributions between *Sotileza* and *Peñas arriba* in the hope of encountering traces of naturalism, then in vogue, and of literary mastery of other nascent themes and ideas at the end of the century. No originality and no outstanding performance characterize the Peredian writings outside the two durable novels after 1885, with a possible exception of the interesting *Pachín González.* Pereda, after *Sotileza,* was an anachronistic (and antagonistic) figure for the defenders of naturalism and the young men soon to emerge more fully as the Generation of 1898; and the acceptance of his masterpiece, in some small part, was due to the mutual affinities between several naturalists and this novel. *Peñas arriba,* of course, supplied in 1895 a rallying call for the declining values of the nineteenth century, under sharper attack; and the book marked an apogee of the century's movements in literature and thought as well as a model of polished, poetical Castilian style.

However, Pereda's conservatism and traditionalism, without the merits and support of intrinsically superior publications, opened the floodgates to the rising tide of opposition, protest, and disillusionment with the concepts of his age and his generation. Before his death in 1906, and almost immediately afterward, Pereda's name and fame were anathema to the Generation of 1898, to the new styles around the period of the First World War, and to the groups in the 1920s, so that criticism is slight in terms of quantity and consistently adverse, except for the few enthusiasts of "el ingenioso hidalgo montañés" ("the ingenious Highland hidalgo") — a typical exuberance

by his biographer, José Montero. Little impartial material, consequently, exists for students of Pereda during this stage, 1906 - 1933,
although valuable biographical and analytical items provide a firm
ground for investigators. The chasm widened during those years
between the archaic ideas and outmoded techniques of Pereda and
the new interests of writers and critics; neglect rather than disagreement and disparagement seemed to be this writer's fate.

In 1933, however, during the centenary celebrations of Pereda's
birth, an unexpected reaction, though hardly overwhelming, came
with the praise of Azorín for the novelist of the *Montaña* as one of
the most powerful contributors to the European nineteenth-century
novel. Since then, there have been more solid critical articles and
studies on Pereda, still not laudatory on many occasions, but with
attention granted his role in the national literature of the preceding
century. Cossío, Eoff, and Montesinos, among other notable
scholars, have published their conclusions about the significance of
the Peredian opus. Pereda has also found favor officially in Spain
after the Civil War because of a supposedly ideological and political
resemblance between his philosophy and that of the present regime;
in many instances, Pereda is closely associated with another favorite
figure for the Spanish establishment, Menéndez Pelayo, as representatives of authentic *españolismo*, "Spanishness."

Attention, then, in the domain of criticism has increased slowly
but qualitatively, not always favorably, and with a keener eye to
Pereda's strong point and durable value, style, in order to determine
a more appreciative reaction to this author's best writings. Likewise,
the place of this novelist in the twentieth century, historically and
aesthetically, and his more equitable stature within his own times
have been the concerns and questions of critics since 1945. Some interest, but no great enthusiasm and certainly no reversal in
noticeable or striking measure of Pereda's role and importance, seem
to be the verdicts of these contemporary judges. Nor has Pereda
fared any better with popular audiences, the readers whom he
wanted to interest and whose decisions affected him always, causing
changes (good and bad) in his plans for the next book. Nevertheless,
the novelist of the *Montaña* has evoked a sincere love of the land, a
sympathy for the poor toilers of his native province, and a rejection
of the excesses of twentieth-century progress, materialism, and
change. Pereda is urging the defense and maintenance of a simple
life, of the beauties of nature, of an unwritten moral code inherent in
mutual respect and charity, and of a strong religious faith — a uni-

versal program illustrated in the little world of the *Montaña* and expressed unfailingly and as an absolute requisite in exemplary, impec-
cable form and style.

Notes And References

Chapter One

1. The biographical data about Pereda's life follow the same patterns in all the principal sources with each critic adding some new details but without startling revelations or major discoveries. The most authoritative references for these standard facts are: Enrique Menéndez Pelayo, "Biografía de Pereda," in *Obras completas* (Madrid, 1922), vol. XVII, originally published in *Diario Montañés* of Santander, May 1, 1906; José Montero, *Pereda* (Madrid, 1919); Jean Camp, *José María de Pereda* (Paris, 1937); and Ricardo Gullón, *Vida de Pereda* (Madrid, 1944).

2. No biographer delves into these formative years for Pereda, that is, the years before the age of twenty, inquiring about his readings and the influences of friends and background; and Gullón, for example, is rather inventive about Pereda's boyhood and adolescent activities, which were probably similar to those of any young man at this time and place.

3. The disappearance of this writing exercise, perhaps deliberately destroyed by Pereda because of its probable banality, has also given rise to the guess that the work may be a short play (some doubt also exists about the precise title); commentators give no more than a slight mention to this first enterprise.

4. José María de Cossío, *La obra literaria de Pereda* (Santander: Sociedad de Menéndez Pelayo, 1934), p. 62.

5. Gullón seems to be the most sensitive and cognizant about this relationship and vital support, referring often to the older brother's interventions and speculating about the impact of Juan Agapito's death on José María.

6. This short but admittedly significant visit by Pereda to France has never been adequately investigated by biographers and critics; the question remains about the exact influence of this sojourn on the writer's ideas and his general attitude toward new literary modes.

7. Salvador de Madariaga, *Spain: A Modern History* (New York: Frederick A. Praeger, 1958), p. 68.

8. This enduring friendship between the directly opposed novelists is surely one of the most fascinating and revealing literary acquaintances of

nineteenth-century Spanish culture; the correspondence from Pereda to Galdós has been reproduced in Soledad Ortega, *Cartas a Galdós* (Madrid: Revista de Occidente, 1964); their respective speeches of acceptance to the Royal Spanish Academy were published in *Discursos de Menéndez Pelayo, Pereda y Galdós* (Madrid: Viuda e hijos de Tello, 1897).

9. The principal source for the correspondence is María Fernanda de Pereda y Torres Quevedo y Enrique Sánchez Reyes, *Epistolario de Pereda y Menéndez Pelayo* (Santander: Consejo Superior de Investigaciones Científicas, 1953); the studies by Miguel Artigas, "De la correspondencia entre Pereda y Menéndez Pelayo," *Boletín de la Biblioteca Menéndez Pelayo* XV (1933), 83 - 107, and "Pereda y Menéndez Pelayo" in the same volume of the *BBMP*, 318 - 36; and Pablo Beltrán de Heredia, "Algunos documentos inéditos de la amistad íntima entre Pereda y Menéndez Pelayo," *BBMP* XV (1933), 405 - 18.

10. There are practically no details about Pereda's courtship and marriage in any of the biographical references, although Gullón in his *Vida de Pereda* hints that the union was "no romantic and wild passion" and that the role of the writer's wife was very limited within the household, the primary consideration being that of assuring the time and tranquility required by her spouse, (p. 83,) a close reflection of the Peredian ideal in many writings, often rendered via a female character's deviation from this placid role.

11. The reactions of these friends, as well as Pereda's constant need for encouragement (and favorable criticism and some flattery) can be noted in correspondence other than the invaluable Menéndez Pelayo and Pérez Galdós sources, such as the exchanges with Ramón de Mesonero Romanos, Armando Palacio Valdés, Salvador Rueda, and José María y Sinforoso Quintanilla, as they have continued to appear in the *Boletín de la Biblioteca Menéndez Pelayo;* and the many letters in Narcìs Oller, *Memòries literàries* (Barcelona: Aedos, 1962) supplement very significantly the epistolary segments of Cossío's earlier volume, *La obra literaria de Pereda.*

12. José F. Montesinos, *Pereda o la novela idilio* (Madrid: Editorial Castalia, 1969) has been insistent on this influence of Fernán Caballero, attributing Pereda's failures to Cecilia Böhl de Faber's impact; but the acknowledged indebtedness of Pereda has not resulted in agreement among the commentators (Menéndez Pelayo, Pardo Bazán, and the later critics, including Montesinos) as to the extent of the similarities, providing an opportunity to compare and to contrast again the Pereda-Fernán Caballero problem, and the critical theories on the extent and depth of this literary relationship.

13. This novel undoubtedly serves as an axis around which Pereda's critical and popular fame emerged favorably as well as unfavorably, and Montesinos insists upon the formula of this book as the yardstick for the Peredian successes and failures after 1879, the beginning of the *novela idilio,* "the novel as an idyll" (*Pereda*, p. 70).

14. It would be unfair and inconclusive to analyze the respective speeches

of the two old friends outside the full context of the "discourses," albeit in order to separate the necessarily courteous and flattering references from the major summations of their ideas and theses; and the provocative question can be a report on the contrast and the comparison between the prior practice by both writers and their theory about the nineteenth-century Spanish novel, with the additional trajectory of the literary history of novelistic development by Menéndez Pelayo *(Discursos de Menéndez Pelayo, Pereda y Galdós).*

15. *Obras completas de D. José María de Pereda* (Madrid: Victoriano Suárez, 1921), vol. I, prologue, p. lxiii. The dates for the seventeen volumes of this edition vary widely at times, depending upon the particular issue of this authoritative text; and the year of publication should more accurately reflect the actual copy used as a source.

16. Menéndez Pelayo, Camp, and Montesinos have quickly sensed this successful exploitation and development, thereby advancing the progress of the novel beyond Fernán Caballero's episodic effect; and all critics have remarked the failure or fidelity, respectively regarding *Escenas montañesas.* Only lately, thanks to Eoff, Clarke, and the accumulating items of the *Boletín de la Biblioteca Menéndez Pelayo,* has there been an endeavor to indicate and to provide other facets of Pereda's achievements.

17. Montero provides some intimations, more perhaps than the other established sources on Pereda's life, as to the value of any letters during this period, although Camp also explores, from the literary and aesthetic viewpoints, the Peredian turns of these years. The later publications of the correspondence still do not supply sure conclusions about this post-*Sotileza* alteration before *Peñas arriba.*

18. This stoicism can be traced to the very early and adamant ideas of Pereda's background, youth, training and literary orientation, comprehended accurately and broadly by John Van Horne, "The Influence of Conservatism on the Art of Pereda," *Publications of the Modern Language Association* XXXIV (1919), 70 - 88.

19. The episode has been generally regarded by the biographers as a romantic, charming event in Pereda's life without any especial importance because of the author's final years; and more attention has been devoted to the delays, procrastinations, and opposition before the actual nomination. Montesinos gives little space to the artistic summations in 1897, although he grasps the influence of the Galdós-Pereda correspondence; and the more recent study by Anthony H. Clarke, *Pereda, paisajista* (Santander: Institución Cultural de Cantabria, 1969) relies slightly on these respective expressions of the regional, realistic theses.

Chapter Two

1. José María de Pereda, *Obras completas* (Madrid: Aguilar, 1948, 1959), 2 vols., with an "estudio preliminar" by José María de Cossío, will be the edition indicated in this book unless reference is made to another edition. All

quotations and references to the Aguilar edition are placed in parentheses by the volume and page numbers within the text.

2. These *Escritos de juventud* are arranged chronologically in the first volume of the Aguilar edition, pp. 51 - 208; and they should be correlated with their dates, 1858 - 1879, following the publications of the longer works after 1864.

3. Montesinos, *Pereda*, pp. 10 - 11.

4. *Escenas montañesas. Colección de bosquejos de costumbres tomados del natural. Prólogo de Antonio de Trueba* (Madrid, 1864), p. xvii, although the entire brief statement should be read for the possible effect on Pereda as Montesinos is ambivalent about the impact on the budding author also (*Pereda*, pp. 9 - 10).

5. Both Menéndez Pelayo and Montesinos, the earliest and the latest most influential critics, coincide in their attitudes about the role of *Escenas montañesas*, the former noting the high art of these sketches as a continuing model and the latter criticizing the failure of Pereda to pursue these promising vignettes in his novels. Cossío and Camp are basically too laudatory about the quality of all the selections.

6. Menéndez Pelayo in his prologue to Pereda's complete works oscillates between "realism" and "naturalism" in his significant classification, and this term is also indicated by Montesinos as a running comment on the Peredian philosophy at this time.

7. Pereda later inserts his frank opinions in prologues to the novels, avoiding the charge of some intrusive interruptions, although he was never fully able to refrain from interrupting the narrative flow for the sake of his ideas; these are two quotations near the end of "La leva," in separate places (I, 264, 266).

8. The coincidence of this title with Cooper's *The Last of the Mohicans* serves as an interesting point of departure for a comparison between the thematic structure of these two short stories by Pereda and the American novel; and later Pereda's major contribution to sea fiction, *Sotileza*, bears some other curious resemblances to *The Pilot*, especially in the storm as a climactic moment, physically and psychologically, for the characters. Menéndez Pelayo in his prologue to the complete works refers to the Peredian characters in *Sotileza* as worthy companions to the heroes of Cooper's novels, p. xliii - xliv.

9. This recurring concept in the Peredian outlook is sharply detailed in the sequel to the "La leva," with a nostalgic mixture of romanticism and realism by this date, cf. Sherman Eoff, "Pereda's Conception of Realism as Related to His Epoch," *Hispanic Review* XIV (1946), 281 - 303.

10. Montesinos on several occasions in *Pereda* refers to the unfortunate influence of this short story upon the novelist's polemical thrusts in future books, although the critic also realizes that, contrariwise, Pereda would not have written his important work, *Peñas arriba*, (pp. 14, 41 - 43, 248).

11. Menéndez Pelayo, Montesinos, and Clarke feel for different reasons

that "Suum cuique" offers a key to Pereda's strong views, politically and ideologically, without any sure direction aesthetically. Their versions of the weight deserved by this short story occur at different places in the studies on Pereda.

12. Montesinos, p. 18. This background has been further explored by him in: *Costumbrismo y novela. Ensayo sobre el redescubrimiento de la realidad española* (Madrid: Castalia, 1965); and *Introducción a una historia de la novela en España* (Madrid: Castalia, 1966).

13. The pleading tone of Pereda's words in his humorously intended title appeals to the sympathy of his readers for his serious defense of his motives; but the variety of his contributions in the two books should be analyzed chronologically, at least in the order of publication (not always indicated clearly), with a still undetermined date of composition at times as another barrier. No edition of the works of Pereda provides this vital chronology of composition and publication, so that the order of appearance of these writings in book form must be accepted until a surer progress of Pereda's development is investigated.

14. Prologue to the *Obras completas*, p. xxv.

15. Menéndez Pelayo's incisive recognition of Fernán Caballero for "the supreme merit of having created the modern novel of Spanish customs, the novel of local flavor" is connected immediately with Pereda's adherence to her ideals, demonstrated in 1864, with the impression that this Pereda-Fernán Caballero parallelism, now but not always later, followed Don Marcelino's philosophy (prologue, pp. xxxv - xxxvii).

16. The conclusion of Walter T. Pattison in *El naturalismo español. Historia externa de un movimiento literario* (Madrid: Gredos, 1969) analyzes succinctly the problem of Pereda's naturalism as homegrown and un-intended, ideologically, cf. pp. 63 - 83.

17. This debate for Pereda, resulting in his complete turn to the right, seems particularly to irk Montesinos throughout his *Pereda*, with supposedly moral arguments being based on personal anxieties and fuzzy logic.

18. Menéndez Pelayo in the prologue first pointed the way to this foreshadowing of his compatriot's novel as a promise of success (pp. xliv - xlv); but Montesinos sees a confirmation in *Pereda* of an early, swift rigidity toward "the realistic eclogue," pp. 67 - 82.

19. Friendly critics see either a temporary lapse or glide over these failures of Pereda (Menéndez Pelayo and Camp, for example); other commentators find confirmation in the weak texts of Pereda's limitations (Montesinos, Van Horne, and the author's emerging opposition at that period).

Chapter Three

1. At this time, the comparative opinions of Menéndez Pelayo in the prologue and in the correspondence can be studied to observe how they parallel on the surface but reveal a disquieted mood of the critic on the personal level.

2. The volumes of the *Obras completas* by Victoriano Suárez must be consulted for the prologues by Pereda; Cossío in the Aguilar edition unhappily omits these significant few pages before each Peredian work; cf. therefore vol. II of the earlier collection.

3. Prologue to the *Obras completas*, pp. xlvii - 1, with a good balance and a stronger attack provided by Clarín: Leopoldo Alas (Clarín), *Solos de Clarín* (Madrid: Fe, 1891), pp. 245 - 51.

4. *Pereda*, p. 59. The question of Balzacian influence on Pereda is studied briefly in Sherman Eoff, "A Phase of Pereda's Writings in Imitation of Balzac," *Modern Language Notes* LIX (1944), 460 - 66, the conclusions of which are opposed by Montesinos, p. 57; the latter in his analysis of *El buey suelto* considers that Pereda and Menéndez Pelayo really advocated a broad satire against modern marital laxity without benefit of Balzac, pp. 55 - 65.

5. *Pereda*, p. 63. A good classroom edition of this novel is: Edwin B. Place, ed., *Don Gonzalo González de la Gonzalera* (Chicago: Sanborn and Co., 1932), with introduction, notes, and vocabulary; an interesting merit resides in the editor's fairness about Pereda's probing inquiries into the problems of democracy and republicanism.

6. The correspondence of Pereda with Menéndez Pelayo and Galdós, especially, but now with other correspondents also, should be followed chronologically during the period of gestation, completion, and reaction for this novel. Montesinos comprehends the need for revision of some arguments about Pereda as new letters appear.

7. L. de Escalante, "El manifiesto electoral de Patricio Rigüelta," *BBMP* XXVIII (1952), 99 - 105; M. C. Fernández-Cordero y Azorín, "El primer centenario de 'La Gloriosa': La Revolución de septiembre de 1868 vista por Pereda," *BBMP* XLIV (1968), 355 - 414.

8. Pereda has consistently enjoyed, along with his compatriot Menéndez Pelayo, a favorable audience in official Spanish circles after the Civil War, although *Don Gonzalo* has not been selected particularly for any undue attention. The descriptions of the breakdown of society with the tendency to violence and chaos in the Gerona of Gironella after the second half of his long novel and the Peredian analysis of the demagoguery in Coteruco can be profitably analyzed with a possible inspiration for the latter in *Don Gonzalo*.

9. *Pereda*, p. 89. This novel is a key for Montesinos to the "moral" rather than "aesthetic" basis for the Peredian devotion to the novel as an idyll; and the critic seems personally harsh toward the political, ideological traditionalism of the novelist in this "mature" (a Montesinos euphemism for Pereda's conservatism, as Van Horne defines the latter's philosophy at this date) novel, pp. 72 - 90.

10. The changing papal tides, in 1846 and in 1878, with the accessions of Pius IX and Leo XIII, respectively, (both beginning their reigns as more liberal pontiffs than their immediate predecessors) must have disturbed very conservative Catholic circles at that particular moment; Fernán Caballero in the last chapter of *La Gaviota* decries in the character of Mystical Rose, a

"type" or "physiology" of the devout churchgoer, the distressing reforms of the new pope in the middle of the nineteenth century. The interesting problem is the effect that these currents in Rome may have exercised on traditionalist writers, including Pereda.

11. Montesinos indicates the pitfall of the Cossío inclusion of fragments and first drafts of Pereda's letters in *La obra literaria de Pereda*, amplified by Cossío in *José María de Pereda. Selección y estudio* from the *Antología de Escritores y Artistas Montañeses*, vol. XLVIII (1957).

12. Menéndez Pelayo is very firm in his opposition to Pereda's novel — as a novel — in the prologue (pp. lv and lx), as "the least realistic" and skirting a decision on this effort "in the field of the dogmatic novel." The correspondence of this period between Pereda, Menéndez Pelayo, and Galdós (separately but with references to the participants) is a revealing confrontation of the several religious interpretations confronting the Spanish intellectuals: Pereda is extremely harsh in his defenses; Menéndez Pelayo supports his friend but disagrees on some points against an impartial critical sense; and Galdós comes off best for his reliance on tolerance, cool judgment, and warmth of spirit toward literary friends. From these exchanges, the "battle" of *Gloria* appears to have been built up as a polemic by critics and historians, disappearing from view rather quickly in the following decade.

13. *Obras completas* by Victoriano Suárez, prologue by Pereda, vol. IV, pp. iv - v.

14. *Pereda*, p. 112.

15. *Ibid.*, pp. 91 - 114. The gist of Montesinos's long survey of this novel is an agreement with Menéndez Pelayo that Pereda failed at the time with this book. The failure is more evident now, and the attack is made on Pereda for his artistic weakness, although Montesinos hints at his disagreement with the novelist's purposes also.

16. Montesinos, in *Pereda* during the chapter on *Peñas arriba*, inserts his literary quarrel with the novelist concerning *De tal palo*, by stating that the latter "had made the young Peñarrubia die," (p. 242).

17. The prologue by Galdós and the comments in the prologue to the complete works of Pereda by Menéndez Pelayo should be read as a unit to see how they coincide in appreciation of the novel's realism and how they differ subtly about the idealization of rural life in *El sabor de la tierruca*.

18. *Epistolario de Pereda y Menéndez Pelayo*, April 7, 1881, p. 72; *Ibid.*, June 13, 1881, p. 72.

19. A letter to Gumersindo Laverde, October 30, 1881, reproduced in Montesinos, *Pereda*, p. 116, from a photocopy supplied to him by Ignacio Aguilera, director of the "Biblioteca de Menéndez Pelayo" in Santander from the extensive correspondence of Pereda and Laverde in their collections, still unpublished, and a new evidence for Montesinos of the Pereda lacunae in terms of the letters.

20. Montesinos is convinced that the novel and the idyll cannot be harmonized and that *El sabor de la tierruca* leans more toward the idyllic — the

cause for joy by Menéndez Pelayo — with the omission, at least, by Pereda of any thesis (*Pereda*, p. 127). The background for these arguments can be analyzed in: Sherman Eoff, "The Spanish Novel of 'Ideas': Critical Opinion (1836 - 1886)," *PMLA* LV (1940), 531 - 58; Gifford Davis, "The Spanish Debate over Idealism and Realism before the Impact of Zola's Naturalism," *PMLA* LXXXIV (1969), 1649 - 55; and Sherman Eoff, "Pereda's Realism: His Style," *Washington University Studies — New Series Language and Literature* XIV (1942), 131 - 57.

21. Clarke in *Pereda, paisajista* associates *El sabor de la tierruca* and *Peñas arriba* on the same vertical line *(passim)*; and Gerda Outzen, *El dinamismo en la obra de Pereda* (Santander: Sociedad de Menéndez Pelayo, 1935) begins to provide many examples of her thesis about the "dynamic" qualities of the Peredian style with this particular novel as an important model.

22. *La cuestión palpitante*, 4th ed. (Madrid, 1891), chapter XIX, pp. 268 - 69.

23. José Balseiro, "José María de Pereda," *Novelistas españoles modernos* (New York: Macmillan, 1946), pp. 79 - 81, finds an answer in the costumbrista background throughout the novel; Montesinos (*Pereda*, pp. 121 - 22) believes that Pereda deliberately composed the book as a novel of customs without any unity; and Clarke in *Pereda, paisajista* neglects the plot and characterization to bring into focus the author's devotion to description and style (cf. especially the three chapters on nature as landscape, protagonist, and image, pp. 133 - 96).

24. These intrusions mar the complicated plots and slow down to a greater extent the *tempo lento* movement of the novel, and Outzen's thesis about Pereda's dynamism does not always reflect the true picture, leaving aside as she does the whole for the sake of the parts (i.e., words, phrases, and sentences), *El dinamismo, passim*. Nevertheless, the effort to extract these disparate ideas from the many places in the text contributes some suggestions about Pereda's uncertainties, personally, artistically, and as a theoretician of the novel during the nineteenth century.

25. Azorín had varying impressions about Pereda's success in *El sabor de la tierruca*, praising the "large descriptive pictures," "a vast rustic panorama," and an "admirable description" with the reservations expressed about the author's omission of colors for these scenes (*Andando y pensando* [Madrid, 1929], "Pereda," pp. 206 - 07); but Clarke *(Pereda, paisajista)* and Outzen *(El dinamismo)* supply examples of colors within the Peredian complete works. Cf. also: Gifford Davis, "The Critical Reception of Naturalism in Spain before 'La Cuestión Palpitante,'" *Hispanic Review* XXIII (1954), 97 - 108.

26. A survey of this nineteenth-century problem with discussion of Pereda's place is: Iris M. Zavala, *Ideología y política en la novela española del siglo XIX* (Madrid: Anaya, 1971); and the study by F. de Cossío, "Universalidad y regionalismo en la obra de Pereda," *BBMP* XV (1933),

391 - 404, is useful for a broader interpretation of the novelist's aims, perhaps somewhat too favorably inclined to Pereda.

27. Montesinos is unimpressed with *El sabor de la tierruca*, basically granting the novel a historical importance as "the culmination of the first manner of Pereda," *(Pereda,* p. 116); he dismisses this book, unapprovingly and quickly, in a few pages (115 - 27).

28. *Sermón perdido,* p. 77.

29. *Polémicas y estudios literarios,* p. 84.

30. Prologue to the *Obras completas,* pp. lxv - lxvi.

31. *Cartas a Galdós,* February 23, 1883, p. 90; *Epistolario de Pereda y Menéndez Pelayo,* October 13, 1883, pp. 77 - 78, and December 8, 1883, p. 78.

32. José María de Cossío, prólogo y notas, *Pedro Sánchez* (Madrid: Espasa-Calpe, 1958), "Clásicos Castellanos," vols. 144, 145. This reference is found in vol. 144, p. xxxviii.

33. Clarke *(Pereda, paisajista)* explores too briefly at the conclusion the reactions of some members of the Generation of 1898 to Pereda's use of nature (pp. 229 - 33), although the same critic makes prior remarks about Azorín's ideas, especially, regarding Pereda *(passim).* Cf. also: Kurt Siebert, *Die Naturschilderungen in Peredas Romanen* (Hamburg: Hamburger Studien zu Volkstum und Kultur der Romanen, 1932), and R. Seeleman, "The Treatment of Landscape in the Novelists of the Generation of '98," *Hispanic Review* IV (1936), 226 - 38. Jean Camp in his classification of "Le sentiment de la Nature chez Pereda" in *José María de Pereda* traces a loving pattern of natural descriptions by the novelist, *passim.*

34. Montesinos argues this point against Pereda in his analyses of any feminine characters in the novels, and Menéndez Pelayo avoids generally the problem, centering his attention upon the brilliant portrait of the heroine in *Sotileza* (although the critic obviously favors the docile pictures of females depicted by the author as exemplary of the Spanish woman).

35. Ralph Emerson Bassett, *Pedro Sánchez* by D. José M. de Pereda (Boston: Ginn and Co., 1916), with introduction, notes, and vocabulary gives an excellent historical sketch (pp. lxxii - lxxxix), and a wealth of details about this period in the notes (pp. 187 - 236). Cossío, in his less detailed but valuable supplementary explanations at the bottom of pages in his text, complements ably the earlier Bassett edition; and the former critic also contributes a stimulating prologue, mentioning for example the possible Peredian connection with the picaresque genre and a source in the *Gil Blas de Santillana (Pedro Sánchez,* I, pp. xxvii - xxix). Camp in his *Pereda* likewise sees an influence, though much more pronounced than the impact noted by Cossío, on Pereda in *Pedro Sánchez* of the *Gil Blas* (Camp, pp. 160 - 67).

36. Pereda's opinions about Fernán Caballero, whether his own at the time of the action of *Pedro Sánchez* or during the composition of the novel have been confirmed by later criticism as her defects, qualities, and characteristics. Pereda's best literary criticism is in this novel, as Montesinos

admits in *Pereda, passim,* a far cry from the opinions in the *Escritos de juventud.*

37. Camp, Cossío in his edition of *Pedro Sánchez,* and Montesinos in *Pereda* call attention to Pereda's contribution to the Spanish historical novel and to the historical series of Galdós, with increasing recognition of this masterly book by Pereda (a challenge because it was so new, different for the writer, according to Montesinos, *Pereda,* pp. 129 - 47).

38. There are frequent references to Cervantes, especially *Don Quixote,* in the writings of Pereda, the correspondence, and the criticism, with a contemporary basis in Boris de Tannenberg, "Ecrivains castillans contemporains: J. M. de Pereda," *Revue Hispanique* V (1898), 330 - 64, and in the biographical portrayal and comparison by Montero in his *Pereda.* Later adverse comments make fun of Pereda's tilting at the windmills of the present, and Clarke *(Pereda, paisajista)* refers briefly to the argument, pp. 15 - 17. The physical resemblance, coincidental or interpreted, seems to have given rise, later in the author's life, to the literary connection and to the idea for an attack on his approaches to modern problems.

Chapter Four

1. *Epistolario de Pereda y Menéndez Pelayo,* December 5, 1884, p. 86, with other letters to his younger countryman revealing progress, fatigue, and satisfaction, pp. 84, 86 - 88; and the same attitude is apparent in the *Cartas a Galdós* of this time, pp. 90, 94, 97. It is interesting that Pereda relied so constantly on his two literary friends during this "peak" of his novelistic career, probably for a combination of factors, self-assurance, encouragement, and pride.

2. Montesinos omits any references to Clarín's praise of *Sotileza* and confirms his generally unimpressive outlook toward the novelist; but Montesinos also overlooks the double-barreled review by Clarín, laudatory for the book and welcoming Pereda into the ranks of the naturalists. The complete review should be analyzed for this astute report on *Sotileza:* Leopoldo Alas (Clarín), " 'Sotileza,' " *Nueva campaña* (1885 - 1886), 1887, pp. 135 - 49.

3. *El naturalismo español,* p. 63; Pattison gives a very capable running account of the pros and cons of the debate after the publication of *Sotileza,* in particular the eclectic defense of Menéndez Pelayo: "In brief: for Don Marcelino his friend is a naturalist but not in the French fashion. He belongs to the moderate Spanish school and he has not been contaminated with the fatal currents across the Pyrenees" (p. 79).

4. A surety of purpose and procedure marks this period of *Pedro Sánchez* and *Sotileza,* the three-year interval unhindered by psychological blocks and erratic artistry; and these years of great expectations are confirmed by all the available correspondence, in addition to the evidence in the exchanges with Menéndez Pelayo and Galdós. This is the apex of the personal and literary trajectory of Pereda, approximately 1882 - 1885, although precise months are impossible to pinpoint for the initial inspirations and sudden decline.

5. The study of Pereda's priests would reveal an idealization of the clergy, of course, in accord with the novelist's firm faith in the Church; but some unexemplary clerics also appear in the Peredian works (e.g., the would-be seminarian in *La puchera,* the pleasant but rather dull priest in *Don Gonzalo,* and the religious hypocrite, a priestly model, at the very least, in *De tal palo,* among other representatives). Balseiro considers Padre Apolinar one of the three best sketches of priests "in a literary sense . . . as characters, not as religious persons" ("Leopoldo Alas ['Clarín']," *Novelistas españoles modernos,* p. 365). Again, the exact relationship, influence, and conscious or unconscious resemblances between the two novelists appear as interesting problems in this characterization of the priest; the correspondence reveals that Pereda was not so clerical, nor Galdós so anticlerical as one might suspect (an idea accepted by Montesinos and proposed gently by Don Benito in his acceptance speech in 1897).

6. Sherman Eoff, "A Fatherly World According to Design," *The Modern Spanish Novel. Comparative Essays Examining the Philosophical Impact of Science on Fiction* (New York: New York University Press, 1961), p. 41.

7. Menéndez Pelayo, Camp, and Cossío clearly support this thesis in their respective attitudes toward Pereda; and early American recognition of Pereda grasped these features of his world: Hannah Lynch, "Pereda, the Spanish Novelist," *The Contemporary Review* LXIX (1896), 218 - 32; Clyde Glascock, "Modern Spanish Novelists. José María de Pereda," *Southwest Review* VIII (1923), 329 - 53; and Maurine Mays, "A Sociological Interpretation of the Works of José María de Pereda," *The Culver-Stockton Quarterly* II (1926), numbers 3 and 4.

8. Balseiro wonders how unique Sotileza is and how representative she is of the girls of Santander and Spain, respectively, at that time *(Novelistas españoles modernos,* pp. 87 - 94).

9. Edition of *Pedro Sánchez,* introduction, p. lvii.

10. "A Fatherly World According to Design," *The Modern Spanish Novel,* p. 48.

11. The thesis of Eoff holds up well, structurally and thematically, but these psychological similarities are tenuously described between the main protagonists of the English novel *(David Copperfield)* and the Spanish counterpart *(Sotileza).* Eoff mentions vaguely the connection between *Pedro Sánchez* and *Guzmán de Alfarache* with an aside to the possible resemblance between the former novel and *David Copperfield.* The question can be raised about Pereda's interest in the picaresque models during the composition of his two novels during this closely timed period of three years, approximately.

12. All the standard biographers (Menéndez Pelayo, Camp, Montero, and Gullón) are undecided on this point: the exact plans and purposes of the novelist in *Sotileza.* Montesinos finds no clues in the published correspondence, but he hints about some indications in letters "it has been possible for me to see" *(Pereda,* p. 150) without supplying this basis in his critique of *Sotileza,* pp. 149 - 77.

13. Eoff relies on the storm at sea as an important similarity between *David Copperfield* and *Sotileza* in "A Fatherly World According to Design," *The Modern Spanish Novel*, pp. 44 - 45. Clarke *(Pereda, paisajista,* chapters VIII, IX, X) compares and contrasts the storm scenes in *El sabor de la tierruca, Sotileza,* and *Peñas arriba,* and then endeavors to link some of the Peredian descriptions with those of Dickens, Hardy, and Turgenev, in chapter 10. A successor to Pereda can be traced at this stage in the novels of Armando Palacio Valdés (who assumed Pereda's place in the Royal Spanish Academy after the latter's death) with an interesting comparison between *Sotileza* and *José,* written by Palacio Valdés in 1885, a popular novel of fishermen from the northern coast of Spain.

14. Montesinos broadened this metaphor from the narrow sights of Pardo Bazán, referring to the early novels of Pereda, in the use of the term, "garden," to that of an "idyll," taking his new definition from Menéndez Pelayo's praise of the idyllic creation of his compatriot. Montesinos and Menéndez Pelayo are surprisingly in agreement on the conflict between the Peredian idyll and the demands of the novel, a meeting of minds that Montesinos accepts happily in order that he can then attack Pereda, repeatedly and unequivocally, on this issue of the novel. These debates around the terms, "garden," "idyll," and "novel," in the respective analyses of Pardo Bazán, Menéndez Pelayo, and Montesinos, can be extended to include the entire nineteenth-century Spanish novel, as Montesinos has endeavored to do in many invaluable studies on this period (cf. María Soledad Carrasco Urgoiti, "La obra de Montesinos en torno a novelistas españoles del siglo XIX," *Revista de Occidente* IX (1965), 253 - 61).

15. The admittedly prejudiced opinions of Menéndez Pelayo in favor of *Sotileza* are nevertheless utilized by him effectively in this explication of the novel; but he tries to embrace too many items within a short discussion, failing to see the forest because of the trees. This review is an excellent starting point for a needed study of the novel; and in addition to the above article, the review of Clarín can be complemented by: J. Fernández Luján, " 'Sotileza' de Pereda," *Pardo Bazán, Valera y Pereda* (Barcelona, 1889), pp. 45 - 64.

16. The thesis of Montesinos in his "Carta-prólogo," p. xi, and in the chapter entitled "Sotileza," pp. 155, 157, stresses that the sole approach to the novel is through its history and that man, not circumstances, is the proper study of the novelist. Juan Valera's opposition to the regional novel — ironic in view of the Andalusian novelist's classification as a regionalist in many respects by literary historians — and even André Gide's idea of the French novel always as the work of moralists are evidenced by Montesinos against *Sotileza,* pp. 161 - 62, 169.

17. Only one complete translation exists in English to the best of my knowledge: *Sotileza;* a novel by José María de Pereda, translated by Glenn Barr (New York: Exposition Press, 1959). The translator provides very good examples of his puzzlements, dilemmas, and resolutions of the many

problems regarding the language of Pereda in the brief introduction, and Professor Barr's renditions of the dialect, terminology, and peculiar expressions of Santander are always interesting and thoughtful — a true labor of love.

18. This vivid commentary by Menéndez Pelayo is a frequently cited passage from the prologue to the *Obras completas*, p. lxxvii, as one of the most incisive and original reactions to Pereda's compelling artistry in *Sotileza;* and the passage is a good starting point for Outzen's myriad examples of linguistic mannerisms in the whole output of Pereda *(El dinamismo)* where, however, she is disappointingly sparse in her references to the richness of *Sotileza.*

Chapter Five

1. José María de Cossío, "La historicidad de 'Peñas arriba,' " *BBMP* XV (1933), 108 - 21; and *Rutas literarias de la Montaña* (Santander, 1960).

2. *Pereda*, pp. 261 - 62; *Epistolario de Pereda y Menéndez Pelayo,* February 12, 1895, pp. 141 - 42.

3. *Epistolario,* November 18, 1892, p. 137; March 20, 1893, p. 139. Pereda's letters to Galdós during this period are very general, though warm as usual, but without any mention of *Peñas arriba (Cartas a Galdós,* pp. 155 - 74).

4. *Pereda*, p. 262.

5. The overly exploited *Gloria - De tal palo* attack and counterattack has still drawn no more than minor forays into the investigative field of the novelistic productions of these two writers.

6. The essays of Cossío in *La obra literaria de Pereda* on "Sotileza" and "Peñas arriba" are strong defenses and praises of the novelist's techniques and descriptions; and Clarke in *Pereda, paisajista* also supports the descriptive qualities, especially in *Peñas arriba.* Montesinos objects to the prolix aspect of these insertions *(Pereda,* "Peñas arriba," pp. 239 - 62).

7. Montesinos is on very safe ground here, it seems from the enthusiastic tone of the Peredian correspondence during this period before the novel's publication about his ideas for *Peñas arriba;* and the critic presses his attack convincingly against consideration of this novel as one of Pereda's masterpieces.

8. Pereda's views at this time of composition might be equated with those of his contemporaries who were more harshly surveying the ruins of the nineteenth century for a comparative study; and the question arises about Pereda's possible baiting of these "angry young men" by his political and social theories in *Peñas arriba* (despite his moderate and indirect intrusions), although his ideas today do not seem so anachronistic and quixotic despite the nineteenth-century flavor to the novel *qua* novel. Pereda, as is evident from the correspondence, always kept abreast of literary currents, in general, within Spain but not outside the borders; and his views do not seem motivated by the previous belligerency.

9. Montesinos is particularly harsh in his offensive against the Peredian defense in *Peñas arriba;* but the critic, granting his effective arguments and logical reactions, has based much of his final objections on his own political, social, and ideological beliefs. The questions of Menéndez Pelayo about the novel itself, the mood of Galdós at this critical moment of his own artistic development (these familiar faces in earlier times), and the responses of Clarín and Pardo Bazán seem to have been muted by the literary debate about the Academy membership.

10. There is still, oddly, no adequate discussion about this obviously sensitive, awkward point of criticism in regard to *Peñas arriba;* but again, at this present time, the need is for a revision of the role of this novel in the Peredian output and in the historical view of the nineteenth-century Spanish novel (a downgrading revision initiated forcefully by Montesinos, though on other grounds mentioned in the above note).

11. The opinions of Menéndez Pelayo about the majority of Pereda's work can be read now as a unit in: Marcelino Menéndez Pelayo, *Estudios y discursos de crítica histórica y literaria* (Madrid: Consejo Superior de Investigaciones Científicas, 1941), vol. VI, pp. 325 - 97. An example of the typical Peredian justification about this novel is: J. M. Martínez y Ramón, *Análisis de "Peñas arriba"* (Torrelavega, 1908).

12. Outzen and Clarke are hard put in their studies to justify the standing of *Peñas arriba* in literary histories; and they rely almost solely on the details of style (Outzen) and on the use of nature (Clarke) with the latter's attempt to bring Pereda into the orbit of the European novel *(passim)*.

13. Clarke *(Pereda, paisajista)*, *passim*, ranges through the whole nineteenth-century novel, including the ideal of nature in Wordsworth; but this critic mentions only briefly some previously investigated and rather evident relationships in Chateaubriand, Scott, Balzac, omitting any mention of Cooper. Clarke's views are nonetheless original on the concept of nature in Pereda, opening the door to needed comparative studies on the theme and this particular author.

Chapter Six

1. Montesinos wryly quotes from several items of the varied correspondence regarding Pereda's erratic thoughts about *La Montálvez* *(Pereda,* "La Montálvez," pp. 179 - 205), perhaps the critic's best employment of epistolary sources in this study to attack Pereda for his weaknesses, artistically and as a satirist, with severe conclusions about the novel as a "novel of analysis."

2. The arguments between Emilia Pardo Bazán and Pereda swirled around this novel, rather clearly, although Menéndez Pelayo opposed his countryman also; but the latter's reasons were based on the qualities lacking in Pereda according to the naturalists: the inclusion of the sordid and distasteful, present for the Santander critic, cf. also: Pattison, *El naturalismo español.* Professor Pattison has sent me the offprint, chapter nine ("Naturalism and the Spanish Novel"), pp. 299 - 317, for a book which, however, I have

not seen as yet. His essay traces the overall picture of naturalism in Spain, Pereda's place at the time of this movement, and the reaction to the Peredian writings during the naturalistic years, clearly and succinctly.

3. *Pereda*, p. 197. Two other prestigious critics, the first a contemporary of Pereda and the second a twentieth-century interpreter of *La Montálvez*, are: Clarín, "La Montálvez," *Mezclilla* (Madrid, 1889), pp. 115 - 43; and Narciso Alonso Cortés, "De 'La Montálvez,' " *BBMP* XV (1933), 51 - 58.

4. Montesinos appears very close to E.M. Forster's ideas about fantasy (the role of this trait or the absence of fantasy elements in the novel) in the English critic's *Aspects of the Novel*, although Montesinos makes no direct reference to Forster throughout the book on *Pereda*.

5. *Pereda*, pp. 207 - 24.

6. *Ibid.*, p. 209. Montesinos admits on the same page that Cossío (*La obra literaria de Pereda*, p. 291) interprets the representation of this character as being based on a real person, from life in Santander. Montesinos also opposes Lincoln's thesis as a matter of coincidence (cf. J. N. Lincoln, "A Note on the Indebtedness of Pereda's 'La puchera' to Bretón's 'La independencia,' " *Hispanic Review* XI [1943], 260 - 63).

7. Menéndez Pelayo objected to the weakness of the plot in this novel, and he even implies that Pereda reverted to a Romantic imitation, specifically from Sir Walter Scott (*Obras completas de D. José M. de Pereda* by Victoriano Suárez, vol. I, pp. lxxxiii - xc, a review originally published in *El Correo*, February 10, 1889).

8. The respective articles can be conveniently read in Pardo Bazán's *Polémicas y estudios literarios*, pp. 25 - 65, fundamentally the core of the critical problem between the two writers and, in part, their allies and defenders.

9. Montesinos (*Pereda*, pp. 224 - 26) considers that *Al primer vuelo* is slightly (very slightly) better than *Nubes de estío;* he is perplexed about the low state of these Peredian productions, with the books' values so mediocre as to merit only a cursory, required glance from the critic.

10. Montesinos gives a final fillip to this "novel-like reporting," but the few observations are very favorable, surprisingly, because of the contemporary readability of the story (*Pereda*, pp. 235 - 37). The Aguilar edition of the *Obras completas* includes in the second volume, pp. 1355 - 1412, the "artículos y escritos diversos"; but these miscellaneous items have primarily a biographical interest (e.g., "De mis recuerdos," pp. 1410 - 12) or provide another glance at the nineteenth-century demagogue, Patricio Rigüelta, the Peredian literary creation ("De Patricio Rigüelta, redivivo," pp. 1356 - 59). The other sketches are local-color vignettes, short stories, and the portrayal of types. The *Ensayos dramáticos* (Santander, 1869), was published in the very limited edition of twenty-five copies, never placed on sale, and could profit by a critical edition, according to the excellent recent guide: Homero Serís, *Guía de nuevos temas de literatura española*, transcribed, edited and collated by D. W. McPheeters (Madrid: Castalia, 1973), p. 294.

Selected Bibliography

The bibliographical materials about Pereda are limited, and this small amount of extensive, pertinent, and original studies and investigations reflects clearly and unfortunately on his declining interest for twentieth-century readers, critics, and scholars. However, the *Boletín de la Biblioteca Menéndez Pelayo* has been publishing articles (especially letters) relevant to Pereda, directly and indirectly, that can provide a solid historical and documental basis to the renewal of inquiry about Pereda's past role in the nineteenth century and his present place in the twentieth century. Señor Ignacio Aguilera, the director of the library of Menéndez Pelayo in Santander, has stimulated this concern, in print and as a librarian, with a devotion to the *Montaña* and, therefore, to Pereda. In a letter of December 5, 1973, Señor Aguilera writes that a *Manual de bibliografía perediana* by Anthony H. Clarke is close to publication; but I have not seen the book as yet, and I have consequently relied upon previous bibliographical sources. I hope that the *Boletín* and the promised *Manual* will both augment and improve upon the items listed in the "Notes and References" and the "Selected Bibliography" of this book.

This selected bibliography is presented only as a starting point and is not intended as a definitive list of references. Items consulted and deemed useful for this study and the sources (whether important or of limited value) listed most often are the criteria for inclusion in the following pages. The correspondence has been listed as a primary source, of course, but the commentaries by the editors are also classified and discussed under the individual publications of letters.

PRIMARY SOURCES

1. Editions

Obras completas de D. José María de Pereda. Madrid: Librería General Victoriano Suárez, 1921 - 1930. 17 volumes, with varying dates for the individual books, depending upon the volume available in this rather uncertain publication schedule; for example, the volume numbers do not correspond to the chronological appearance of Pereda's works. The texts are reliable sources for references, however, and other editorial choices for separate books of Pereda seem to follow this set.

Obras completas de José María de Pereda. Madrid: Aguilar, 1948, 1959. 2
volumes, with no apparent changes in the several reprintings which are
indicated as different editions, e.g., the edition used herein corresponds
to the above dates for the first and second volumes with the notation
that the books belong to the fifth and seventh editions, respectively.
The works are presented in chronological order, the selections
reproduce correctly without any evident omissions the full materials,
and the printing is free of technical errors. A serious omission,
nevertheless, is the exclusion of the generally short prologues written by
Pereda for many individual books, important critical evidence for a
complete analysis, and a fair understanding of the work in question
(these introductions are provided in the Victoriano Suárez *Obras completas*). The Aguilar edition is augmented profitably by the "Escritos de
juventud" in vol. I and by the "Artículos y escritos diversos" in vol. II,
identified as much as possible by their time sequence and place of first
publication.

Both editions have been utilized in this book since the two supply
different items of Pereda's complete writings; but I have referred to the
Aguilar edition for any references and quotations because this set is
more readily available with an appeal to more popular reading of this
author, one of the aims of the Twayne series. The earlier edition should
be consulted for any questions and doubts about the Aguilar texts with
the previously noted indication of the individual prologues by Pereda.

2. Correspondence

Oller, Narcìs. *Memòries literàries*. Barcelona: Aedos, 1962. An important
    presentation of letters by Pereda to his Catalan friend, the writer, Oller,
    on personal and literary problems, especially around the time of the
    suicide of Pereda's son and the composition of *Peñas arriba*.
Ortega, Soledad. *Cartas a Galdós*. Madrid: Revista de Occidente, 1964. A
    very extensive collection from 1872 until 1905 on this significant
    literary friendship between two very different personalities and writers;
    a major conclusion is that neither individual was absolute and rigid in
    ideas and reactions within these private exchanges.
Pereda y Torres Quevedo, María Fernanda de y Enrique Sánchez Reyes.
    Epistolario de Pereda y Menéndez Pelayo. Santander: Consejo Superior
    de Investigaciones Científicas, 1953. A good model of sound critical
    scholarship with 143 letters of the two most famous citizens from the
    Montaña, dating from 1876 until 1905, serving as a valuable comple-
    ment and comparison to the *Cartas a Galdós;* the notes following the
    letters give thorough explanations about references and the background
    of this correspondence.
Other letters are increasingly valuable as the correspondence becomes
    slowly available, and these materials certainly should be utilized in any
    longer study on Pereda, the man and the writer, with these con-

tributions of especial interest: José María de Cossío, "José María de Pereda," *Antología de escritores y artistas montañeses*, XLVIII (1957), Santander; E. Varela Hervías, "Cartas de Pereda a Mesonero Romanos," *Bulletin Hispanique* LX (1958), 375 - 81; María Concepción Fernández-Cordero Azorín, "Cartas de Pereda a José María y Sinforoso Quintanilla," *BBMP* XLIV (1968), 169 - 340; and the excerpts in Cossío *(La obra literaria de Pereda)* and Montesinos *(Pereda)*, *qq.v.*

SECONDARY SOURCES

1. Books

CAMP, JEAN. *José María de Pereda. Sa vie, son oeuvre et son temps (1833 - 1906)*. Paris: Fernand Sorlot, 1937. A panoramic survey connecting closely the events of Pereda's life with his artistic progress at the same time; a chronological approach with sure data and abundant documentation; the overall attitude and conclusion favor greatly Pereda's novels, historically and aesthetically.

CLARKE, ANTHONY H. *Pereda, paisajista*. Santander: Institución Cultural de Cantabria, 1969. The subtitle, *El sentimiento de la naturaleza en la novela española del siglo XIX*, indicates Clarke's thesis generally throughout the book, although he devotes more attention to this idea in the second half of his study; he attempts to relate Pereda with European novelistic trends, particularly British novelists of the nineteenth century; and he agrees with Montesinos on many points, in particular within the later chapters, but with considerable praise for Pereda as a stylist.

COSSÍO, JOSÉ MARÍA DE. *La obra literaria de Pereda, su historia y su crítica*. Santander: Sociedad de Menéndez Pelayo, J. Martínez, 1934. A primary value of this work resides in the use of letters from Pereda and the direct citation of many of the communications; lengthy analyses of individual novels, particularly *Sotileza* and *Peñas arriba*. The tone is laudatory and shows approval for Pereda by a respected critic with notable objectivity regarding the novelist's weaknesses in his art.

FERNÁNDEZ-CORDERO AZORÍN, MARÍA CONCEPCIÓN. *La sociedad española en la obra literaria de don José María de Pereda*. Santander: Resma, 1970. An excellent investigation of the Peredian vision of the Spain of his time, with his interpretations of the classes and types within these social groups, based on a close reading of the texts with many quotations to support the thesis. Maintains that Pereda showed a broader and more profound knowledge of Spanish society than criticism has previously acknowledged.

GULLÓN, RICARDO. *Vida de Pereda*. Madrid: Editora Nacional, 1944. The emphasis is on the biographical elements in this reliable summary of the generally known facts with a few incursions into the interesting psychological and artistic agonies of Pereda. The background of the works explains clearly the various situations, problems, and reactions. There is little discussion and penetration of the books outside the field of literary history and the author's life.

MONTERO, JOSÉ. *Pereda; glosas y comentarios de la vida y de los libros del ingenioso hidalgo montañés.* Madrid: Imp. del Instituto nacional de sordomudos y de ciegos, 1919. One of the useful, accurate guides to the biography of Pereda, but the overall examination is lacking in objectivity because of the predominant defense and admiration for the novelist with no recognition of adverse criticism and the subject's limitations. The analyses of the works lack new insights and recognition of other writers and their contributions within the same framework of Pereda's philosophy and ideology.

MONTESINOS, JOSÉ. F. *Pereda o la novela idilio.* Madrid: Editorial Castalia, 1969. The most important contribution to criticism about Pereda by a masterly authority on the nineteenth-century novel, who reacts against the favorable, at times eulogizing, studies of Menéndez Pelayo, Montero, Camp, Gullón, and Cossío. Downgrades Pereda's artistry as a novelist with the conclusion that he failed to produce works of first-rate category for the most part; the objections have been counterbalanced somewhat by the continuing articles on Pereda in the *Boletín de la Biblioteca Menéndez Pelayo* as well as the additions of Clarke and Fernández-Cordero Azorín.

OUTZEN, GERDA. *El dinamismo en la obra de Pereda.* Santander: Sociedad de Menéndez Pelayo, J. Martínez, 1935. Translated from German by María Fernanda de Pereda y Torres Quevedo. An attempt to demonstrate an exciting quality of Pereda's works by the selection of many examples from the books. The method is the *explicación de texto,* although the definitions of the "dynamic" are nebulous at times and too many categories of this term cloud the central argument. Provides valuable insight into Pereda's role as a stylist, with a completely positive reaction to the novelist's language.

SIEBERT, KURT. *Die Naturschilderungen in Peredas Romanen.* Hamburg: Hamburger Studien zu Volkstum und Kultur der Romanen, 1932. A brief introduction to the use of nature in Pereda's works, limited to the evidence of the texts. Clearly written and well organized. It is augmented and expanded by Clarke's later study of "the sentiment of nature."

2. Articles

BALSEIRO, JOSÉ. "José María de Pereda." In *Novelistas españoles modernos.* New York: Macmillan, 1946, pp. 54 - 116. A critical balance maintained toward Pereda with commentaries ranging usefully beyond the discussion of any particular books by the novelist. Contains a wise selection of notes and bibliography.

BASSETT, RALPH EMERSON. *Pedro Sánchez by D. José M. de Pereda.* Boston: Ginn and Co., 1916. Introduction, notes, and vocabulary. An edition intended for American schools that can be employed advantageously for an understanding of Pereda in general, the period of this novel, and the language of the writer; an example of investigative research and reflective analysis of the literary problems.

Cossío, José María de. "Estudio preliminar." In *Obras completas de José María de Pereda*. 2 volumes. Madrid: Aguilar, 1948, 1959. Vol. I, pp. 7 - 47. A short but fair and authoritative summary of this critic's attitude toward Pereda as expressed in the former's longer articles and books; a good starting point for the comprehension of Cossío's positive, though impartial, stance.

————. "Prólogo." In *Pedro Sánchez*. 2 volumes, 144, 145. Madrid: Espasa-Calpe, 1958. "Clásicos Castellanos." Vol. 144, pp. vii - xxxix. The notes complement ably the text, although the comments are few in number; the general ambiance precedes Cossío's incisive explanation for his belief that *Pedro Sánchez* is, if not the best, certainly close to the most outstanding novel of Pereda.

Eoff, Sherman. "A Fatherly World According to Design." In *The Modern Spanish Novel. Comparative Essays Examining the Philosophical Impact of Science on Fiction*. New York: New York University Press, 1961. Pp. 21 - 50. A speculative but stimulating, original approach to the discussion of an idea in the field of comparative literature; interesting likewise for the interpretation of similar possibilities in the Spanish novel, especially.

————. "Pereda's Conception of Realism as Related to His Epoch." *Hispanic Review* XIV (1946), 281 - 303. The examination of a misinterpreted point about Pereda — the man within the age — and the need for a fair statement about his views at that time. Contains moderate conclusion about Pereda's true, valid place as neither so reactionary nor so anachronistic as critics of the following century have insisted.

————. "Pereda's Realism: His Style." *Washington University Studies - New Series Language and Literature* XIV (1942), 131 - 57. Pereda's stylistic ventures reflect correctly his interpretation of realism, within the generally accepted standards and at the same time with the fusion of the author's individualistic beliefs and some costumbrista traditions; a clear, precise report on the detailed reading of the author's books.

Glascock, Clyde. "Modern Spanish Novelists. José María de Pereda." *Southwest Review* VIII (1923), 329 - 53. Interesting for an American reaction to Pereda and for the implied relation between the Spanish novelist's love of the *Montaña* and the regional lore of the Western United States.

Menéndez Pelayo, Enrique. "Biografía de Pereda." In *Obras completas de D. José María de Pereda*. Madrid: Librería General de Victoriano Suárez, 1922. Vol. XVII, pp. 305 - 556. This lengthy biography is actually the work not only of Menéndez Pelayo but also of four other friends of Pereda, and the material was first published in *Diario Montañés* of Santander, May 1, 1906; the whole approach is very descriptive and favorable toward Pereda but the bibliographical items beginning on page 498 to the end of the biography are indispensable; this endeavor is probably the point of departure for all the following criticism, in particular, for the facts of Pereda's life.

MENÉNDEZ PELAYO, MARCELINO. *Estudios y discursos de crítica histórica y literaria.* Madrid: Consejo de Investigaciones Científicas, 1941. Vol. VI, pp. 325 - 97. The complete writings of Menéndez Pelayo about Pereda are found among this whole opus, providing the compendium of the diverse opinions over the years as Don Marcelino, particularly, penned the expected good review. It is required reading for understanding all later criticism, pro and con Pereda. Menéndez Pelayo's views are in many stances acceptable and correct with a surprising number of telling marks against Pereda.

————. "Prólogo." In *Obras completas de D. José María de Pereda.* Madrid: Librería General de Victoriano Suárez, 1921. Vol. I, pp. v - xc. The long essay on Pereda, the reviews of *Sotileza* and *La puchera*, with the deliberate mention about omitting the review of *La Montálvez* (a revealing indication of this critic's attitude) provide the first step in this major Peredian criticism. Menéndez Pelayo's philosophy, his friendship with Pereda, and his association with the *Montaña* must always be remembered in studying this essential material together with the previously mentioned articles by him concerning Pereda.

PATTISON, WALTER T. "Pereda ¿naturalista a pesar suyo?" *El naturalismo español. Historia externa de un movimiento literario.* Madrid: Gredos, 1969. Pp. 63 - 83. This excellent commentary on a repeated problem of Peredian criticism offers the convincing argument by a noted critic that Pereda is the "hombre-cumbre" or the most representative figure of this epoch but that resemblances between naturalism and Pereda's writings are not signs of influence by, and imitation of, French writers.

PEREDA, JOSÉ MARÍA DE. *Discursos de Menéndez Pelayo, Pereda y Galdós,* leídos ante la Real Academia Española en las recepciones públicas del 7 y 21 de febrero de 1897. Madrid: Viuda e hijos de Tello, 1897. One of the most important and comprehensive manifestoes of nineteenth-century Spanish literature, above all for the development of the novel. Consists of three brief articles in a small volume that should be included in the *Obras completas* of Pereda as well as in the editions of the other two speakers. It is a generally omitted source because of the late date (1897) for the literary formation and production of each individual speaker in addition to the end-of-the-century occasion.

PLACE, EDWIN B. *Don Gonzalo González de la Gonzalera.* Chicago: Sanborn and Co., 1932. Contains introduction, notes, and vocabulary. An edition, like that of Bassett for *Pedro Sánchez,* prepared for American schools but which supplies worthwhile articles at any level for an analysis and comprehension of the life and the works of Pereda. Evidences a very sure grasp of the implications of the Peredian theses in this novel.

TANNENBERG, BORIS DE. "Ecrivains castillans contemporains: J. M. de Pereda." *Revue Hispanique* V (1898), 330 - 64. Personal impressions of Pereda after a visit to the writer in Santander with some of his thoughts on the books; a general consideration of the works, chronologically and within the larger trends of the day.

VAN HORNE, JOHN. "The Influence of Conservatism on the Art of Pereda." *Publications of the Modern Language Association* XXXIV (1919), 70 - 88. The connection between Pereda's ideology and his art is penetratingly probed and ascertained without any decision on the author's part in favor of Pereda's political, social, and religious conservatism early in his life and at the outset of his writing endeavors, which constituted a set of beliefs firmly rooted and resistant to change.

VÉZINET, F. "José María de Pereda." In *Les maîtres du roman espagnol contemporain*. Paris: Hachette, 1907. Pp. 129 - 66. An interesting companion to the reactions of Boris de Tannenberg for the French reception of Pereda. It is cognizant of his main themes and ideas and favors a wide reading of his stories and novels as highly representative of Spanish novelistic developments and as the accurate portrayal not only of the region of Santander but also of the national scene.

Index